CW01161192

# THE WARM ARCTIC

# THE WARM ARCTIC

Norman Price

Book Guild Publishing
Sussex, England

First published in Great Britain in 2008 by
The Book Guild Ltd
Pavilion View
19 New Road
Brighton, BN1 1UF

Copyright © Norman Price 2008

The right of Norman Price to be identified as the author of this work has been asserted by him in accordance with the Copyright, Designs and Patents Act 1988.

All rights reserved. No part of this publication may be reproduced, transmitted, or stored in a retrieval system, in any form or by any means, without permission in writing from the publisher, nor be otherwise circulated in any form of binding or cover other than that in which it is published and without a similar condition being imposed on the subsequent purchaser.

Typesetting in Times by YHT Ltd, London

Printed in Great Britain by CPI Antony Rowe

A catalogue record for this book is available from The British Library.

ISBN 978 1 84624 230 4

*This book is dedicated to Benjamin Howell, my eldest grandson who accompanied me to Iceland and Greenland (Chapter 10). He will carry my baton of adventure into the future.*

# CONTENTS

| | | |
|---|---|---|
| Preface | | ix |
| 1 | **The Arctic** | 1 |
| 2 | **Spitsbergen** <br> A small expedition's encounter with this harsh region and others working on the island. | 9 |
| 3 | **Greenland** <br> A visit to the west coast of the world's largest island. | 33 |
| 4 | **Canada's Nunavut** <br> A winter's experience amongst the Inuit and those working to help them. | 53 |
| 5 | **Canada's Mackenzie River Delta** <br> The trek from Inuvik to Aklavik that didn't happen. | 81 |
| 6 | **Alaska** <br> On the shores of the Bering Straits. An old gold mining area and the people that make it their home. | 117 |
| 7 | **Russia's Chukotka** <br> A visit to 'the furthest corner of Russia' and the warmth of living within the community. | 143 |
| 8 | **Murmansk** <br> Russia's Arctic city and seaport on the Kola Peninsula. | 171 |

| | | |
|---|---|---|
| **9** | **Finnish Lapland** | 187 |
| | The woods and lakes in the land of the Saami reindeer herders. | |
| **10** | **Iceland and East Greenland** | 207 |
| | An amazing adventure with a grandson. | |
| Postscript | | 249 |
| Index | | 251 |

# PREFACE

Of all the people who live in or visit the Arctic, some will love it and some will hate it, but I doubt that there are any who are indifferent.

The Arctic can be fickle and flip from gentle and beautiful to wild and savage. It is spectacular and alluring but it has a dark face, which it displays without warning. There is little that is certain other than that its winters are most uncomfortably cold and that the people who live in this unique region have exceptionally warm and open hearts.

This book evolved from a love affair, when one man, out of curiosity and a search of adventure, set foot in the North and became infatuated with the people and their environment. The tantalising allure of this combination became irresistible and called him back again and again to explore fresh venues and facets.

So began a journey through all four seasons that circumnavigated the Arctic Ocean, dipping into lands and communities along the way and, indeed, into the Ocean itself.

Norman D. Price

# THE LANDS SURROUNDING THE ARCTIC OCEAN

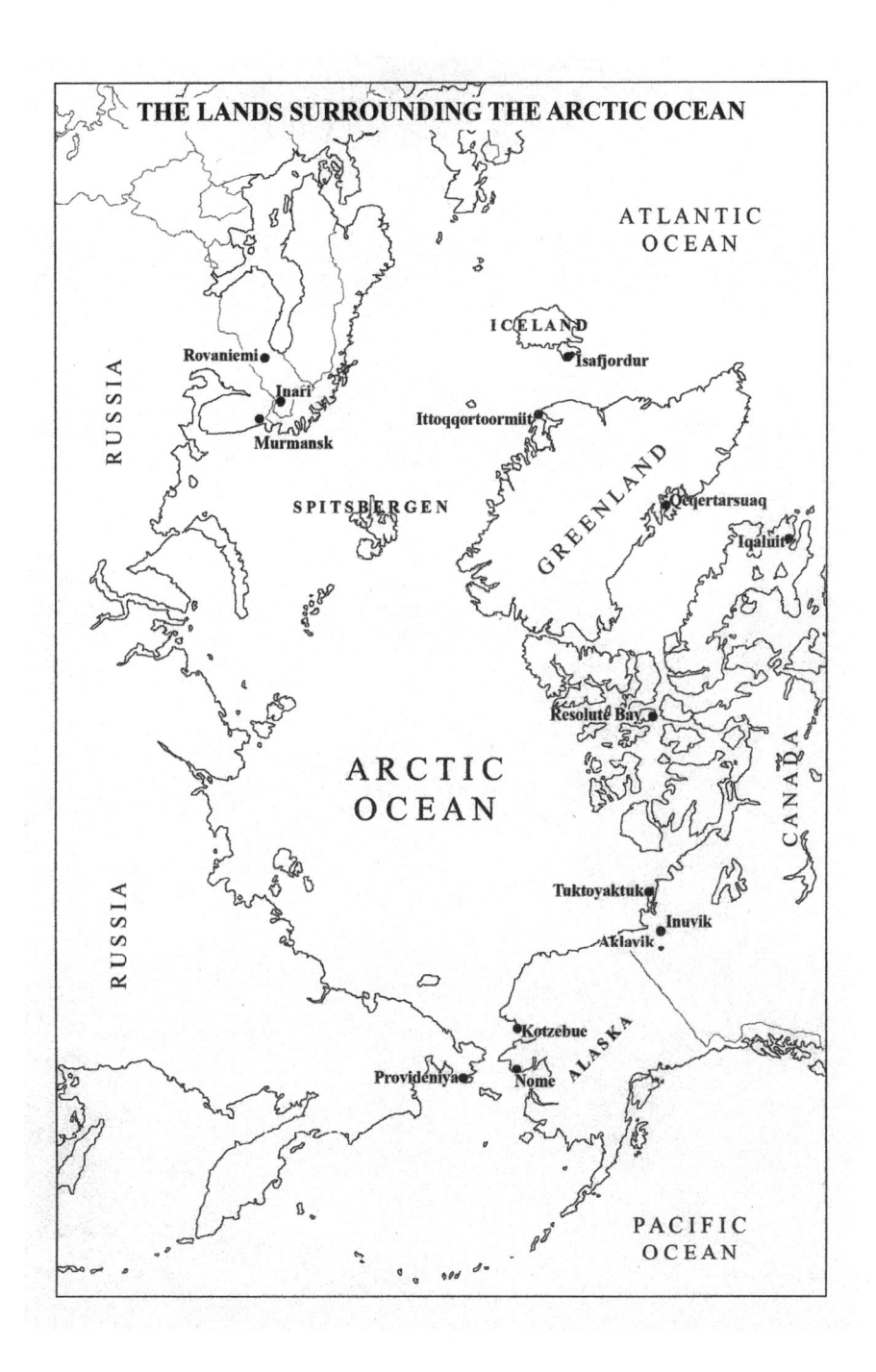

# Chapter 1

# THE ARCTIC

The Arctic is a vast area and occupies nearly 8% of the planet and 15% of earth's landmass. Having said that, it is an area very difficult to define with precision. It is best to think of it more as a concept than a precise area. 'A region of short, cool summers and long, cold winters' is an apt description of the Arctic, but its demarcation from the temperate zone is more universally accepted by 'academics' as the limit of the tree line or the permafrost – which roughly coincide with each other. That demarcation line does not simply follow the Arctic Circle and in places can be as far north as the northern tip of Norway and yet dip as far south as 55°N (i.e. nearly 800 miles to the south of the Arctic Circle in Ontario, Canada), the same latitude as Newcastle upon Tyne in England.

The landmasses that comprise the Arctic today were not as they were in the geological past. They have moved with the drift of the continental plates, like rafts in a viscous sea. 500 million years ago those lands may have been more than 3,000 miles away from the North Pole and the influence of its former locations of the distant past is still felt. When located in the temperate or tropical regions, these lands were covered in lush vegetation. Although now treeless in the High Arctic, that lush vegetation has formed rich deposits of coal and oil. Man's present search for, and exploitation of, those resources has brought industry to many places in the Arctic and, with it, considerable changes.

The extent of the flora is often a delight and surprise to a new visitor. In the summer the 24 hours of daylight permit dense carpets of Arctic wildflowers to grow and also have a profound effect on the riches of the sea. Marine algae proliferate, feeding the smaller waterborne creatures. This attracts the fish, which in turn attract the seals and, finally, at the top of the food chain, the polar bears. Because of the permafrost, melting snow does not drain away and myriad lakes and ponds form on the land. These lakes and ponds support a rich insect life that miraculously survives the winter. The insects attract vast flocks of immigrant birds to nest and raise their young with the abundant supply of food. Nature has balanced it all very finely and any disturbance of the rhythm can have a considerable knock-on effect. If, for example, the snows are late clearing from the breeding grounds of the migrant birds, the number of nesting sites is reduced. With the consequent reduction of breeding birds, the insects on which they feed multiply and the Arctic foxes, the normal predators of the birds, have to look to the lemmings for their food supply. The number of lemmings is in turn reduced.

Man, too, was attracted to the north by the hunting and fishing. Besides the polar bears and the Arctic foxes, there are reindeer and caribou, musk ox, seals, walruses and whales. The indigenous people generally can be divided into two groups: the Eurasian Group, living along the northern reaches of Europe and Asia, and the Western Arctic Group, living in North America, Canada and Greenland, with a small number on the eastern tip of Russia.

The Eurasian group, which include the Saami (Lapps) and those of Arctic Russia, spread directly from the south and followed the rivers that run from south to north from the temperate lands about a million years ago. Except for the Saami who also spread into northern Scandinavia, these people make up many of the ethnic minorities of Russia. In the Polar Regions, there are some 19 tribes varying in number from the Eskimosy or Yupik,[1] with only about 1,300 members to the Komi (322,000) and Yakuty (296,000).[2] The different tribes that make up this group are distinct and their various languages mutually unintelligible. Their apparent cultural similarities are probably due to the

---

[1] The Yupik are akin to the Western Culture but are included here as they live in Asian Russia
[2] 1970 figures – Source: Narodnoye khozyaystvo SSSR

similarity of conditions and methods of solving common problems rather than a common cultural source.[3]

The Western Group comprises those who had their origins in Mongolia. These people are culturally very similar and their dialects are mutually intelligible. They have been given the collective name of Eskimo. The earliest inhabitants of North America and Canada were there many thousands of years before the coming of the white men. Evidence dates from 12,000 years ago, but the migrations probably started even earlier. Some anthropologists argue that the migration commenced as long ago as 40,000 years. They came from Asia and the gateway is generally thought to have been over a land bridge, now known as Beringia, that at one time joined the Asiatic northeast to Alaska. The immigrants spread over the new land, with some continuing as far south as South America. The earlier immigrants tended to shun the tundra regions and moved south of the tree line. The dwellers of the true Arctic regions appeared sometime before 2200 BC and by 2000 BC had spread rapidly across Alaska and the Canadian Arctic Archipelago to reach northernmost Greenland. This explosive expansion was all the more remarkable as they achieved it without leaving evidence of sledges or boats. These were the 'Small Tool people'. Their small chipped artefacts were derived from the Neolithic period of the region generally known as eastern Siberia. They maintained a subsistence economy, living off the mammals of the land and the sea and catching fish from rivers and lakes; in time they learned to hunt seals through the frozen sea in winter. They developed into what is known as the Dorset culture, a name given to them after some of their remains were found at Cape Dorset on the southwest extremity of Baffin Island. By 400 BC a new culture, the 'Norton culture', also from Asia, brought new hunting skills and better tools. Its representatives first appeared in Alaska and then moved across northern Canada as far as Greenland – as had the 'Small Tools' people. They displaced or absorbed the Dorset culture to form the predecessors of today's littoral Eskimo. They had better hunting

---

[3] But see Chapter 5

skills, using the kayak for seal hunting and the umiak (a larger, skin-covered open boat) for hunting the whales. Then, as now, they generally led a simple subsistence life, developing the skills to thrive in the demanding conditions of the Arctic. In the mid-seventeenth century, the conditions of the extreme north deteriorated and the Eskimos were forced further south towards the Arctic Circle.

This is a convenient point to discuss the use of 'Eskimo' as a collective name, as opposed to the self-designation of each of the dialects. In general terms these self-designations, such as Yupik, Inupiat, Inuvialuit and Inuit mean, 'the people', but since the sixteenth century, Europeans have used the collective term 'Eskimo'. It had its origins in Montagnak, an Algonquian language. At one time it was believed that it meant 'eaters of raw flesh' and to this day there are many who feel this is derogatory and 'politically incorrect'. However, this translation is probably erroneous. The name is somewhat obscure but is believed to make reference to snowshoes.[4,5] The Canadian Eskimo and, to a lesser extent, the Greenland Eskimo are unhappy about being referred to by this name and prefer to be called Inuit. The Inupiat of Alaska refer to themselves as Eskimo and the Russian Yupik call themselves Eskimosy. Rather than cause offence to any group, this book will use the local preferred term whenever possible, but when talking about the Western Culture collectively there is no convenient alternative to the name Eskimo.

These people who settled in the North learnt how to deal with their environment and are better able to live there because of the climate and the advent of ice. Whilst snow and ice will frequently bring the temperate lands to a standstill, the people of the North are able to exist in that climate *because* of the cold rather than in spite of it. It is the snow and ice which give greater freedom of movement over the rough tundra. Rivers freeze and turn into roadways for easy travel. Soft, wet, boggy ground becomes rock hard and the covering of snow enables hunters to track their prey.

---

[4] Encyclopaedia Britannica 4:558:3b
[5] See also Chapter 10

Snow blocks are readily available for the building of igloos and the winter can even provide a means of navigation. In Russia's Chukotka, the first permanent snows of the winter follow a strong northerly wind so that, under the falling snow, the grasses are flattened pointing towards the south. The natives of Chukotka have long since learnt to navigate by digging under the snow to assess the position of the grasses and establish north and south.

The ice is the friend of the Eskimo, rather than their enemy, but then they know the ice and its ways as well as a Londoner knows how to read a city street and they have many different words to describe the snow in all the subtleties of its different forms. I was told that when the ice is thin, the sea ice is much safer than freshwater ice. Thin freshwater ice can just split and give way but when the sea ice is still thin, 'It's sort of rubbery and moves about but stays together,'[6] my Eskimo informer told me. Seals are hunted through their breathing holes. Manmade holes permit crab fishing from spots that would be inaccessible without the ice. The crab fishing, as described to me by an Alaskan Eskimo from a camp near Safety Lagoon, seems to be relatively simple. 'Just tie the bait onto a line and lower it to the bottom. When a king crab takes it, it won't let go and you just haul it out.' Wolves and caribou leave their tracks in the snow, which can be followed by hunters.

Blubber, meat and fish were eaten when raw (and most nutritious), while partially digested lichen from a caribou's stomach is a delicacy. Driftwood – the only wood available – is carved and pegged to make harpoons and sleds. Where there is no wood, caribou antlers are pieced together. In an emergency, Inuit-built sleds from frozen fish or hides-sleds could be eaten if necessary.

In the past, as autumn waned, many Inuit gathered in groups of 100 or more on the ice to build winter snow house villages. When stormbound, an entire village might gather in a large snow house to take part in a drum dance, watch wrestling matches or witness a shaman's attempt to quell a storm. Today, in the winter, the Inuit live in modern homes in communities.

---

[6] Chapter 6

## THE WARM ARTIC

The Inuit have 100 words for various types of snow but not one word for chief. Power lies in the community's acceptance or rejection of its members. There are no bad hunters, just 'unlucky' ones. In the past, when all luck ran out, people died. Today they are less vulnerable.

Intensely spiritual, many Inuit shared an unshakable belief in the supernatural, and their daily lives were directed by concerns over human and animal souls, monsters and deities. They relied on shamans and medicine men to protect them from evil spirits. In many areas of the Arctic today, the Christian Church is now well established

Despite their constant struggle for survival, the Inuit lived life one day at a time, with a constant cheerfulness that puzzled early European explorers. But the Inuit had an explanation: 'If you knew what horrors we often have to live through, you would understand why we are so fond of laughing.'[7]

The Arctic is far from being a desolate waste of snow and ice and has its natural or renewable resources that sustain the indigenous people. As stated earlier, the Arctic makes up some 15% of the world's land mass but its population is only 0.3% of the inhabitants of the earth. With such a low population density they can live off the land. Those resources are, however, quite inadequate to make any significant contribution to the food supplies of the rest of the world, the one exception being the fishing from the rich marine life in these cold waters.

The immigrants came later to the north. One of the earliest was Eric the Red from Iceland. He set up a colony in Greenland in the tenth century and may well have been in the south of Greenland before the Thule Eskimos drifted down from the north. Eric the Red's colony made a promising start, but dwindled and vanished after 400 years.[8] It was not until it became a colony of Denmark that immigrants settled successfully in Greenland. The immigrants of northern Russia are of European stock. In pursuit of

---

[7] 'The First Canadians' in *Reader's Digest Atlas of Canada* (Montreal: Reader's Digest Association, 1981)
[8] Chapter 3

furs, and then more rapidly with the advent of Russian imperialism, they started to emigrate east and north and reached the Pacific two centuries ago. The immigrants in Alaska and the Canadian north came later. The Inuit generally refer to them as the Kabloona and this is a convenient term for use in this book. The Kabloona immigrants now consider the Arctic their home and many truly care for the North, its environment and the welfare of its entire people. It is dangerous to generalise, but it was my experience that the Russian immigrants to the Arctic also cared for and protected their aboriginal Arctic neighbours.

The visitors are a recent phenomenon and have become more frequent with the simplification of travel. They are so many and various that it is hard to be specific but some are once-only visitors: tourists, adventurers, explorers, journalists, researchers and business or government personnel. Although they often lack tact and care and, if not carefully monitored, can do harm to the environment and damage the long term welfare of the others, their presence is becoming ever more important.

I first saw the Arctic from the shirt-sleeved comfort of an airliner flying at some 30,000 feet over Greenland. As a professional airline pilot, I had visited many countries around the four corners of the globe but my face was never pressed as hard to the flight deck windows as on those occasions when my route took me over Greenland. From high level it seemed to beckon and challenge me to test its surface and explore its cold demeanour, but it was not until I had hung up my flying cap and briefcase for the last time that I was able to take up the challenge to enter this intriguing world which has now so captivated me. It is from the island of Spitsbergen in the Svalbard archipelago that we start our journey through the lands which surround the Arctic Ocean.

# Chapter 2

# SPITSBERGEN

*A small expedition's encounter with this harsh region and others working on the island.*

It was the search for adventure that took me to Spitsbergen, but to give it purpose I had put together a small team to make a genuine scientific study. It was a proper expedition that had received the approval of the Royal Geographic Society and it had the title 'Svalbard Acid Rain Project 1987' – an expedition best described as 'Small Budget'. We were indeed going to make a study of the acidity of the snow and water in the rivers and lakes. I was the expedition leader and my Science Leader, Myles, was a limnologist and school teacher. The other five members were school leavers ranging from 17 to 19 years old. We were all very excited as our aircraft descended through the overcast to give us our first view of the island. What we saw was intimidating but quite typical of a High Arctic summer: dull and grey, the choppy waters of the fjords telling us that it was also very windy.

Longyearbyen is the only airport on the archipelago. Before it was built, aircraft flew in during the winter and landed on the frozen tundra. In the summer, the only way in was by sea. Now there are regular air services to provide for the resident population and give the islands a new importance – tourism, though the only tourists who would find it acceptable would be those seeking adventure. They would find themselves in the Arctic with the inherent logistical difficulties of equipment, supplies and travel and the serious problems of survival. The tourists who visit are more likely to be on short visits under the control of experienced operators rather than the hordes who wreak havoc on the environment of gentler climes. The Norwegian governor is likely to maintain a tight control over the activities of the tourists and be watchful for the protection of the vulnerable fauna and flora.

Spitsbergen is well into the High Arctic. It is the largest of the islands of the Svalbard archipelago, the most northerly point of which is 81°N. Although only 620 miles (995 kilometres) from the North Pole, the warming waters of the Gulf Stream temper the climate and it is not as savage as might be expected for such a latitude. Temperatures below −30°C, or for that matter above +10°C, are rare. The name 'Spitsbergen' means 'Land of Pointed Mountains' and it is justified. Its terrain is indeed spectacular and largely Alpine with peaks up to 5,600 feet (1,717 metres). The coast is heavily indented with fjords. Some 60% of the archipelago is covered by an ice-cap dotted with Nunataks.[1] The name 'Svalbard' for the archipelago is also appropriate. It means 'On the Edge of the Cold'. Its northerly shores are on the sea ice of the Arctic Ocean. Because of the Gulf Stream, however, the southerly shores are generally ice free from June to October. Its isolation as an island distant from any major land mass has given it the questionable status of being devoid of an indigenous or native population. There is however, a very large population of polar bears, who are not the cute furry creatures depicted on Christmas cards. There are adult males weighing as much as 1,500 pounds, particularly savage and very much on the top of the food chain. At no time during the whole of the six weeks we were on the island, did we come across a resident Norwegian outside the town of Longyearbyen who did not carry a high powered rifle. With great difficulty I had managed to acquire a licence to purchase a rifle in the UK and an export licence to take it with us so that we too could be protected from any predatory bears.

Despite their isolation and sparse population, the islands have had a long and sometimes eventful history. They were first mentioned in the Icelandic Sagas of the twelfth century as being '12 days' sailing' from Iceland. They were probably also known to

---

[1] Eskimo or Inuit name given to the tops of the mountains poking through the ice

Russian sailors, but it was not until the Dutch navigator William Barents found the archipelago in 1596 that it was drawn to public attention. In the early seventeenth century the English and Dutch whalers came to the area and some vestiges of their activities are still to be found. Later, the Russian and then Norwegian fur trappers arrived to hunt and trap seal and walrus, reindeer, polar bear and arctic foxes, the Russians being the first to overwinter on the islands. The discovery of a variety of minerals, including coal, gypsum, lead-zinc and marble, gave the islands even greater commercial significance and prospectors became frequent visitors. Coal is the most important of their minerals and the only one to be exploited, but the first mines were not opened until 1904. With mining came the first permanent settlements. The administrative and principal town of Longyearbyen got its name from Alfred Longyear, the original American operator of the mines. As the competition for the commercial values of the island intensified the question of sovereignty became urgent and eventually, by the Treaty of Paris 1920, it was granted to Norway, but other signatories to the treaty retained their rights to mining and carrying out scientific work. The Treaty of Paris expressly excluded military activity because of the strategic importance of the islands, sitting as they do on the edge of the frozen Arctic Ocean. At the time of the 'Cold War' between the East and the West that strategic importance was particularly acute. All shipping, and that includes naval vessels and atomic nuclear submarines, entering the major Russian port of Murmansk and the North-East Passage across northern Russia has to pass between Svalbard and the Scandinavian mainland. The coal on the island was important to both Norway and Russia but on Spitsbergen it was of particular interest to the Russians, not just for its mineral value, but because the mining activities gave them a right by treaty to maintain a presence on a group of islands that held an important strategic position for their shipping. The figures published for the 1970s show that the Norwegian community numbered about 1,000, while the Russians varied between 1,800 and 3,200.[2]

---

[2] *Armstrong, Terence, Rogers, George* and Rowley, Graham, *The Circumpolar North* (London: Methuen, 1978)

This resident population of Norwegians and Russians operate and work on the mines. There is a scattering of Norwegians who make up the administrative force, police, environmental and wildlife officers. There are no figures to indicate how many of these residents were clandestine military personnel. Visitors like us are generally scientists and adventurers. The combination of the 'Cold War' and the large Soviet presence on this Norwegian Territory would later provide us with both amusement and sadness.

For an adventure visit, Svalbard was challenging in that we were very much on our own. Everything necessary for our extended stay had to be brought in. The only exception was fuel, purchased from a depot in Longyearbyen; other than that, if anything had been forgotten the expedition would have to manage without or be abandoned. Careful planning was vital. Our stores and equipment had been sent previously by sea freight. We had chartered a boat to take us from Longyearbyen to our base camp at Brucebyen at the top of the Billifjorden, a large fjord terminating at a huge glacier, the Nordenskiöldbreen. The boat, *The Iskongen*,[3] was waiting for us at the docks, its skipper a burly Norwegian. His first mate was an Englishman who, the year before, had been the skipper of his own boat but had had the misfortune to sink it when he struck some rocks in the inland waters. The only other crew man was a young Norwegian deck hand. All our supplies were loaded on board.

As we pulled away from the dock we had a chance to see something of the town from off the coast. It was small. There was an area of brightly painted little houses, a cluster of buildings used for the administration of the archipelago – the Governor's offices, the police and wildlife departments – and a coal fired power station on the edge of town. But the most striking feature was the extensive bucket chain system suspended from pylons. This carried the coal from the adjacent mines to the point where it could be loaded onto cargo ships and dispatched to Norway, or some other country. Longyearbyen could not be accused of being pretty. The fjords were surrounded by high hills extensively

---

[3] The Ice King

patched with snow, the tops of which were eroded flat, and it was easy to imagine what it must have been like when glacier ice filled them to the level of the mountain summits.

*The Iskongen* chugged its steady course into the main fjord, the Isfjorden,[4] a wide stretch of water reaching to the Greenland Sea and the Arctic Ocean 40 miles away to the west. We were then able to see the panorama of mountains and peaks, glaciers and high bird-cliffs. It was a pleasure to remain on deck. The air was clean and fresh and, although the day was grey and overcast, it was not too cold. As we entered the Billifjorden, we could see the intense bird activity along the cliffs. Northern Fulmars followed alongside our ship. The young Norwegian deckhand told me that sometimes these birds land on the deck and if the ship was heaving and rolling, the fulmars became desperately sea sick and quite helpless. He would just pick them up and throw them back into the water where they quickly recovered. It sounded an odd story to me but I had no way of checking the reliability of his tale.

Amongst our equipment was a small inflatable boat that had been loaned to us, complete with outboard engine. This was to get us around the fjords and, at the end of the expedition, return us to Longyearbyen. During the five or six hours that it took to sail to Brucebyen, we unpacked and inflated the boat and fitted the engine, all ready to ferry us ashore when we got to our destination. It didn't look a very big boat, but we thought it would do the job. The skipper watched us from the wheel house and, before we got to our landing site, he said, 'I don't seem to have a booking for your return trip.'

This was a small budget expedition and we were scratching around for money. The cost of chartering *The Iskongen* for the return would hit us hard financially.

'Oh,' I happily replied, 'at the end of the expedition, we will have consumed all the supplies and our plan is to return to Longyearbyen in our own craft.'

The skipper looked at our little boat and then at me. 'Well if you change your mind, try to get a message to me somehow.'

---

[4] Ice Fjord

He knew what was likely to happen. We were blissfully unaware. *The Iskongen* dropped anchor a few hundred yards off the shingle beach at Cape Napier. We launched the inflatable and ferried three of the lads ashore. Two of them put on immersion suits and waded knee deep in the shallows whilst the inflatable ferried the stores and equipment to them and they carried it onto the beach. In a short space of time we were all ashore surrounded by rucksacks and crates. *The Iskongen* raised its anchor and headed back to Longyearbyen. We were alone on a remote headland. The expedition was about to start in earnest.

The Norwegian police had details of our plans, location of our base camp, expected movements and the expected date for our return. I was quite confident that we had made our plans carefully and covered most, if not all, contingencies. I was, however, acutely aware that we had neither radio nor any other form of communication, apart from a heliograph that could be used to attract attention, if anyone was there to notice. If we had to get a message to the skipper of *The Iskongen*, I did not know how that was to be arranged. The only possibility of making contact with the outside world would have been via the Russian coal-mining settlement of Pyramiden situated five miles across the fjord.

We had chosen this location carefully. Off the beach up a short rise were the three huts of a British science base which had been abandoned many years earlier. There were two lakes either side that would provide us with fresh water, and we were well positioned to trek to various sites to gather data for our science project.

From the beach to the old science base there were some rails and a little truck we could push. After securely mooring our inflatable boat off the beach, we used the truck to ferry our equipment and provisions to the huts, then stood and looked about us. From here, across the lake, we had an excellent view of the glacier and two rather magnificent Nunataks standing proudly out of the surface. Around the shores of the lake there was relatively lush vegetation dotted with hardy little flowers known locally as Reindeer Roses. The water was perfectly still and reflected the scene like a mirror. It was all very grand and attractive.

The Governor had stated that we must make use of tents for accommodation, but the two larger huts were unlocked. They were not in good repair. The smaller hut was locked but in very good condition and obviously well maintained. I decided to ignore this one and use the two unlocked huts, one of which would make a good mess hut as it offered much more room than a tent for communal activities, our equipment and stores. The second we used as a dormitory.

Our science objective was the study of acid rain. At the time of our visit, there was much concern about the acid rain generated by European industry wreaking havoc on the environment. There was a wealth of data on the extent of the acidity on mainland Europe, but virtually no information on the natural levels of acidity on areas unaffected by industry. Svalbard was particularly interesting because the general wind patterns of the north protected it from any drifting pollution from industrialised Europe. Our method was to gather samples of snow at different depths, melt water and lake water and record the pH of a pristine environment to form a base line against which pollution could be compared.

Expeditions into the wilderness areas of the world, like Spitsbergen, are many and various. They range from the large budget, well equipped teams run, or sponsored, by governments or military organisations, to the small team, low budget groups. What they all generally have in common is a membership prepared to share discomforts and dangers and work together towards a common goal – an ideal that bonds together its members and underpins the enjoyment and lasting excitement of most expeditions. Each member has to practise the art of sharing and tolerance to avoid conflict within the group and in the process will discover that that is the way to get the most out of the experience. Our expedition fell into the small team, low budget category, but we did not skimp on zeal and enthusiasm.

Our life would be simple. We intended to trek to the locations selected for our research, dig snow pits, take samples from melt water and streams and from a number of lakes and bring them back to base camp for analysis. We were self-sufficient. We mixed our science and adventure with enthusiastic abandon. We tried to climb the extensive loose scree slopes that formed from the fractured rock at the base of the surrounding hills, but it was a case of taking three steps up and slithering four steps down. We took our inflatable to the snout of the glacier and then followed the glacier streams to various locations to collect water samples. I had never walked on a glacier before and was very surprised to find that it was not dissimilar to walking along a gravel path. It was firm and crunched under foot but its appearance made it easy to imagine we were walking along the tops of clouds. We carried crampons but there didn't seem any need to use them. My only concern was that the engine of our boat was not proving as reliable as I would have liked. On a number of occasions it would fail and it took quite a bit of persuasion to get it going again.

As a team, we had to learn to understand each other's foibles and eccentricities. There were some big age gaps to bridge. I was the oldest at 55; Myles was 30 and the rest were in their late teens. I knew that my propensity to snore at night could be a problem to others but nothing was ever said. One morning, however, I awoke to find myself surrounded by shoes! I later learned that the others had been trying to silence my snoring, but I was too good a sleeper for that to be effective. Occasionally, the lads would move out into tents to get some peace and quiet. When it came to fitness and strength, the youngsters were way ahead of me. I couldn't carry as much and I couldn't move as fast. My only way of keeping their respect was to have frequent swims in the fjord with the glacial ice floating past. That the lads balked at – and so, for that matter, did Myles. Although our accommodation was quite primitive, I tried to maintain as high a civilised standard as the circumstances permitted. The younger members seemed to feel that an expedition was an occasion when restraints should be set aside and total freedom from convention should reign. It was clearly going to take us a little while to settle down together.

In the crystal-clear Arctic air, we could see the Russian coal-mining community of Pyramiden quite distinctly from our base camp; and no doubt they could see us, or perhaps notice the smoke from our stove. In the silence of a still day we could even hear their yellow MIG-18 helicopters starting their engines and often saw them shuttling due south on the opposite shore to and from their main base at Barentsberg. It is quite remarkable how far a small sound will travel in a near perfect silence.

One morning, one of the helicopters from Pyramiden made an unusual detour across the fjord and flew low over our camp before setting the normal course south. They had obviously come across to have a closer look at us. We waved happily at the aircraft as it flew overhead. Two days after this incident, Myles was away with three of the lads collecting samples and I remained with the other two at base camp. We had earlier noticed a three man detachment of Norwegian police speeding toward the head of the fjord. They were the first people to breach our isolation, but they didn't stop. Not long afterwards, one of the lads called me and said that a little landing craft flying the Soviet flag had pulled up on our beach. Our life was beginning to get very crowded. Eight Russians made their way up the beach towards our camp. They were like everything that a bad movie could depict, almost a spoof.

One of our lads had our rifle slung over his shoulder. 'Shall I waste them?' he asked with a grin.

Really! The teenagers could be quite childish at times.

'Let's go and greet them,' I responded.

Our visitors were a motley bunch dressed in heavy coats and broad-brimmed hats, but one of their number wore a dapper suit complete with tie. I noticed that he sported incongruous black polished 'winkle-picker' shoes of the type that had been fashionable in England in the 1950s. They were hopelessly out of place on the Arctic tundra. He seemed to be leading the way.

'Come and have tea with us,' I invited.

The dapper man waved a bottle at me and said, 'Tea – no. Cognac!'

At that time I had little experience of integrating with Russians, but I did know that if drinking was to be the order of the day then a great deal of alcohol was likely to be consumed.

I whispered to one of the other lads who had gathered outside the hut, 'Get back and hide all our liquor supply.'

I didn't want to be anti-social and ungenerous, but our liquor was otherwise likely to vanish and we had no way of buying any more. We welcomed them into the hut we used as a mess and produced what drinking vessels we could muster. Introductions were made. The other members of the Soviet party seemed to be directors of one department or another. The dapper man was the only English speaker and translated for the others. At that time, I had not learned to speak Russian, so English had to be the language for communication. The cognac flowed. Toasts of friendship and brotherhood were made. There were smiles all round and *bonhomie* glowed between us. I pondered the reason for the visit. Why should they pay us a social call? The Norwegians had warned us that the Soviets were very suspicious of strangers and we should keep away from their settlement if we were to avoid trouble. I knew there was friction between the Norwegians and the Soviets. It had to be more than a social call, I reasoned, but I bided my time – and enjoyed their cognac.

When half the bottle had been consumed, their questions started – in the most genial and inoffensive tones. How many of us were there? What was our nationality? What were our objectives? And they peered into our equipment boxes and flipped through our science notes. Rather than being offended by this ill-concealed inquisition and search, I found the situation comic. I realised they were just worried that our expedition might pose some sort of a threat to them. I decided the best approach was to put their minds at rest. Candidly, I gave them a conducted tour of our humble domain and showed them plenty of evidence of our scientific plans. I was right to do so. Once they were reassured, the questions ceased and by the time the bottle of cognac was empty we had been invited to their settlement the following day. I may have demeaned myself by being almost obsequiously frank, but in return I had gained a colossal bonus, and I was well pleased with the outcome. I was already looking forward to getting a view of the Soviet community generally denied to so many others.

Before our visitors took their leave, the Norwegian police patrol came into our camp. As soon as they saw the Soviets, they reacted aggressively. One officer raced down to the Soviet landing craft and another stood in the doorway of our hut. I had met this officer in Longyearbyen and judged him to be very friendly, but this time he was stiff and tense. I went over to him.

'How many of them are there and how long have they been here? Have they been wandering around?'

He almost barked the questions at me. It was intimidating and I answered as best I could, but I was enjoying my *rapport* with the Russians and did not want it disturbed. The police officer eventually turned away, warning me to keep an eye on them. When the Russians eventually departed, I walked with them down to the beach to see them off. As I returned to our huts, I saw two of the Norwegian police officers keeping watch from the top of a nearby cliff. It was sad to witness this display of hostility. There was obviously an undercurrent of suppressed hostility between the two communities, but I didn't want to be a party to it.

The next day, as arranged, we crossed the fjord in our little inflatable boat and were greeted on the beach at Pyramiden by the same dapper man who had visited us. With him stood Olga. Olga was the resident teacher from their school. She was middle-aged, short in stature and very 'square' in appearance. She looked like the archetypal schoolmistress. Her spectacled eyes were gentle and she had a ready smile. She spoke excellent English in a very soft voice and was to be our guide for the day.

The settlement was typical of the Arctic towns of Russia. Pyramiden was efficient and well-equipped. It possessed a sports arena and stadium, heated swimming pool, hospital, library and cinema. The miners had a minimum posting of two years and many of them had brought their families with them. Olga's school provided for the education of the numerous children whom we saw in the town. The presence of women and children gave the community a homely feel. The settlement also had a farm with cattle and pigs and a huge heated greenhouse that produced not only vegetables but the flowers that Russians so love. With the artificial warmth and 24 hours of summer light, the growth in the greenhouse was prolific. The dung from the cattle was used to add humus to the barren soil so that there was even a patch of grass growing in the square in front of the community hall. In the centre of this verdure was a statue of Lenin. Olga told us that although the minimum posting was two years, many of the inhabitants stayed on for very much longer. They even had a resident of 92. Their health record was excellent with rarely so much as a common cold. Only the occasional accidents justified the existence of the hospital.

Pyramiden was of stern countenance – even grim to Western eyes. Longyearbyen was softer in appearance, having colourful buildings and being less rigidly set out, but I doubt that it was any better equipped or even as efficient. Wherever Olga took us, simple gifts were presented. At the sports area, where a football match was in progress, we were served cakes, and tea from a samovar. A supply of milk was given to us at the dairy, and bread from the bakery. Even in the library, the librarian found a small book written in English and presented it to me. Although the text was an insufferably dull dissertation on the Soviet policy and achievements in nuclear electrical generation, I have kept it safely as a token of friendship from the member of one community to a visiting stranger. In subsequent travels to Russia, I have found this geniality typical once you have been accepted by the community. At the end of the day we felt warmed by their hospitality and, clutching the rare treasurers of fresh bread and milk, we returned to our little boat and sailed back to our base camp.

When Myles and the other three returned from their field trip, we told them of our experience. They too wanted to visit Pyramiden but, conscious of the warnings by the Norwegians and the events that led to our receiving an invitation from the Russians, I advised them to try to make immediate contact with someone in authority before wandering about the town. I suggested they seek out Olga. This advice was not taken, however, and they simply started to wander about the town. In a very short space of time, they found themselves surrounded by a group of 'well-built men' and Olga, who explained that they were uninvited and unwelcome. They were escorted back to their boat and sent packing. No doubt their diary entries about Pyramiden reflect a different impression from my own.

We lapsed back into our isolation and work, but we were not

always alone. Our base at Brucebyen by the Nordenskiöldbreen glacier, where its snout dropped into the fjord, was quite an attraction. It was a grand and dynamic location and we had the occasional visitors: sometimes Norwegians from Longyearbyen taking a weekend break; sometimes adventurers on guided tours. Apparently Brucebyen was part of their circuit. The adventurers would fly into Longyearbyen, then spend the next ten days journeying around the fjords in two very large twin-engine inflatable craft, visiting various locations and camping on the tundra. One morning, I was seeing off Myles in our inflatable and had stripped off and was swimming and pushing the boat out of the shallows into deeper water when the visitors arrived. I think they were a little surprised to see me naked in the water. They were dressed in survival immersion suits. On one occasion the visitors camped by our base camp and we had a chance to chat to them. After tactful enquiry we discovered the tourists were paying two and a half times more for their ten days than it was costing us for the six weeks we had on the island.

Very occasionally we came across other travellers, usually in small groups, but we met one individual travelling alone. He was a teacher from Germany who came to Svalbard every year, sometimes even in the winter, to recover his sense of equilibrium between school terms. In the summer – such as it is – he brought his kayak and paddled around the shores in the icy waters camping on the beaches. One day I found him sitting on a rock watching a little bird, an aptly named turnstone, flicking over the pebbles and picking off morsels of food from beneath. We became friends and have remained so ever since. Whilst the search for personal space makes the loneliness of the Arctic so attractive, its isolation encourages a wonderful bond with chance strangers. Meetings are usually enthusiastic and warm. We would even deviate for as much as a mile from our respective routes just to shake hands and say 'hello'.

Once, whilst four of us were motoring up a fjord for the start of a long trek, we spotted a small hut above the shingle beach. As we approached, two men came running down to the water's edge waving vigorously at us. We waved back, but their vigour continued unabated and, thinking they might be in difficulties, we turned ashore. It turned out that the hut was being used by a Polish science group from the University of Warsaw. We were ushered into their very comfortable quarters, fed tea and biscuits and treated most royally. They were not in difficulties. I suppose they were just pleased to see fresh faces.

After our refreshment with the Poles, we carried on to complete a very tough one day trek. It took us over thirteen hours to cover the eleven miles to our destination. My group was to carry a tent and sufficient supplies for a week to a location by a large lake. Myles would follow later and spend the time collecting and analysing samples of water and any life found in the lake. The route entailed a climb up a glacier and across a mountain ridge, then down onto the north-facing tundra by Austfjorden leading into the Arctic Ocean. From the head of the fjord, where we moored our boat, it was an easy walk for a few miles across flat stony tundra. I was amazed to see how the tiny wildflowers managed to grow out of patches of rocks. Scattered along the surface were lumps of coal washed out of the earth by erosion. The next bit was the worst: we had to climb over towering mounds of moraine to get onto the glacier surface. The moraine was formed by the infinitesimal forward movement of the glacier and was composed of a wet sticky mud embedded with rocks. It wasn't too bad when we were able to step from rock to rock, but if we had to put our feet in the mud it clung to our boots like glue and it was difficult to drag ourselves free. By the time we had cleared the moraine and got on to the glacier I had pulled a muscle in my back and it was giving me 'gyp'. Nevertheless, I had no option but to press on; I'm ashamed to say that I treated it by swallowing a handful of pain killers, while the lads kindly offered to carry some of my load.

We had been advised by experienced Antarctic expeditioners to carry small plastic sledges designed for children. They were strapped onto the back of our rucksacks and weigh very little, but once on the icy glacier or snow surfaces, we were able to use them to tow behind us and take the weight of the rucksacks off our backs. It was remarkably effective. Without the rucksacks on our backs the crust on the areas of snow we traversed was able to carry our weight, while the sledges trundled behind us on tethers like obedient dogs. From the top of the mountain ridge we were even able to sit on the sledges and toboggan downhill. We arrived at our destination exhausted. Thirteen and a half hours is a long time to be carrying loads. We put up the tent, had a hot meal and the lads crashed out. This was the only time that I felt the advantage of age. I was no less tired than my younger colleagues, but there was work still to be done and I felt I could keep going. The youngsters had carried some of my load, so the least I could do in return was to let them sleep and get on with the camp chores before turning in myself. Aside from cleaning the mess kit, I had to collect fresh water and set things up for the next morning. By the time I crawled into the tent they were deeply asleep. If I snored that night, it didn't seem to disturb them.

Without the heavy loads, our return progress was eased and we were better able to appreciate the grandeur of the scenery. We were surrounded by high pointed mountains and snow fields. Strangely, at the highest point of our route we were joined by a glaucous gull. This bird was probably as surprised to see us as we were to see him; it circled us for some time as it followed our progress back to the boat. I was glad to get back across the moraine which proved no easier to traverse.

Our boat was waiting for us on the beach and we had about five or six miles of fjord to cross to get back to base. The weather had become overcast and there was now a bit of a wind, but it was not significant enough to worry us or delay our return. We made reasonably good progress at first but with surprising speed the conditions deteriorated: the wind got stronger and the waters more choppy. By the time we were half way across, the wind was howling and large waves were breaking over the bow and flooding the cockpit with water and bits of ice. Fortunately, we were wearing immersion suits. It was pretty miserable and alarming but, providing our engine kept going, we would be all right. Our course took us into the wind so, to cope with the conditions, two of the lads hung forward over the bow to stop it lifting; the other handled the engine to steer the boat, and I did my bit by holding the fuel tank clear of the flooding hull with one hand and bailing with the other. I looked back at the cliffs behind us – tall and rugged with rocks at their foot. They were down-wind so in the event of that temperamental little engine failing we were going to be blown back into them. I was not amused by the situation, but there was precious little we could do about it. We were committed and had to press on. I wondered what the lads were thinking. It was not until we were safely back at base camp that one of them commented: 'All we needed to complete the day was a killer whale to start making love to the boat.' Every expedition should have a man like him on the team.

Most of our boat rides were a pleasure. We travelled sufficiently off shore to avoid any rocks but not too far out in case of engine problems. Many of the high cliffs are bird colonies comprising either northern fulmars or puffins. The puffins were the most curious of our progress. They would swoop down from the cliffs and, if we slowed the boat a fraction, were able to fly alongside. They were so close we could see every detail of them as they came just beyond arm's reach. Their beady eyes examined us most carefully before they tired and turned away. Sadly, there was too much movement of the boat to be able to take any photographs of these intimate encounters. It was on one of these rides down to Gåsodden Point where the Billifjorden meets the Isfjorden that the engine decided to fail just before the point. It refused to re-start. The wind was blowing down the Isfjorden and we began to drift away from the land. The cause of the failure was a mystery so I had no idea what to do to entice life into that dead lump of metal. As we drifted into the main fjord we fitted the oars and tried to row towards a tiny island where we could pull the boat out of the water and examine the engine. It was the first time I had attempted to row an inflatable and I found it very difficult to handle. The craft had no keel and, without an effective engine, no directional stability. It must have been a comic sight. Our gyrations in lieu of a course made it clear we were going to miss the island and I could see that we were likely to finish up drifting into the Greenland Sea. It was really all rather depressing. I made one last desperate crank of the engine and it burst into life. I headed at once for the beach at Gåsodden Point and did not stop until we ran aground. Having got safely ashore, I stripped the engine down, examined the spark plug, blew through the fuel lines, but could find nothing wrong. As far as I could tell it was just temperamental.

I now knew what that burly skipper of *The Iskongen* knew all along. Our boat was quite unsuitable for getting us back to Longyearbyen. The Norwegian vessels we had seen were all larger but, more important, they were all fitted with twin engines or carried a spare engine. We were going to have to get a message back to the skipper of *The Iskongen* and tell him we needed to book him to take us back. At base camp, my decision was agreed by all. We had just enough money in the kitty to cover the return charter and it was going to be money very well spent. But how were we going to get a message back, I wondered.

Not long after the incident of engine failure I heard the steady whoosh of rotors – the sound of a helicopter. There were very occasional over-flights by police and scientists using the helicopters based at Longyearbyen. I went outside and spotted it in the distance, coming our way. With the sun roughly behind it, I was perfectly placed to use the heliograph. It descended steadily towards us. The others had joined me and stood with their arms in the air and their legs astride, the international ground to air signal that we wanted to be picked up – the most appropriate signal I knew. The helicopter landed by the huts and a police officer stepped out.

'Do you need to be picked up?' he asked.

I told him we did not need immediate rescue but it was vital to get a message back to the skipper of *The Iskongen* and ask him to pick us up on the 26th of August.

'OK' he said. 'I can try and arrange that for you.'

As it happened, he and the pilot had intended to land at Brucebyen in any event. I think they were just checking up on our expedition and making sure we were not in difficulties or getting up to mischief. We entertained them with coffee. The pilot noticed the heliograph hanging from my neck.

'We spotted that more than ten kilometres away,' he said, nodding with approval.

I have carried that same heliograph with me ever since. Five days later we came back from a field trip and found a scrap of paper weighed down on our mess table with a stone. It read:

To Svalbard Acid Rain Project
m/s 'Iskongen Will Arrive
To Pick You Up'
26ᵀᴴ August!
Best Regards The Governor's Office
PLEASE CLEAN UP AFTER YOU!!!

In the 24 hours of daylight time became irrelevant and our schedules disintegrated. Conventional timing for everyday life became quite random. On one trek, my diary records: 'We had a hot drink before going to bed at about 4.00 a.m. I awoke at seven o'clock but I wasn't sure whether it was 7.00 a.m. or 7.00 p.m.! The sun is in the east so I presume it is a.m.' It just didn't seem to matter. Three o'clock in the afternoon was much the same as three o'clock in the morning. With the exception of breakfast, we did generally eat at the same time and this maintained a sense of brotherhood. There was plenty of adventure to be found during our stay on Spitsbergen. There were deep crevasse fields to be explored and mountains to climb – with caution, as the rocks were generally unstable. Every field trip was an adventure. Whilst the lads were off trying to climb the big Nunataks, Myles and I spent 48 hours in a tent on the glacier taking it in 6 hour shifts to record pH readings of a glacier stream every 30 minutes. During our six weeks we had a full range of weather conditions. My diary records a range from warm, still, clear and bright under a cloudless sky to freezing temperatures, strong winds and heavy rain or snow. We took it all in our stride, but the greatest difficulties were encountered during the warm spells. On one trek, the temperature rose to +13°C. It was nice to wear lighter clothes, but we found that the snow became soft and would not hold our weight; the crunchy gravel-like surface of the glaciers turned dangerously slippery so that even standing was difficult. The rivers that fed into the fjords went from ankle-depth streams to fast, knee-deep torrents that were treacherous to ford. The worst was the softening of the moraine that guarded the terminals of the glaciers – such as we had experienced on that long thirteen and a half hour trek. Occasionally, we saw the stocky little reindeer unique to Svalbard. They are smaller and thicker set than the other species of reindeer and caribou found in the Arctic. The mature animals were cautious and gave us a wide berth but the younger ones were curious. They would move down wind to test our scent and inch carefully towards us. If we sat very still and they were satisfied we were not going to harm them, they would come very close, sniffing the air as they came. When their curiosity was satisfied, they returned to grazing and ignored us. It was charming that wild animals who had little experience of man could be so fearless.

The creatures that weren't so charming were the Arctic terns. They nested on the rocky ground where their eggs were well camouflaged. From a distance it was quite impossible to spot their nests; but if you got too close the seemingly empty sky would suddenly fill with angry and aggressive birds that attacked like hornets. It was like being an extra in Hitchcock's film, *The Birds*. We were fortunate, however, in not having to cope with the adventure of meeting one of the thousands of polar bears living on the islands. Others have met polar bears and some of those have died as a result of such encounters. In the museum in Longyearbyen they have the rifle of a trapper who disappeared in the days before Christmas 1926. Apparently, he was walking over to the home of a friend to celebrate Christmas with him when he was confronted by a bear. His gun jammed and he was unable to protect himself. Nothing was ever heard of him until his rifle and skull were fortuitously found some fifty years later. There is a round of ammunition still jammed in the breach.

By the end of August the sun was noticeably lower in the sky and although it did dip below the horizon there was still 24 hours of daylight, but the evenings were getting very gloomy. Summer was at an end. Soon it would be time for us to pack up the expedition and return home. We had become settled in our hermitage at Brucebyen and there was a feeling of emotional regret amongst us when we saw the little cutter, *The Iskongen*, return to pick us up. It was not until we got back to civilisation that we realised how our appearance had deteriorated – we looked like the scruffiest vagabonds.

We had a few days in Longyearbyen before we were scheduled to fly out. Myles and the lads left me at the camp site in Longyearbyen whilst they went across to the other side of the fjord to camp and explore. I wanted to find out more about the town and its history and regularly walked the four miles from the camp site to explore and talk to its residents.

I climbed up to one of the abandoned coal mines above the town. It seemed odd that the entrances to the mines were well up in the side of the hills rather than deep underground. I sat alone amongst the derelict buildings taking in the scene and thinking of the history of this little town during the Second World War. The non-military aspects of the Treaty of Paris were ignored during hostilities and the islands were occupied by a German garrison, who thus had access to the coal and a base from which to threaten the supply convoys into Russia. They also set up a weather observatory to gather vital meteorological data. In August 1941 an allied force of mixed British and Norwegian commandos raided the islands, rendered the mines inoperative and evacuated the civilian population to England. Then, in 1942, a small Norwegian force attacked and expelled the German garrison and retook the islands. In September of the following year the German battleships *Tirpitz* and *Scharnhorst*, accompanied by 10 destroyers, came into the fjords and completed the devastation of the mines by bombardment. For all I knew, their shells might well have caused the dereliction of the mine entrance where I was seated. The meteorological station had remained hidden until the end of hostilities so the Germans continued sending their reports and managed to avoid detection. Eventually, after the war and when life was beginning to return to normal, the German commanding officer came into town to surrender to the allies. The only person he could find to accept his surrender was the skipper of a Norwegian trawler. Neither knew the correct protocol so they agreed that the handing over of the German officer's pistol would be sufficiently symbolic. By this simple ceremony the small meteorological unit had the dubious distinction of being the last German force to surrender to the Allies.

The museum and the curator were a wonderful source of information. I learned that despite orchestrated culture and sports events among the Soviets and the Norwegians there continued to be friction between the two groups. I had already witnessed some of that at Brucebyen. Certainly the Norwegians were an easy going community and the government officials always helpful, but people in Longyearbyen were quick to make derogatory remarks about their Soviet neighbours. Like most disputes between neighbours, complaints were based on fact but tainted by distorted emphasis and suspicion. For example, the curator of the Norwegian museum complained that the little Soviet museum in Pyramiden contained reference to neither Norwegian presence nor activities on the islands and this suggested that, in truth, Norwegian sovereignty was not truly recognised. Another example was provided by an airport manager who said that whilst he could run daily scheduled flights and numerous charters between Longyearbyen and the Norwegian mainland with a staff of three or four persons, the Soviet airline, Aeroflot, was demanding a staff of 12 to run one flight a month. This, he hinted darkly, was a typical Soviet ploy to swamp the island with their people. Certainly the Soviet communities preferred to keep to themselves and did not welcome uninvited visitors, which exacerbated the suspicions against them. With the East-West Cold War still simmering, one would have had to be naive to ignore the fact that the strategic importance of the islands to both parties would encourage opportunism and paranoia. With hindsight, however, it seems to me that the suspicions of the Norwegians resulted in part from a failure to take account of Soviet administrative inefficiency and a certain natural insularity of the Russian people who sometimes fail to record the history and achievements of other nations.

Happily, in times of crisis, the true spirit of the Arctic prevails between the communities and they quickly unite to form an effective, integrated rescue team. Whilst I was on the islands, a chartered helicopter operating with a Norwegian science team crashed in a remote part of the archipelago. The crash triggered an automatic distress signal from the safety equipment of the downed aircraft. This was picked up by a Russian satellite system which instantly relayed it to Moscow. Moscow telexed the details to an international rescue centre in Paris. Paris relayed them by radio to Longyearbyen and within an hour of the helicopter hitting the ground a rescue team was alongside the wreckage attending to the injured. Sadly, one passenger died of his injuries, but the co-operation of the rescue services could not be faulted. On another occasion, when a cruise ship was on fire and in distress close to Svalbard both Norwegian and Russian helicopters based on Spitsbergen worked efficiently together to get all the passengers and crew off and to safety. In times of trouble, the Arctic people will band together and look after each other, and the Russians and Norwegians were no exception.

From the curator of the little museum and her exhibits, I was able to learn more about some of the expeditions in which Spitsbergen has figured. In 1926 Roald Amundsen flew his airship, *The Norge*, from Spitsbergen to Nome in Alaska, across the Arctic Ocean and over the North Geographic Pole. One expedition trekked from northern Canada to the North Pole and then, as the ice began to break into large pans, drifted on the ice towards Spitsbergen. Some expeditions have failed ignominiously. A Spanish team of motor cyclists arrived determined to ride scramble bikes to the North Pole. They admitted defeat only 100 metres from Longyearbyen's airport, much to the amusement of the locals. The tyres they were using were quite unsuitable for ice. One would have thought the motorcyclists could at least have had a trial run in the Pyrenees, or taken them to some Alpine region and tested the equipment. What gave the local Norwegians the best laugh was a winter expedition from a Mediterranean nation. They arrived in January, well kitted out for the cold, but quite oblivious to the fact that at that latitude, the sun would not rise. They were in what Arctic people call 'the dark period'. Their leader was desperately trying to establish how they had been the victims of a monumental natural disaster.

Our expedition was at an end and I reflected on it. Our scientific data got good feedback from scientific sources over the subsequent years.[5] What was more important to me was the fact that we had eventually gelled as a team. We had all learned the satisfaction which comes from pulling your weight and helping each other in difficult circumstances, and we had all learned to keep our temper and remain tolerant of each other. I think the expedition was a success.

---

[5] Our report is lodged with the RGS and the British Library

# Chapter 3

# GREENLAND

*A visit to the west coast of the world's largest island.*

Greenland is a country that abounds with grand statistics. Its land is the nearest to the North Pole. It is the world's largest island. It has the greatest ice cap in the northern hemisphere. The icebergs that calve from its ice cap have sunk more ships than those from any other – one was responsible for sinking *The Titanic* in April 1912. Any endeavour to write descriptively about such a country runs the risk of sinking into a morass of grandiose statistics. Nonetheless, they are worthy of mention and it would be wrong to omit those which give a reliable picture to the reader.

The geographic North Pole sits in the frozen waters of the Arctic Ocean, and the most northerly tip of land at latitude 82°39' N is Greenland's Kap (Cape) Morris Jesup. The country stretches 1,659 miles (2,670 kilometres) from this northern point to its most southerly tip, Kap Farvel, at 59°46' N. If this, the world's largest island, were to be moved so that Kap Morris Jesup was over London, Kap Farvel would be south of the Atlas Mountains in Algeria. The country's gigantic ice sheet is a dominating influence on all aspects of Greenland: its climate, geography, industry and its people. It is, in places, 10,000 feet (3,077 metres) thick, a mass so heavy that the weight has pushed the land surface under the ice to some 1,000 feet (308 metres) below sea-level. Whilst it is very much smaller than the Antarctic ice cap, scientists have nonetheless suggested that if the water locked up in Greenland's ice were to melt and be released, there would be sufficient to raise the level of the world's oceans by something over 20 feet.

This vast ice sheet is mostly cradled inland by mountains and gives rise to its local name – The Inland Ice. Greenland is generally mountainous and some of the mountains are spectacularly high, the two highest being in the South East. They are Mt Gunnbjørn at 12,139 ft (3,740 metres) and Mt Forel at 11,024 ft (3,400 metres). Between the mountains and the sea is land free of permanent ice. This land is deeply indented with fjords and forms ideal protective harbours.

Unlike Spitsbergen, Greenland does not have the benefit of the warm Gulf Stream to temper its climate. The reverse is true and although Cape Farvel is as far south as the Norwegian capital of Oslo its climate remains truly Arctic. The currents from the Arctic Ocean spill into the Greenland Sea, carrying its ice with it. This ice continues to flow with the currents down the east coast of Greenland, past Cape Farve, then northwards up the Davis Strait, so that it is well into June or July before the coastal waters are navigable. The inland ice causes cold katabatic winds to blow outwards. In the summer there are the typical coastal fogs of the Arctic that chill to the bone, whilst away from the coast, when the sky is clear and the air still, the sun can be fierce and surprisingly hot in sheltered nooks and crannies.

Again, unlike Spitsbergen, an indigenous population has for some 4,500 years enriched Greenland. Like the other Eskimo of Alaska and the Inuit of Canada, they had their origins in Mongolia and their cultural ties with their Alaskan and Canadian cousins are obvious. Although the coastal strip between the seas and the Inland Ice comprises only about 15% of the whole island, its area is equal to that of England and Italy combined. Yet today its meagre population numbers only some 55,000 people spread between 100 settlements and towns. Ninety per cent of this population lives on the west coast. At one point only about 16 miles separates it from Canada's Ellesmere Island and in the geological past it was part of the North American tectonic plate until it split along a line now marked by the Davis Strait. Its geology is therefore very similar to that of northern Canada but its political roots have been deep in Europe for many centuries and this has had a great influence on its people. It is only in the north-east that one will find a few of the true Thule people who originally populated this vast island. Of the rest of the population, 10% is European and the remainder are of mixed Inuit and Danish ancestry with a handful of other immigrants. Although the majority are of mixed Inuit and European stock, they prefer to be called Inuit or Greenlanders. To distinguish them from the Inuit of Canada, this chapter will refer to them as Greenlanders.

Some sources say that the ancient Greeks and Irish were the first Europeans to know Greenland. Certainly the name given to the ancient Eskimo, the Thule people, has its origins in the Greek language.[1] Greenland's involvement with Europe probably started with the colony set up by the Norseman, Eric the Red, who was outlawed from Iceland and, in the year 982 AD, sailed west to seek the land that was rumoured to lie there. He found it and after three years of exploration he was satisfied that the land would support a colony. He is said to be the one to give the island its name. He returned in 986 AD and settled on the west coast. This region of Greenland was then uninhabited – although there was evidence that a previous culture had existed. His colony was successful and it was from here that Leif Ericsson, his son, sailed to North America in the year 1000 – but that is another story. After 200 years there were perhaps some 3,000 persons in the Greenland colony, but then they began to meet with bands of Thule people moving down from the north. The two cultures were not in harmony and both the Icelandic annals and Inuit traditions record evidence of hostile exchanges. About this time, the thirteenth century, the weather conditions deteriorated and by the fourteenth century, the colony was in difficulties. Contact with Europe, then suffering from the Black Death, was lost. By the time the English maritime explorer Sir Martin Frobisher reached Greenland in the sixteenth century, the Inuit were in sole possession of the land. Whatever happened to the Norse colony has never been satisfactorily explained, although traces of their settlement remain.

In later years, whalers from various nations visited the country,

---

[1] Thule is a Greek name for a place or people on the very limit of possible travel

charted its coast and traded with the Inuit. In 1721, the Norwegian missionary Hans Egede started the first European colony at a place where the present capital Nuuk now stands. Egede found no trace of descendants of the Norse colony, but his new settlement survived and spread, introducing Christianity to the Inuit. At the time this new colony was started, the states of Norway and Denmark were united. When that union was eventually dissolved the possession of Greenland was given to Denmark by the Congress of Vienna in 1815. It remained a colony until 1953 when Denmark's constitution was amended to include Greenland as an integral part of the Kingdom. In May 1979 Greenland was granted Home Rule and in 1982, by referendum, voted to withdraw from its membership of the EEC. The principal reason given was that the common directives of the EEC were often unsuitable for Greenland, a place so radically different from the rest of Europe. The Greenlanders now prefer to call their country Kalaallit Nunaat – Land of the People.

The Greenlanders' traditional form of transport in winter is by dog sledge. When the ice breaks, they use boats. There are no railways on Greenland. The larger towns do have road networks, sometimes with fleets of buses, and even taxi services, but no roads stretch beyond the limits of the individual towns. The Greenlanders are experienced seamen and, as virtually all communities are on the coast, there is a reasonably good service of small ships and ferries which ply the coastal waters when ice permits during the relatively short summers. The principal form of long distance travel over the island, however, is by air. After the Second World War there were only three airports that could accommodate transport aircraft so an extensive fleet of large helicopters was developed by Greenlandair. Thus virtually all the communities could be connected and served.

Greenland's unique landscape and efficient transport system effectively lends itself to tourism for all who are adventurous at heart. To be assured of efficient logistical support for trekking into the mountains I chose to travel into this part of the Arctic with a well-known Danish organisation.

Together with my adventurous companions, we set foot on

Greenland at the airport of Sønder Strømfjord.[2] Sited just north of the Arctic Circle, it was built during the Second World War as a staging airport for ferrying flights between the Americas and England. It is now the country's main airport. There I noticed a group of tourists waiting to take the flight back to Denmark. Next to them I felt puny and I couldn't help noticing how pallid we all were by comparison. Their skin was tanned and they radiated health and fitness. I envied them.

We had a little time before we moved on to our first destination and went for a walk to stretch our limbs. Like everything else about the Arctic, my first experience of Greenland came as a surprise. It was early July. There wasn't a cloud in the sky and the fierceness of the sun caught me unawares. I had expected it to be cool, or at least mild, but it was hot – very hot – and I could feel my skin burning in the sunshine. I had been warned to expect the mosquitoes there to be a nuisance, but the creatures that descended on us were unique. 'They are big enough to mate with chickens and have been known to carry off polar bears,' a droll American pilot working for Greenlandair had told me. It's not true of course, but as the mosquitoes swarmed over us, frantically probing for blood, I did not feel his comments were so far removed from fact. Unless you had an allergy to their bites, they were only a nuisance and otherwise quite harmless. The local people seemed to ignore them and I found a good quality insect repellent very effective. Although the insects still swarmed over any exposed flesh, they never settled on areas treated with the repellent.

At this latitude, Greenland was still blessed with a reasonably rich vegetation, albeit dwarf in stature. Around the airport were a few willow trees, but none stood more than shoulder high. Later, when we moved about Disko Bay and the island of Qeqertarsuaq we found birch trees clinging to the ground to avoid the elements. They were virtually without height. Only a very few plants in sheltered places grew as much as knee height. I even found a rhododendron so small that a branch and flower I carelessly

---

[2] Now better known as Kangerlussuaq – 'The Long Fjord'

broke off from the main plant could sit within my hand. Later, during long treks, we were able to find clumps of a form of wild celery that was delicious and refreshing to eat.

On one of Greenlandair's helicopters we flew 200 miles north to the town of Qeqertarsuaq[3] on the island of Qeqertarsuaq. The name means simply 'The Big Island'. From the helicopter we looked down into the many fjords indenting the coast. Strangely, some of them were choked with ice while others were totally clear. I could see nothing to account for this. Between the fjords, the fingers of land were mountainous and we could assess the type of terrain that was later to tax us so physically. Away to the east, the ice cap shimmered in the bright sunlight. Out to sea could be seen remarkable mirages where the icebergs were reflected in the sky immediately above them.

Qeqertarsuaq is one of Greenland's larger towns with a population of about 900. The terrain was predominantly rocky with little soil. 'How could anyone call this country Greenland?' I mused. We collected our belongings and marched, in some semblance of order, to a hut on the edge of town. This was to be our base whilst on the island. It did not take long to explore the little town. In my diary, I described it as 'a shamble of very nice colourful huts set in a surround of litter and assorted rubbish. Huskies were chained up everywhere. Except for the dogs, it seemed a bit of a ghost town. There were lots of buildings but no people.' I later found a small co-operative store that seemed to sell most essential items which, in this society, included hunting knives, rifles and ammunition. A sheltered harbour catered for the larger fishing boats and the smaller motorboats used for seal hunting. There was a church and a school. Sledges sat on the rocks outside most homes and boats of all sizes were either moored in the water or pulled up next to the houses.

As each family seemed to have a team of sledge dogs, the dog population far exceeded the number of Greenlanders. A rough estimate would be nearly 2000 animals and, as evening approached, they all began to howl. One dog would begin, then another

---

[3] Danish name Godhavn

joined in. One howling pack would set off another until their howls reverberated off the surrounding hills in a crescendo of sound. It was an eerie chorus to lull us to sleep in the perpetual daylight that was summer this far above the Arctic Circle.

I awoke early that first morning, immediately alert to the magic of our location. My companions were still just bundles in their sleeping bags as I dressed quickly and walked a short distance out of the town and along the beach, revelling in the clarity and purity of the air. The sand was jet black. I presumed that it was volcanic in origin. Grasses and sedges grew above the high tide line. Off the coast, icebergs of various sizes drifted towards the Davis Strait. Scattered along the beaches like seaweed were broken pieces of ice. Their blue-white colour made them stand out in sharp contrast to the black sand. There was no wind. The sun that would not set in the 24 hours of summer daylight was well up in the sky and gave an illusion of warmth. On an impulse, devoid equally of bravado and logic, I stripped naked, waded into the water and began to swim amongst the bobbing pieces of ice. Initially the sensation was that of being stung by nettles. This was quickly replaced by one of invigoration and I swam strongly for a short way parallel to the beach. Common sense dictated that I should not stay in such cold water more than a few moments, so I soon got out, dressed and went for a run along the beach to generate a little extra warmth. I did not feel chilled; in fact, I positively glowed. Cold water against skin produces an increase of blood supply to the body surface. As I had been warm before the swim and had dressed quickly in good thermal clothing immediately after getting out of the water, the effect was a sensation of warmth rather than chill. Breakfast was being prepared by the time I got back to the hut and it was particularly enjoyable.

The cold clear waters off Greenland are ideal for shrimps and the sea is rich with them, mostly around Disko Bay. There are large trawling fleets operating from Qeqertarsuaq and Ilulissat[4] on the main island. During that first morning, my exploration of the town took me to a shrimp-processing factory by the harbour

---

[4] Danish name Jackobshavn

mouth. There seemed to be neither formalities to be observed nor restrictions on my movements – I just walked in. A shrimp trawler was tied up to the factory's jetty, unloading its catch onto a conveyor belt that lifted it into the building where the crustaceans were processed. First they were boiled in large vats, then passed through automated machinery that shelled and cleaned them and fed the processed shellfish onto an inspection belt, where a number of Greenlandic girls picked out the substandard stock and any extraneous material. The girls were dressed in white overalls, their hair enclosed in head-dresses. Generally young, they were immediately conscious of my presence but raised no objections. They chattered steadily among themselves with the occasional fits of giggles, but they kept on with their work and only occasionally did they lift their eyes to me. I felt inadequate because I knew neither Inuktitut nor Danish, the two languages spoken in Greenland, and could not communicate easily with them. Had I been with the group, one of the Danish leaders would have made himself understood for me. However, on this occasion I felt it would have been a disadvantage. People, wherever they may be, react to groups differently from the way they would to individuals. With a group there is a reserve, a holding back, a sense of difference that inhibits the intimacy that can flow between individuals. On this occasion, I was pleased to be alone and thus more readily accepted as an individual by these girls. No words flowed between us, but there was a rich communication with the eyes that radiated a friendly curiosity and left me feeling charmed and, I confess, a little shy.

Much of our time in Greenland was spent trekking in the mountains or along the coast to absorb the country's stark beauty and feel the loneliness of the surroundings. Such treks were spectacular, invigorating and demanding, but more intriguing for me were the occasions when I found myself integrating with the Greenlanders. The more I mixed with them, the quicker the stereotype image of 'Eskimo' dissipated and was replaced with a recognition that I was amongst a sparse rural community, the individuals of which would have fitted comfortably into almost any other rural society in England or, probably, anywhere else in the world. Their desires and needs were the same as most other people's; only the uniqueness of their environment dictated their methods of achieving them.

Many of the everyday activities of these rural people were the same as those one would expect to find in any other coastal rural community: collecting provisions or fresh water, cleaning and maintaining their homes, repairing their boats and fishing. At certain times of the year, catching a particular local fish[5] presents nothing in the way of a challenge. These small fish, measuring about six to nine inches in length, virtually give themselves up to capture. I thought of the legends of lemmings throwing themselves off the cliffs of Norway into the sea; here, on a beach by Qeqertarsuaq, the *angmassat* seemed to thrust themselves onto the sand in an equally illogical pursuit of death and all one needed to collect them efficiently was a hand net. They were gathered from the beach, dried and used to feed the fishermen's dogs. I never found out whether the Greenlanders ate the fish themselves.

As a group, we had some spectacular treks into the mountains and temporary camps at other locations along the coast. I thought I was fit before setting off to Greenland, but I had a real struggle keeping up with the others on the climbs through the hills and mountains. There were no tracks or trails. Outside the town there was just virgin land. We picked our route by eye, choosing the terrain that looked easiest on the way to wherever one wanted to go. Because of the permafrost surface water could only flow away in the rivers. It could not sink into the subsoil so, off the rocks, the earth was wet and spongy in the valleys. We found it much more comfortable following the contours of the hill sides where the ground was drier.

Sometimes we would take a day trip and pick our way to the top of a mountain ridge whence we could get superb views out into Disko Bay to watch the icebergs drift slowly and majestically northwards along the coast into Baffin Bay. In places they were tightly packed into a conglomerate of white ice; in others they were scattered and isolated. One or two seemed as big as small

---

[5] I understood this fish to be called 'angmassat'

villages. Their movement was not perceptible and it would be months, or even years, before they turned south with the current back into the Davis Strait and then into the Western Atlantic where their movement would be monitored by the Canadian and United States Coast Guard as they drifted south into the shipping lanes.

July, being early summer, we were blessed with good weather during our time in Greenland. The skies were clear and the sun fierce but on occasions patches of fog drifted in. When we descended from high ground where we had been in the sun, entering the fog was a very chilling experience. We could not take any weather condition for granted.

Some of our treks took us along the coast. On these walks we passed towering cliffs, some of which showed erosion by the sea 100 or so feet (30 metres) above sea level. Most curious!

'Was the sea level much higher in the geological past?' I asked our guide.

'No,' was his reply. 'It is because in the past this area had an icecap that forced the level of the land down. That is when the erosion took place. Now that the icecap has retreated, the land, relieved of the weight of ice, has risen back up to its present height.'

Such an obvious example of geological movement was awe-inspiring.

After a few days, our group travelled by a small supply boat to Saqqaq[6] on the mainland. The word means 'Sunny Side'. The passage took only a few hours but it was a most memorable journey. The sea was packed with ice and although our little ship was designed for such conditions it could only progress by picking the channels of clear water and nudging its way through any ice blocking its way. At frequent intervals one of the crew members climbed the mast to assess the easier route and would shout down his observations to the skipper at the helm. Although the day was sunny, it was bitterly cold because of a light wind and the forward motion of the ship, but not one member of my party retreated

---

[6] The old spelling is Sarqaq

indoors to the warmth of the cabin. This was an experience we were not going to miss.

Saqqaq is a community of barely 200 inhabitants[7] nestling on some rocks by a natural harbour. It had a church and a community hall. As a group we were self-sufficient, which was just as well as its co-operative store seemed to carry less stock than the average British newsagent. I think the only thing we contributed to the village was the rent for a small wooden building as our base camp. I loved Saqqaq and to this day think of it as my personal Shangri-La.

A senior elder in the town had an unexpected and indulgent occupation. This was tending his greenhouse. It was sited on some level ground behind his home and in it a variety of flowers and vegetables was grown. With great pride he escorted me around his treasures explaining that it was 'his hobby and absorbing interest'.

'Where do you get your seeds from?' I asked.

'Oh, I have to get them by mail order, but it is very difficult and takes a long time,' he explained.

He did a lot of propagation from cuttings and his prized possession was an Alaskan Rose. It was not a richly scented species with lush growth but, nonetheless, a remarkable plant to be found growing at that latitude and in that environment. It was, he boasted, the most northerly rose in the world. Whether or not his boast was justified I do not know, but his enthusiasm captivated me. His vegetables even included such delicate plants as tomatoes and beans. Outside, in a cold frame, grew sturdy rhubarb plants revelling in the 24 hours of daylight that provided a vigorous growing period. The big Russian greenhouse on Spitsbergen[8] had the advantage of a large power station nearby and it was fitted with heating and lighting so that the plants could cope with the long Arctic night, but this man's modest greenhouse seemed no different from any other domestic greenhouse one might find at more temperate latitudes – except that through the glass could be

---

[7] 180 people (2005 figure)
[8] See Chapter 2

seen a spectacular display of icebergs sailing almost imperceptibly by. I can offer no greater explanation for his success than the passionate care he devoted to the plants which somehow defeated the harshness of the Greenland winters.

There are many wonderful examples of exotic plants growing wild on the tundra, but almost all are in miniature, so I was a little taken aback when I chanced on a graveyard and saw from a distance that most of the graves were richly covered in large colourful flowers. As I moved closer I was surprised to see that these included daffodils, tulips, carnations, irises, lilies and a variety of similar blooms. On examination most proved to be of plastic, though some were silk. This struck me as a curious comment on the Greenlanders' opinion of their own flora which I had found so attractive.

As a group we continued our walks and treks into the mountains. I elected to go on a five day excursion – the longest so far – and it turned out to be my most challenging. Because of its length, each of us was carrying much heavier loads of food and fuel than usual, but when we set off I didn't think the additional weight was going to cause me too many problems. Our tour leader took us along a valley for some hours where the going was relatively easy. We then started to climb a steep hillside to a lake he had found on his map. It was some 1000 feet (308 metres) up. I was about 20 years older than the rest of the group and perhaps a little over weight – the life of an airline pilot tends to be a bit sedentary. This combination very quickly began to tell and I started to trail behind. I couldn't turn back, for we were too far into the trek, and I couldn't dump the load, as everything was essential. I had to keep going with as much tenacity as I could muster. The others arrived at the lake a good hour before me and had already set up a camp – minus the tent I was carrying. I felt humiliated to have performed so poorly. I was also extremely tired, but I stayed awake long enough to have a decent meal before crawling into my sleeping bag. I looked about me. It was a truly beautiful spot. It might have been devoid of tall or lush vegetation but there were clumps of diminutive flowers between the rocks and in various places patches of deep moss. The high peaks of the mountains still carried a mantle of snow. The lake itself was small and half covered in ice, the water's suspended glacial flow giving it an unusual pale blue appearance that was most attractive. I was trembling with fatigue and ached in every limb. I realised that I was in a dangerous state for a middle-aged man and, for the first time in my life, became convinced I would have a heart attack and be beyond reach of proper medical aid. As I pulled the sleeping bag over my head, I had only two thoughts: one, that it was a pity to kill myself at so relatively young an age, but if I had to go, it couldn't be in more beautiful surroundings, and two, that my dear wife was going to be upset and I was very sorry about that, but our children were off our hands and I knew she would cope with life alone. The oddest thing was that I was totally calm and resigned to my fate and without any fear. It was with the greatest surprise that I awoke the next morning feeling refreshed and ready for another day trekking in the mountains. It was indeed a beautiful day and I felt that, from now on, life could only be a bonus. I did not then know that my subsequent travels in the Arctic would bring far greater challenges, dangers and hardships and I would develop a fitness and fortitude to face them with resolution. Breakfast that day was wonderful beyond belief. The rest of that long trek took us between high peaks, down slopes strewn with boulders, and along rivers where unusual rock formations towered above us. Every day was tiring, but I never again felt that utter fatigue which had so nearly wiped me out on the first day. I should add here that, when I returned home to England at the end of my Greenland adventure, I had lost some 15 lbs in weight and needed a piece of rope to keep my trousers up.

One day back at Saqqaq, when I was walking through the village, I saw a woman drawing water from a communal tap. She had her very young daughter with her and each had a pail, which they had just finished filling. They picked up their load and headed for home. The young girl was managing, but it was a terrific load for such a youngster.

'Can I help carry your daughter's load?' I offered, hoping that the mother could understand English.

'No', she responded. 'My daughter must learn to be strong.' It could be that the mother did not want any form of involvement with a stranger, but I think the truth was simply what she said. In a small community like that, all, including young children, must learn to work and make their contribution to the unit. Their determination impressed me.

Most of the people of the Arctic still depend on hunting and fishing for both their subsistence and income[9] and the community of Saqqaq is no exception. So many of us in Europe have a wide choice of food and clothing and we are generally able to rely on an earned income to provide for ourselves and family. This luxury can produce a sanctimonious attitude towards hunting and the hunters. I have no love of killing and try to remain at peace with nature and God's creatures, preferring not to dwell on the means by which food arrives on my plate at meal times. This peace of mind was rudely disturbed when I came upon a family of Greenlanders who had just returned from a successful seal hunt. The animals were being deftly skinned and butchered on the rocks by the water's edge. The fact that these were a common unendangered species of seal did nothing to temper my shock at seeing their fate but, after contemplating the scene, I became more pragmatic and rational. The seals had been shot with a rifle so their death would have been quick. The clothing of the family appeared to have been made of cotton and nylon. They had used an open fibreglass boat fitted with an outboard engine to hunt their prey. Some of the hunters wore rubber waterproof boots and overalls. The women wore earrings. All wore watches. A transistor radio stood on the rocks and played music. I could see no reason why this family should not possess these simple items and could think of no practical alternative method by which they could have provided for themselves and acquired these possessions without making their living from hunting the sea around them and trading in their produce. I still have no love for killing but am now ready to defend the rights of the indigenous people of the Arctic to hunt, and profit from, the fruits of the sea.[10]

---

[9] See Chapter 4
[10] Note my conversation with the Inuit Roy in Chapter 5

An important part of the Greenland diet is whale meat. The skin of the animal is considered a great delicacy. In the days before imported foods it was probably their most important source of vitamin C. In Qeqertarsuaq I saw a man come through the little town selling whale meat from a wheelbarrow. In Ilulissat, the whaling boats tied up on the quayside and sold their catch directly to the townspeople gathering on the dock. I mused that the bureaucracies in many countries would never tolerate such a casual way of distributing food to the general public, but here, perhaps because of the cool climate and the natural approach to life, the people did not seem to come to any harm.

The Greenlanders' life of hunting is deeply ingrained in their culture. To disturb that culture abruptly is to invite trouble. An example of this can be seen in the ghost town of Qutdligssat on the north-east of Qeqertarsuaq Island, a short but chilly ride from Saqqaq in an open boat. Coal had been found on the island and an attempt was made to exploit this mineral resource. The Danish KGH[11] agency, then administering Greenland, set up a mine, with facilities for the locally recruited miners and their families. A community was built, complete with houses, a school, shops, a community centre and a hospital. The mine did not succeed, however, and was eventually abandoned. The KGH agency, mindful of its responsibilities to the community it had created, collected the miners and their families and took them to Ilulissat, the nearest large town, where they were given accommodation and welfare support. No doubt the agency's intention was honourable and caring, but it had failed to take account of the effect of its actions on the culture of the people. Uprooted from that way of life, then transported into an industrial and subsequently urban existence without the facilities to return to traditional pursuits many suffered a loss of identity and fell victims to idleness and drink.

When I was in West Greenland, the town of Ilulissat was the second largest on Greenland, after the island's much larger capital

---

[11] Kongelig Grønlandske Handel (Royal Greenland Trading Company)

city, Nuuk.[12] Ilulissat has the vestige of a shopping street and a museum. The museum was built in a modern style and brightly coloured. Outside and in front was the reconstruction of an ancient sod and stone house, a striking comparison between the ancient forms of living and the comforts of the modern buildings. The less authentic, but no doubt practical, addition of a casement window rather spoilt the illusion of a genuine building. Modern apartment blocks have since been put up, but around the edges of the town are examples of a more traditional style of dwelling.

I was glad to have experienced the smaller communities of Qeqertarsuaq and Saqqaq before moving to Ilulissat. It would be difficult to describe it as a large city, but the troubles of an urban community were perhaps in evidence. Its citizens were friendly and quick to respond genially to a stranger's approach, but they lacked the warmth and openness of the people of the smaller communities. For the first time I saw some evidence of drunkenness in the streets. These drunks, however, were not aggressive nor a nuisance to others. Their expressions were vacant and their gait was reminiscent of small boats endeavouring to sail across a strong current, so that their direction of travel did not always coincide with the direction in which their bodies faced.

One day, I chanced upon a wedding at the Church of Zion and witnessed a similar rejection of the local flora in favour of artificial replicas from abroad as I had observed in the rural graveyard. The bride carried a bouquet of silk flowers of temperate species instead of the attractive miniatures that abounded locally. The costumes, however, were sufficient distraction from the anomaly of artificial flowers. At this wedding, the bride and groom, and most of the lady guests present, wore national dress. The groom's outfit consisted of a hooded white smock, black trousers, and the seal skin boots known as 'mukluks'. The smock and trousers appeared to be made of cotton, or similar fabric. The bride, and most of the lady guests, wore brightly coloured costumes. The style of these was uniform, but the designs, colours and patterns were individual. Their bodice and sleeves were composed of multi-

---

[12] The town of Sisimiut (Danish name Holsteinsborg) now claims to be the second largest

coloured beads covering a fabric blouse. Their pants were of sealskin and these fitted into the tops of their highly decorated white mukluks. There was a colourfully embroidered cummerbund about the waist and the tops of the mukluks were fringed with lace. All but one of the ladies wore white mukluks. The exception was an older woman whose mukluks were red.[13]

Ilulissat, though urban, was fascinating. One day I walked out to Semmermiut at the back of the town, where there were high cliffs that looked across the Ilulissat Fjord. In the fjord were majestic icebergs calving from the inland ice. I had been told that in the distant past, during times of starvation when the hunting failed, the older women who contributed the least would relieve the pressure of the food supplies by jumping to their deaths from this point. It was stark and lonely on those cliffs and in the low light, still air and calm I could easily imagine their ghosts about me.

The Ilulissat fjord is one of the most spectacular locations for ice. At a number of points, the inland ice, under the relentless pressure generated by its own weight, oozes out of its cradle of mountains and calves into the fjords. The Ilulissat is one of the most magnificent, choked with ice that is sometimes moving at the rate of about eight feet a day. That may not seem much, but when you consider these icebergs are the size of hills, you realise that it is very impressive indeed. With a sound reminiscent of distant thunder the mountains of ice creak and groan their noisy way down the fjords to the sea, then float majestically into the Atlantic. To sail between these enormous bergs that tower some 200 or more feet above the water is an awe-inspiring experience, particularly in a small boat. In the late summer, the temptation to get too close is fraught with danger. Chunks of ice the size of houses break off without warning and fall into the fjord, creating spectacular waves that would swamp any boat nearby. Five of us, including our tour leader Jørgen, hired a small boat to take us into this wonderland. Our skipper stayed well away from the large

---

[13] I did not manage to establish the significance of the red mukluks

bergs but he did bring us in sufficiently close to dazzle us with their grandeur. It was a sight I shall never forget and my spirits soared.

Floating on its own was a flat table of ice about 40 yards across, with its top no more than six feet out of the water. The temptation was too much for me. The air was still and the sun was strong. The conditions were perfect. I persuaded the skipper to pull alongside and let me off onto the ice table. After I had stripped off, I got him to back away a reasonable distance, lowered myself into the water and swam back to the boat. I confess it was an act of unmitigated bravado and the sense of smugness took a long time to evaporate.

A day or two later, we heard that a French team were going to perform a stunt. A Frenchman was going to be flown over the fjord and, wearing a thermal wet suit, would jump from the helicopter into the water. A rescue boat was to stand by with a medical team in attendance. Film and television crews would record the event. Our team leader had met them in the Ilulissat hotel and they had told him about their plans.

'Oh,' said Jørgen, 'one of my party goes swimming naked there every day!'

At the town's museum, I talked to an information officer. She was a Dane who had lived in Greenland for many years and tried to pass on to me her local knowledge of the area. I mentioned the drunkenness and she conceded that it was a problem that was proving difficult to solve. A limitation of the sales of alcohol did not seem to be effective.

'I don't suppose you have much serious crime here,' I observed.

'Oh yes we do,' was her immediate response. 'It was only three, or maybe four years ago that two hunters got into a drunken argument and one shot the other. It was terrible. There is terrible crime here in Greenland.'

I nodded gravely in response. Every killing is tragic, but if the killing she referred to had occurred in the temperate world, it would hardly have received a mention in the newspapers. Rather than being horrified by the event, I took comfort in the thought that there was at least one place in the world where a single drunken murder in a three or four year period was considered evidence of serious criminal activity.[14]

Back at Sønder Strømfjord we waited for the flight to take us back to Europe. The plane came in and amongst the arriving passengers was a party of tourists with rucksacks and walking boots. I looked at them and thought what a pallid and puny bunch they were. Beside them my group was tanned and radiated health and fitness. I thought how wonderful it was to be as healthy and fit as we were.

Tourism continues to develop in Greenland. They now even have their own web page on the Internet.[15] I am happy for the source of much needed revenue that this will bring the people, but am a little fearful of what it may do to them and the environment. I hope that only those who care about the environment will be attracted to this island that has so fascinated me.

It was with considerable pleasure some twenty years after my visit to Greenland that I was able to return with my wife. It was her first time in the Arctic and she deserved to experience it in a measure of comfort. Cruise ships were now plying their trade into the region, so we chose one that took in Ilulissat and organised an excursion by small fishing boats into the ice-filled Ilulissat Fjord. I had often told her about my visit but she found the experience awe-inspring – and, once again, it awed me. During my first visit, I had gathered material about the town in the form of photographs and a description of the fjord in winter when it was frozen solid. Now, 20 years later, I asked the Danish skipper of our boat when the sea froze over.

'I've been up here for ten years, and I've never known it to freeze over,' was his reply. Could global warming have made such a difference so soon, I wondered?

We were blessed with clear blue skies and the same strong sun I had experienced before. After our trip amongst the icebergs when it was cold, I took my wife for a walk to Semmermiut. She too learned that it could be surprisingly hot in the Arctic. This return

---

[14] Compare this with the Canadian Chapter 4 and Chapter 5
[15] http://www.greenland-guide.gl/default.htm

## THE WARM ARTIC

trip on a cruise ship with my wife gave me the opportunity to see something of the southern part of Greenland as we went down past the capital Nuuk and the southern town of Qaqortoq.[16] It came as a considerable surprise how lush the south was by comparison. I realised for the first time that the Norseman, Eric the Red, had had every justification to call the country 'Greenland'.[17]

---

[16] Danish name Julianehab
[17] My visit to East Greenland is recorded in Chapter 10

# Chapter 4

# CANADA'S NUNAVUT

*A winter's experience amongst the Inuit and those working to help them.*

Canada has one million square miles of territory that can truly be described as Arctic. The climate is harsh and typically continental. The Rocky Mountains in the west block the mild and moist westerly or south-westerly Pacific air that might otherwise ameliorate the severity of this region. It is covered with tundra composed of mosses and lichen. The permafrost stretches as far south as latitude 55°N. Some areas have snow cover and ice fields for most of the year. It is indeed a cold and savage wilderness.

The white man, or Kabloona,[1] was a late arrival to the Canadian north.[2] Until the twentieth century, his interests were in the pursuit of furs in the forests south of the tree line. To the north, his principal interest was the search for the North West Passage. Sir Martin Frobisher led the way in 1576 and was followed in the seventeenth and eighteenth centuries by other adventurers. Eventually, the Royal Navy took up the search for the North West Passage in the middle of the nineteenth century with an expedition led by Sir John Franklin. This ill-fated expedition was eventually lost without survivors. In searching for Franklin, the process of mapping the Arctic Archipelago was begun, but not completed until the employment of aerial photographic reconnaissance after the Second World War.

---

[1] Kabloona is the Inuktitut word for any person who is not Inuit
[2] Chapter 1 gives an account of the indigenous peoples' entry to the Arctic

## THE WARM ARTIC

Few places in the world are as isolated as the Arctic and sub-Arctic wastes of Northern Canada. In the early years of the Kabloona's penetration of the area, it was only the Royal Canadian Mounted Police (representing the government), fur traders and missionaries who ventured into this wilderness. Theirs was an unique existence and they referred to the rest of the world as 'the outside'.

Furs were always important to the Inuit. Their very survival depended upon the warmth of the skins of caribou, polar bear and seal. Although they now use the modern technical fibres brought by the white man, there is no doubt that the thermal properties and comfort of good furs are superior. In Canada's north, fur was the only product of significance that could be exchanged for imported goods. With the European quest for fur, the Inuit, like those from south of the tree line, took advantage of the demand. They could improve their hunting and chances of survival by bartering furs for guns, ammunition, and other modern hunting equipment. They could also improve their standard of living with better homes and modest luxuries which could now be afforded. In time, their bartering with skins and furs developed into a cash economy. This, their only source of an independent income, was shattered when the overzealous 'Animal Rights' movement in Europe destroyed the market in furs. How were the independent Inuit going to buy clothing made from fibres, heat their home with fuel oil, or buy guns and ammunition with which to hunt if they lost their source of income? In protecting the un-endangered seals of the arctic the 'Animal Rights' movement in Europe had successfully endangered the modern independent Inuit. These self-reliant people were now faced with returning to the more primitive conditions of living and hunting with ancient tools to maintain their independence, or seeking employment with the Kabloona and/or help from social organisations and, in doing so, prostituting the very independence that had made them such remarkable people.

By the 1930s it was recognised that the extreme north of the isolated North West Territories was so bereft of population and so generally neglected there was a danger of foreign powers claiming that the archipelago was 'terra nullius' and making territorial claims. The inducement to do so was the promise of mineral resources – particularly oil – and the strategic importance of the islands for military purposes. To counter this, the Canadian government induced the Inuit to return to the extreme north at Resolute Bay and Grise Fjord. With stoicism, those communities have survived and developed although, even today, neither can boast a population of more than 200 persons. Involvement with the white men and the encroachment of the twentieth century caused a loss of identity, culture, traditions and even language, particularly where there was a significant white population which tended to overshadow Inuit culture. The relocation of the Inuit to Resolute Bay and Grise Fjord exacerbated this process.[3] Now the sense of nationalism amongst the Inuit of northern Canada is strong. Some 80% of the population are Inuit. They have pressed hard for a land claim on the territory they call their own and have been successful. On April 1st 1999, the Northwest Territories divided into two parts: the Eastern portion known as Nunavut (which means 'Our Land' in Inuktitut), and the western territory which retains the name of 'The North West Territories'. With a population density of 0.009 persons per square kilometre (compare the United Kingdom's figure of 228.0 and China's 102.0),[4] Nunavut is not an independent nation, nor is it intended to be. Its creation will give its people better mineral and royalty rights and better representation in wildlife management, resource management and environmental control, and a capital transfer of payment of funds to the people and other fiscal benefits that will perhaps permit them to maintain their independence into the twenty-first century.

It was a chance remark made by a Norwegian on Spitsbergen that sent me to this Arctic wilderness. It had been summer – for what that was worth – and this Norwegian had expressed some reservations about the summer visitors he had met on the island.

---

[3] This contention is supported by a criminology research study by Professor Darryl Wood of the University of Alaska, 'Research on Crime in Canadian Inuit Communities,' Basis for Doctorate, (October 6, 1997)

[4] Philip's Universal Atlas (London: G. Philip & Son, 1981)

'It's all very well coming up here in the summer,' he said, 'but it's the winter that sorts out the men from the boys.' I congratulated him on his grasp of English idioms but quietly mulled over the implication that, as I had not yet spent any time experiencing the Arctic's winters, I might well be a boy and not a man. It was a challenge I could not let pass.

In the research library of the National Meteorological Office in Bracknell I discovered that Resolute Bay has a cold weather record far more severe than Spitsbergen and even more severe than many of the research stations on Antarctica. January, February and March are the coldest months. At latitude 74°45′ N, the sun barely manages to drag itself up to the horizon at noon on the 6th of February. By the middle of February the midday sun is just high enough to give light for photography and fits neatly into the middle of the region's coldest period when the mean temperature would be −33°C.

Resolute Bay was a good choice for other reasons. It is easily accessible by air and there is a resident Inuit community with whom I could try to mix and to whom I could turn for help if I was in trouble. Furthermore, a co-operative store is available for provisions. I have to admit that I was also influenced by the fact that there was a resident nursing station in the community should I fall victim to the cold. As Resolute Bay was on the route for those hardy souls who attempt the treks to the North Pole, the community had an excellent expedition outfitter[5] that might be able to supply me with items of equipment. Bazel and Terry Jesudason ran the outfitters and generally organised everything from Bed and Breakfast to getting aircraft and supplies to the North Pole itself. They proved to be very helpful.

I set off with a tent – and a hot water bottle – to discover whether I was to be classified as a man or a boy. On the flight north from Montreal I sat next to some Canadian Naval Officers who had some duties to perform at Resolute Bay. They asked what I was planning. I told them. There was silence for a minute or two. 'Jeese!' was their response. They then told me what they

---

[5] The business no longer operates as an expedition outfitter

called an old Eskimo joke: 'Two polar bears met outside an igloo. One said to the other, "This is the sort I like best; all crunchy on the outside and chewy on the inside."' That gave me something to think about. How would the polar bears react to a tent? The skies were clear for most of the flight and I was able to take in the vastness of the snow covered scene below. It seemed endlessly devoid of any visible sign of vegetation or man. Cloud cover started to build up as we approached our destination. I got a few glimpses of the frozen surface of Lancaster Sound which forms the main entrance to the North West Passage and then I lost sight of the surface as the cloud thickened. It was obviously very blustery as we got down to lower levels. The air was turbulent and I could feel the wind-sheer as the aircraft lurched its way towards the runway. The pilots were obviously having a hard time keeping the airspeed stable as I could hear very large shifts in engine power setting as they tried to adjust for the gusts. I'm sure they were as pleased as I was to get the aircraft firmly on the ground.

Before I left England, my great fear had been that there would be a recurrence of the occasional freak conditions when the temperature in February had been as high as $-3.9°C$. I need not have worried. On arrival, the meteorological office at the airport recorded a low of $-38°C$ and a wind speed of over 40 miles per hour with gusts up to 50 or 60 miles per hour. I reckoned that was a wind chill equivalent of $-62°C$ or below.

Maybe I carry with me preconceived ideas when I set off on my travels and, of course, such ideas are usually wrong and can be dangerous. The community at Resolute Bay itself was much as I had imagined, however: a circular collection of mostly small wooden houses situated at the end of a road four miles from the airport. It was set on mainly level ground between a low range of hills and the coast. The coast was not obvious because the sea was frozen to a depth of some six feet and, as the tide was moderate and the seabed relatively free of rocks, the surface of the ice was comparatively smooth. It was the smoothness of the sea ice alone that distinguished it from the land. A layer of snow covered everything. Every thing is so novel in the Arctic that I am surprised when I venture up north and on this occasion it was the thinness of the depth of snow that surprised me. I had thought that waist depth would be the norm but, except where the drifts had accumulated around some obstruction and packed deep and firm, the surface snow was only an inch or two deep with blades of grass and stones poking through the surface. I didn't expect this, but I should have done. The high Arctic is a cold desert with very little precipitation. The intense cold keeps the snow in crystal form and prevents it from soaking into the ground or evaporating. Strong winds, like the one that had greeted me, swirl and spin the hard flakes and move them around so that as fast as they are blown away from one spot, the crystals are replaced from elsewhere. In the strong wind, the blowing crystals of snow give the surface the appearance of being molten with an ankle deep milky flow in which everything and everyone appears to be standing. There is the illusion of an infinitely wide but shallow, fast flowing river flooding the land. In my previous experiences in the Alps and elsewhere when the snow was deep and crisp, I had heard it crunch underfoot, much like footfalls on a gravel path, but here where the snow had accumulated and packed down with the wind it is so dry that it squeals like an injured pig when walked on. It is a most uncanny and eerie sound.

With some difficulty, I set about putting up my tent on the edge of the community. An Inuk[6] man picked his way over to see what I was doing. The deep hood of his parka was pulled close about his face.

'An ice house is warmer,' he ventured.

'I don't know how to build an igloo,' I replied, hoping he would teach me but he made no offer.

I got the tent erect and started to unpack my rucksack, thinking the best thing I could do was to crawl into my down sleeping bag, try and make a hot drink and endeavour to get warm again.

'What sort of heater do you have?' he asked.

'I haven't got a heater,' I replied sheepishly.

'I wouldn't do that if I were you,' he responded and walked away shaking his head in consternation.

---

[6] Inuk is singular; Inuit is plural

What was left of my already thin confidence promptly evaporated.

Before leaving England I had, of course, taken advice from as many experienced Arctic men as I could find, but to work out the logistics of carrying out simple every day functions in those conditions requires personal experience of the Arctic winter and I had no previous experience. I had been assured by medical men and Arctic travellers that when the cold becomes life threatening, the discomfort is such that there is no question of sleeping and dying in your sleep. A person who was simply asleep would be awoken by the discomfort and perish only if he could do nothing about his situation. That was one small comfort. A much greater comfort was that a mere 150 yards away was Bazel and Terry's building and I knew that it was well heated and the doors were unlocked. I could always crawl in there if I got desperate.

My first night was the worst I have ever suffered. Tired from my efforts, I crawled into my sleeping bag to try and get warm. By the light of a candle I was mesmerised watching my breath rise a foot or two as a thick mist, freeze into flakes of ice and settle back onto my bedding to form a thin layer of snow. The hot water bottle that I had packed as an after-thought turned out to be my favourite piece of expedition equipment. It was positively life saving. In those temperatures, exposed flesh starts to freeze in less than a minute and many simple tasks could not be accomplished whilst wearing gloves. The warmth of the hot water bottle was a quick and convenient way to stop hands freezing. Filling it with warm water had been one of my initial tasks, but still I could not get warm. My movements became sluggish and I realised what an incredible achievement it was for those early Arctic dwellers to adapt to these conditions and thrive. Simple tasks had become a real problem. The stiffness of my chilled hands made it difficult for me to close the zip of my sleeping bag and that made me more sympathetic of the arthritic elderly who cannot tolerate the cold and have difficulty buttoning a cardigan.

I had just drifted off into an exhausted sleep when something like an air-raid siren sounded just a few yards away from my tent. For a moment I thought this was the day of judgement and it must be Gabriel's horn summoning me before my maker. At that moment, the flames of Purgatory, or even Hell itself, seemed to me an attractive alternative to the interior of my tent. I did nothing. The siren stopped and slumber eventually returned.

I managed to sleep fitfully through until the following morning and then that sound – like the squealing of injured pigs – told me that people were approaching my tent.

'Are you all right in there, Norman?'

It was my Inuk friend and some others who were staying with Bazel and Terry.

'No. I'm frozen,' I replied.

But the fact that I could speak was sufficient to reassure them that I was perfectly all right. I came out of the tent clutching a hot cup of tea I had just brewed on my little primus stove. I was beginning to thaw and the tea was working miracles for me. There were three of them: the Inuk I had previously met, another Inuk and a Kabloona whom I later learnt were social workers doing a job in the area. I was beginning to feel that life was returning to me and the four of us talked for a bit. Apparently, the siren that had awoken me during the night went off at 11.00 p.m. each evening to summon children back to their homes. The Inuk social worker wore a jacket but had neither hat nor parka and he stood there hopping from one foot to the other trying to stay warm and shield his bare ears from the icy wind. He was clearly uncomfortable.

'I didn't think you guys got cold,' I said.

'Oh, yes we do!' he replied, and I began to feel a little better knowing that I was not the only one feeling miserably cold.

After my breakfast, I went in to see Bazel as I now had a better idea of how to increase my level of comfort. I hired a large Arctic pyramid tent so as to give myself more room and asked what he could suggest to improve the insulation of my bedding. I knew that bear skins, particularly polar bear skins, were the ultimate choice of bedding, but they were too precious to lend to the likes of me.

'Caribou skins are the answer,' he said without hesitation.

I remembered the Norwegians saying that reindeer skins were excellent and the caribou are almost identical to reindeer. I borrowed two caribou skins. One went under my legs to protect the sleeping bag from the ice and the other over my legs. Bazel and the Norwegians were right: the caribou skins made all the difference; they are nature's electric blankets. I won't say that I was blissfully comfortable but, thus equipped, and beginning to adjust to my environment, I was able to elevate my thoughts from pure survival to the real business of learning something of the place and the people about me.

In discovering how to cope with this environment, all sorts of other difficulties came my way. They were the sort of difficulties that those, like me, who are accustomed to the more genteel temperate zones of the world, may not expect. The first time I used my camera, I got a nasty shock when the cold metal stuck to my eyebrow and I had trouble freeing it. I found that the ink in my ball-point pen froze and I was forced to use a pencil for making notes. I had brought a reasonable quantity of raisins to eat as a quick high-energy snack, but when I put them in my mouth, I found they had frozen to the texture of gravel and become very difficult and unpleasant to eat. The Mars bars that I enjoy had to be attacked with an ice axe before I could eat them. My toothpaste froze solid and had to be boiled before I could clean my teeth. So too the syrup I had brought to sweeten my morning porridge. On the plus side was the ease of dealing with liquid spills: just wait a few moments, then pick up the frozen liquid and throw it out of the tent! In temperatures where exposed flesh freezes in under a minute even the most basic aspects of living in a tent required careful thought and planning.

Bazel and Terry were models of Canadian hospitality. Terry was a native Canadian and looked after the Bed and Breakfast side of their business. Bazel was a Tamil born in Madras, who had trained as an engineer and emigrated to Canada many years previously. They had married in Yellowknife and decided to set up the expedition business in Resolute Bay. They had built up a good reputation throughout the world of expeditions and adventure tourism and it was thus I had found them. It was still too early in the year for the treks to the North Pole, and far too early for the usual adventure tourists so, aside from the visiting social workers, they were not particularly busy. Hot coffee was always to hand and anyone in need of a cup could walk in and help themselves and socialise with anyone else who was passing.

The two social workers who had paid me a visit on my first morning, the Kabloona called Cliff and the Inuk named Innukie, were enjoying Terry's coffee when I popped in and they were happy to talk to me about their work. This part of the north was something of a problem area. 'Hard drugs' and 'career opportunities' seemed to sum up the two major problems. Hard drugs had found their way up from the south and spread like wildfire amongst the Inuit communities. The abuse was so extensive that family groups who had managed to resist the pressures were in the minority and frequently marginalised by the rest of their kinfolk. When living in low density population areas, people are very dependent on each other, so to be marginalised by the majority of the community was making life intolerable for those who wanted to avoid the drug scene. The question of career prospects was nearly as depressing. The opportunities for subsistence living were steadily waning and, although education had improved dramatically, those children who had intellectually enriched themselves and gone south in pursuit of higher education and professional training had no chance to use their skills in the restricted communities of their homes. They were destined either to break from their families and move away from the homeland they loved so much, or suffer the frustration of having earned skills and education that would remain unused. Cliff and Innukie were quite despondent and could see no way forward. The one heartening feature was the earnestness of their desire to do what they could for the people they so obviously cared about. Whatever sense of pride and nationalism it was that urged them forward to a state of near independence, they were still going to need men like Cliff and Innukie who were dedicating their lives to helping them.

On St. Valentine's Day, the 14th of February, a general celebration took place in the community hall. There was music and dancing. The youngsters had put on their party clothes and people of all ages came to join in the fun. What, in my ignorance, I found most remarkable was that the activities were totally *unremarkable*.

Had I been in an English village communal party, it would have been little different. For example, in addition to the music and dancing, there were such things as raffles and, as a fund-raising activity, various people, my self included, volunteered to have custard pies thrown at them whilst people bid for the right to throw those pies. The more I looked around, the more the scene resembled the rural activities of my own English village. I came to the conclusion that if any of these Inuit came to England only their Mongolian features and laconic drawl would distinguish them from the rural English. I marvelled at the youngsters. The girls wore party dresses that were flimsy and generally bare shouldered. As the evening progressed they grew more and more excited and chased each other around the hall and then out of doors. If I remember correctly, the wind was still blowing and the temperature very low. There is no way I would have ventured outside without my thermal clothing, yet these children in their thin party frocks were rushing around outside. They eventually returned after a minute or two; their faces were pink but they seemed unhurt by the exposure to the elements.

It was Terry who introduced me to a most remarkable couple in Resolute Bay – Ray and Florence Sliney. Florence had quickly heard of my arrival in Resolute. She was the principal of the community's school and was most anxious to give her more senior pupils some experience or contact with the world beyond Northern Canada. Would I give a talk to her senior pupils? It was hardly something I was prepared for, but I was delighted to try and contribute something to the Arctic in any way that I could. The next morning, at an agreed time, I found myself in a bright and well equipped little school, standing before a handful of the more senior pupils trying to tell them something about a world far removed from their own and answer their questions. What I told them would hardly be of interest to readers of this book, but I tried to paint a picture of life in a temperate climate where the population density was some 2,500% greater than theirs. It was hardly an erudite performance and I have a sneaking suspicion that I learned more than I imparted. To finish I was given a chance to ask my own questions.

# THE WARM ARTIC

'How many of you will be going on for further education?' was my first question.

All but one put up his hand.

Mindful of what I had been told by Cliff and Innukie, my second question was: 'Do you intend to return to Resolute Bay to stay when you have finished your education?'

This time all put up their hands.

Ray and Florence invited me to have dinner with them a few days later and I was delighted to accept. Their house was well appointed and nicely decorated. In its cheery interior it was difficult to comprehend the savagery of the winter outside. During dinner, I began to realise what an extraordinary couple my host and hostess were. They were living proof that you do not have to have the physique of Tarzan and Jane to be tough and adventurous. Florence was slim and elegant and had a fine bone structure. Ray had obviously been powerful in his youth, but I doubt that athletics had ever featured strongly amongst his activities. Both were charming and excellent hosts. The story of their life together held me spellbound. Florence was a trained teacher and Ray a refrigeration engineer when they met. As a young couple they had bought their own light aircraft. From their home in Winnipeg, Florence took flying lessons and they set off in their little machine to explore their native Canada. I believe the aircraft was a Piper Cub, a very small two-seater with limited power. I think I would prefer something more robust were I to venture any distance by air. In any event, the little aircraft served them well and they came to no harm. When eventually they moved to British Columbia, they sent on all their possessions by freight but decided to fly to their new home in their own aircraft. However, their little machine was not powerful enough to climb to a height that would take them over the Rocky Mountains so they chose their weather conditions carefully and followed the road and railway through the passes between the towering peaks until safely over lower ground. The urge for travel and adventure was too strong to resist and they eventually decided they must see the world. They sold their business, put what savings they had together and flew to Chichester in England. There they bought a small sailing boat and took some lessons on how to sail it and how to handle their dinghy. The tides in Chichester harbour are known to be very strong and Ray regaled me with stories of learning to row the dinghy whilst it was tethered on a long line to the quay so that he was not swept away. When they felt sufficiently confident with their little boat, they set off across the English Channel, down the European coast and into the Mediterranean Sea. There they spent six months preparing themselves for the Atlantic and beyond. In the next 12 years, they crossed the Atlantic Ocean, navigated the Panama Canal and Pacific Ocean. They visited the islands they chose and, when finances demanded, looked for employment wherever they could find it. They took tourists on cruises, taught English in schools, and worked at whatever else they could – including labouring on farms picking crops – so as to finance their journey. On one occasion, when anchored by one small community, they suffered a violent storm and their boat was seriously damaged. They had no insurance cover and did not have the funds for its repair. They were stuck. But the little community took pity on them. From their own pockets the people clubbed together and donated sufficient funds to cover the cost of the repair. When, many years later, Ray and Florence told me this story, their voices filled with emotion.

Before their travels ended, Ray and Florence were able to make peripheral excursions to India and Nepal. At the end of the 12 years, they found themselves in Japan but their little boat, having suffered all that the elements could throw at it, was showing its age. They sold it and made their way back to Canada. Florence returned to teaching. A posting took them to Canada's far north where they realised the inadequacy of the school, so they set to and reorganised the establishment at Resolute Bay. After my visit, I learned that they subsequently moved to Iqaluit, now Nunavut's capital city, where they took over a much larger school. Whilst there, they realised that the white-man's education conducted in English was causing the young to lose their native tongue, Inuktitut, and it was becoming a problem for the young children to communicate with their elders, because some of the grandparents could not speak English. They could see the cultural gulf that was developing between the young and their heritage and Florence struggled to have Inuktitut taught in all grades to reverse this trend. Before leaving Iqaluit, she had managed to get Inuit teachers in all her classes from grades one to six.

As an aside I would mention that on one of my flights back from the Arctic I was seated next to a lady teacher from Vancouver. I told her I had met Florence in Resolute Bay. Did she know of her? My companion had not met Florence but she certainly knew her by reputation and recited the published awards and accolades she had received from Canada's teaching profession. Florence and Ray have now retired from the north to a small town in Alberta where they spend their summers trekking in the Rocky Mountains and helping with the running of a local school. They are a truly remarkable couple.

When I was in Greenland,[7] I had come to the conclusion that serious and violent crimes were very rare events. I had hoped that here in Resolute Bay the people would be similarly law abiding and gentle. That was surely the norm for all people of the Arctic. Certainly in Canada's Nunavut I had no feeling that I had to watch my back in the same way one does in so many of the large cities in the temperate and tropical zones of the world. Everyone treated me in the friendliest way – the very young, the older men in particular and all age groups of women were most genial – but, although I never sensed aggression, the young men tended to be supercilious and were quick to try and belittle me. I was later to learn from the Royal Canadian Mounted Police (RCMP) in Iqaluit that, although property was generally respected and the Kabloona were perfectly safe, there was a considerable amount of violence among the Inuit themselves. 'Knives and hatchets stuff' was the graphic phrase used by an officer at their headquarters. I have not been able to discover any reason for this domestic violence – nor the supercilious attitudes of the young men – and am left wondering whether it is drugs, or the frustrated sense of nationalism and loss of identity that must bear the blame for this uncharacteristic behaviour. If it is the latter the creation of

---

[7] See Chapter 3

Nunavut may prove a panacea. If the former, Cliff and Innukie will have their work cut out for many years to come. I was comforted by a story that I believe is more characteristic of the Inuit:

> A man killed his wife and, after serving a seven-year gaol term, was incorporated into the community again by a very forgiving and sensitive elder council. He made a complete turn around by giving up drinking, remarried and became a prominent leader in the community. The Inuit way is not so much to punish an offender but to try and lead the person to a more productive and useful life. They believe a 'return to the land' and community pressure can do this.[8]

Whilst taking advantage of Terry's coffee machine, I met an officer of the RCMP who had not long been posted to Resolute Bay. He was the only officer in the area and had been spending the morning going around the homes introducing himself to the inhabitants of the community and getting to know everyone on his beat. His beat was probably the size of England, but with such a low population density, getting to know everyone may not have been all that difficult. I had the feeling that if one got into trouble he would be a good man to have around. The atmosphere was very genial and we chatted for a while and talked about his work. By the way he spoke about the people of the area, he obviously cared for them. He was, however, an extraordinarily tall and powerfully built young officer.

I had to ask: 'If you have to make an arrest, do the Inuit tend to put up a fight?'

'Nope. They aren't that stupid,' was his succinct reply.

I couldn't help liking the man.

In my wanderings around the community and its environs one day, I noticed a building marked 'Department of Renewable Resources'. On the outside the skin of a polar bear was stretched, drying on a frame. I noticed the skin was fitted with a 'tag'. The building had normally been locked, but on this occasion someone was inside. I entered to find a very young Kabloona officer of the

---

[8] Related to me by Florence Sliney

department arranging his desk. He was not too busy to talk to me about his work. In most other countries he would have been called a game ranger from the game department, but I suppose that the wild animals should not be thought of as game and, in truth, they are one of Canada's resources. The duties of this man included monitoring the condition of the wild animals and the extent of the hunting. Polar bear skins fetched very high prices in the market place, particularly in the Japanese market where a skin could sell for some $10,000. The bears needed protection and it was this young man's job to see to that protection in the area.

'How do the Inuit accept government dictates to control their hunting?' I asked.

'They wouldn't, so we don't,' was his response. 'I know what levels of bear kills would be approved by the government as sustainable. My function is to get the elders to sit around this table and talk about how they are going to sustain the bear population and regulate the kills. If they haven't thought about all the points, I get them to think about it and work it out. That way, they regulate themselves and will ensure that their own regulations are obeyed. My job is to see that their decisions conform pretty well to governmental standards.'

I was most impressed with the wisdom of this approach and would have dearly loved to sit in on a meeting.

I asked him about the 'tag' on the skin outside. I was told it was a way of keeping a tally on the number of bears killed. Sufficient tags were issued to the community for the agreed limit of kills. Every bear killed had to be tagged and when all the tags had been used up for the period, there was to be no more hunting. Even a bear killed in self defence had to be tagged and the elders of each community had to decide from which allocation that tag must come.

Evenings are long drawn-out affairs in the Arctic winter. The wind had eased and I was trying to stretch my legs in the gloom by walking out to sea for a short way. Bazel had assured me that the ice was perfectly safe to walk on but warned me not to go too far without a rifle for fear of encountering polar bears. I was still within sight of the community when I saw the light of a snowmobile coming towards me from out on the sea. It was pulling a sledge with a young man sitting on its cargo. The driver stopped and stood up, obviously wanting to talk, so I went over to him. The driver of the skidoo was the elder of the two and he looked very pleased with himself.

'My son is a great hunter,' he said. 'He has just killed his first polar bear.'

The father's pride in his son's achievement was very touching. I went over to the young man on the sledge, who seemed no more than a callow youth, shook his hand and said, 'Well done!'

I thought his head would split in half as the grin spread over his young face. The excitement and happiness of the two was so infectious I wanted to share it with them. It was as if one of my neighbour's children back in England had just won some great academic accolade. Not only would the flesh of the bear provide for the family, but the pelt was a valuable commodity and would bring them some financial security.

Later that evening I could not help dwelling on the apparently insoluble conflict between the community's need to progress into the twenty-first century and the importance of maintaining ancient cultural values. Perhaps the emergence of Nunavut will provide the solution and I pray that there will be many like Ray and Florence, Cliff and Innukie, that tall 'Mountie' and the young officer from the department of renewable resources, who really care for the people and devote their working lives to helping them. Within Nunavut the Inuit will be making the decisions, but I suspect they will still need help from the south.

I had now experienced a deep winter in the Arctic. I had made many mistakes and some of my equipment was not up to the job, but I had learned a good deal, albeit my body had suffered. My feet were mildly frostbitten. I had taken mountaineering boots, rather than specialist Arctic cold weather boots and my feet took seven weeks to recover. The cold had burnt the skin off my fingertips when I had tried to handle very cold metal. I had slowly learned how to cope with living in extreme cold conditions, but in the process I had nearly asphyxiated myself by not having enough ventilation in my tent and I had even managed to set fire to it when my numb fingers had let fuel spill onto a burning stove. But I *had* learned to manage – and was getting better at it day by day.[9] Although I would not recommend living in a tent during the Arctic winter if there were an alternative, I believed that I could cope and felt ready to face the question of whether I was a man or a boy.

There was still much more for me to experience in the community but being mid-winter, little was going on and my cameras were giving trouble in the severe conditions. I decided, therefore, to return in the spring of the following year when the weather would be milder and I would be able to concentrate on the photography and specific activities.

In April of the following year, I went back to the Canadian north. It was spring and the sun reached higher into a brighter sky than I had experienced in the February gloom at Resolute Bay the previous year. The warmth of the midday sun was beginning to be felt. But warmth is a relative term. The thermometer ranged between a tolerable −20°C to −30°C, rather than between an uncomfortable −30°C to −40°C.

This time I included Iqaluit in my itinerary. Since Nunavut came into being, Iqaluit is the capital city. It is situated at the head of Frobisher Bay on Baffin Island. When I arrived the sea was still frozen and there was a firm covering of snow everywhere. I stayed in a boarding establishment out at Apex, some four miles outside the town. The sea ice covering Frobisher Bay was different from that off the coast of Resolute. There is, I am led to believe, a 40 foot tide and the sea bed is littered with large rocks. At the beginning of winter when the sea starts to freeze, the rise and fall of the tide pounds the young ice on those rocks and leaves their imprint on its surface. By the time the bay is completely frozen, the surface is a misshapen field of lumps and bumps.

By world standards, Iqaluit is not a large city but it was buzzing with activity. There were some cars and taxis, but snowmobiles

---

[9] For a full assessment of camping difficulties in conditions of severe cold, see the author's report 'Arctic Winter Camp Expedition, Resolute Bay – 1991', Royal Geographical Society, Kensington Gore, London

predominated. The drivers of these noisy little machines seemed to be even less disciplined than the motorcyclists of the temperate parts of the world. They were certainly driven with more vigour. Lots of people were moving about in the streets. On the edge of the town I watched an Inuk hunter come in on a dog sledge. The animals were exhausted and dropped down when he pulled them to a halt. I was impressed that the first thing the hunter did was to see to the welfare of his dogs. After he had attended to all his essential duties, he was prepared to chat.

'Why the dogs? Why not a snowmobile?' I asked.

'Snowmobiles are fast,' he replied. 'I used to have one, but they are expensive to buy and run. Dogs don't have mechanical breakdowns and leave you stranded on the ice; and dogs can give warning of bears and smell out the breathing holes of the seals. A snowmobile can't do that.'

He obviously believed that not all modern technologies were better than the traditional ways.

In the city there is a splendid little Anglican cathedral dedicated to St Jude. In 1970, the Queen turned the first sod to commence its construction. The building is white, circular and domed, designed to represent a gigantic igloo. Its steeple rising from the apex of the dome also makes it reminiscent of an inverted wine glass. Inside, the Inuit theme is continued. The altar rails are replicas of the kamisk sledges that are used to pull freight. The lecterns are short upright sledges. The altar step is covered in sealskins and the cross behind the altar is made from the tusks of the narwhal, the unicorn of the Arctic seas. The font, made from a local stone, was a gift from the Queen. The curtain behind the altar was decorated with Inuit themes by the children of the local school.

Outside, in front of the cathedral, is a playground where a number of children were playing. On that day the weather was bright and sunny but there was a cold wind. I talked to a young Inuk lady carrying a child in the folded back hood of her parka. The day was pleasant but still very cold, with the thermometer indicating closer to $-30°$ than $-20°C$.

'Do any of the children get injured by the cold?' I asked.

'No,' she replied. 'If it gets really cold, we keep them inside.'

I wondered what her interpretation of 'really cold' was.

I was taken to see a small workshop manufacturing items of jewellery from caribou antler, walrus ivory and similar material. There were four Inuit craftsmen using modern electrically driven drills, much like the old fashioned dental drills, cutters and other fine hand tools. I was introduced to them and they all agreed that I could take photographs whilst they worked. I asked that they ignored me as best they could whilst I took the pictures. Their conversation was in a slow, drawling Inuktitut that I could not understand. I hadn't been there long before a telephone rang and a lady worker was summoned to take the call. The others carried on and eventually the lady returned. She settled silently back to her work and all was quiet for a few minutes. Then, still concentrating on her work, the lady began speaking in a most mournful hesitatant voice. The others fell completely silent. The woman droned on and I judged by her tone that the telephone call had brought some tragic news. Ought I to stop taking photographs? I wondered and I paused, undecided what to do. Her face was totally expressionless and she continued for another sentence or two, then they all roared with laughter. I was so relieved that I joined in – I wish I knew what the joke was.

Whilst still in Iqaluit, I eventually arranged for someone to take me out on his snowmobile and let me photograph him building an igloo. After a false start with a young man who changed his mind at the last minute, an older man agreed to build me an igloo for $100. His name was Geosah. Mr Geosah was a portly gentleman with a round smiling face, probably 55 years of age. He looked to me just like an artist's impression of Mr Pickwick. He called for me at my lodgings and indicated that I should sit on the kamisk sledge to be pulled by his snowmobile. More by gestures than words, he pointed out that our combined respective bulk was beyond the capacity of the seat of his machine. We set out down the bay for some 10 or 20 miles to find a suitable spot. The day was overcast and dull but not too cold. Mr Geosah had a permanent beam on his jovial face. Although his English was very limited and I spoke no Inuktitut, we seemed to take an instant liking to each other and quickly built up a good rapport. I can't remember what we laughed about, but we seemed to spend a lot of time laughing together – simple jokes mostly, but clearly he was making a big effort to be pleasant to me and I was trying to be pleasant to him.

I am told that when there are a couple of Inuit working together and time is of the essence, an igloo shelter can be erected within ten minutes. Mr Geosah was working alone. He kept stopping to explain what he was doing and give me a chance to photograph the important steps of the construction, so it took quite a bit longer than normal. He first chose a spot where the snow was reasonably deep and compacted. He next marked out the site by shuffling round in a circle that was about nine feet in diameter. Using a carpenter's saw, he cut out blocks of snow, lifted them into place, sliced – rather than chopped – them to a good fit with a machete and pushed them together.[10] The blocks seemed to go home with a click and immediately set rigidly. After getting up the first course of blocks, he cut a step into the wall so that the subsequent courses went up in a spiral. Further blocks were cut from the inside of the igloo. This material was not only on site and no distance to carry, but the process effectively lowered the floor so that fewer courses of blocks were needed and the finished structure would be stronger with less area exposed to the wind. In a reasonably short time he was up to the top of the dome and just had to plug the hole to complete it.

He cut a suitably large block, looked at me and grinned, and said, 'If you make it bad, this is when it all fall down.'

And he lowered the block into position to complete the building. Mr Geosah's igloo did not fall down.

Mr Geosah looked pleased with himself and I was delighted to have witnessed the ingenuity of this ancient craft. The igloo he had built for me was quite a remarkable structure. Outside it was not much more than three feet tall. The entrance was a hole cut in the blocks at ground level. On crawling through the entrance hole,

---

[10] Without modern metal tools, the Inuit would have used knives and saws made from whalebones

there was a step down of another three feet, thus giving a six foot man room to stand up.

My companion got a stove going to brew some tea and then started rummaging in the stores box on his sledge. For the first time, he frowned and showed irritation.

'Ah! My wife has forgotten the sandwiches,' he said. 'I should give you food.'

He looked so crestfallen that I felt sorry for him. I had not expected any form of food or drink but clearly he intended to give me a good service and felt he had let me down. He was genuinely upset. Perhaps, after his labours, he was hungry. I managed to reassure him and we settled on the snow outside the igloo to drink our tea.

Then I broached a subject that is never far from my mind in the Arctic.

'If you are in an igloo, what do you do if a bear approaches?'

'If a bear gets too close, you take your rifle and shoot it,' was his blunt reply.

'But if you don't have a rifle, what do you do?' I expanded.

'Still not difficult,' he answered. 'One man goes to one side of the bear and the other man goes to the other side of the bear. The bear no likes this and runs away.'

'But if you don't have a rifle and you are alone?' I persisted.

Mr Geosah hesitated for a moment or two and then smiled broadly. 'Ah. Not so good,' was his best offer.

The next day I flew north to Resolute Bay and this time stayed with Bazel and Terry in warm and comfortable accommodation.

About two or three miles from the community is the remains of a dwelling built in about 1400 AD when the Thule people inhabited the area. The principal diet of those inhabitants was the big whales then found in the region, but by 1650 AD the climate had cooled and the whales moved away forcing the people to turn to other prey for their survival. Eventually, deteriorating conditions compelled the early inhabitants to leave. Now all that remains visible of this dwelling is the whalebone structure of the roof which has been partially restored by a government agency and preserved. When it had been inhabited, skins, probably of seal or walrus, would have been stretched over the whalebone. Beneath would be a pit forming the dwelling area. I sat beside it for a while wondering whether those earlier Thule people were really any different from the Inuit who now lived in the heated and well insulated wooden homes just around the point of the bay. Without the skin covering over the roof, snow had filled the area and I could not tell whether the pit of this ancient dwelling remained, but, at best, life in such a small and lonely home in this vast wilderness would have been Spartan and the thought reinforced for me the remarkable character of the people who had become adapted to living here.

Being April, it was the period when expeditions venture off into the Arctic wastes to pursue their various objectives. At the time I was there, a Spanish expedition was out on the ice and they had left a man with Bazel and Terry to act as base camp manager and radio operator. His name was Louis. It was all part of the service that Bazel and Terry offered. I didn't have too much to do with this chap but one morning he borrowed Bazel's car to drive to the airport. It so happened that I had some business at the airport so I went along for the ride. The vehicle had to be warmed by a circuit connected to the mains electricity. After twenty minutes the car was ready. Louis and I climbed in and he started the engine, selected first gear and let out the clutch. The vehicle vibrated but did not move forward. Louis looked puzzled and tried revving the engine harder. I realised that, as we were parked on ice, the wheels were getting no traction and spinning. Clearly he had never driven on ice before. I suggested he use minimum power and only let in the clutch very gently. He looked at me as if I had gone mad. I had obviously said something that was contrary to all he held dear. I assured him it was the only way we were going to get moving and, eventually, he accepted my suggestion and we got under way. We looked at each other and smiled. At that point I should have told him I was walking and jumped out. He turned onto the road and 'put his foot down' as I expect was his custom when driving in his home town in Spain. The road was built on a steep embankment some four or five feet above the surrounding land to help prevent drifting snow obliterating the surface, but it was still covered in snow and ice. Having got moving, the snow tyres gripped sufficiently to let the vehicle accelerate and we hurtled along this elevated highway at high speed. I had prepared myself for many risks travelling in the Arctic, but to die at the hands of a Spaniard driving on ice was not one of them. For the first time in my life I was speechless. I clutched my seat and prayed. We survived.

I must say I thoroughly enjoyed the walk back. If I kept well away from the road, I would not be at risk from my Spanish friend; moreover, the sky was clear and there was absolutely no wind. At the meteorological office, I was told the temperature had sunk to −42°C but I felt perfectly warm and comfortable walking. In fact, with the effort of walking and wearing a down-filled jacket, I started to get too warm and realised I was beginning to perspire. My hi-tech clothing would wick any moisture away from my skin to the outer layers of clothing, but any form of moisture would be dangerous when I stopped exercising. It would freeze. To prevent the build up of excess heat and to let any perspiration evaporate, I unzipped my down jacket and let it hang loose with only my dark green fibre-pile jacket providing insulation. I walked happily on taking in my surroundings before I noticed that the green fibre-pile was turning white. Ice crystals from my frozen perspiration were building up on my chest. I felt like a 'Robin White Breast'. By the time I got back to the Bay the crystals had built up to a depth of about a quarter of an inch. They simply brushed off my jacket when I arrived.

The next day Bazel arranged for me to join a seal hunt. The hunter who was to take me out was probably a descendant of the Thule people who had built that whalebone structure half a millennium ago. His name was Pijamini and he was from Gris Fjord on Elsmere Island, some two hundred miles to the north-east. He worked for Bazel. He was a man of similar age but less portly than Geosah. He also lacked his bubbling warmth and good humour. I was instructed that I had to be very careful about movements when on the ice. The seals had many breathing holes in the sea ice. They were cautious when rising for air because that was when they were most at risk from attack by bears. Although noises unconnected with the ice, such as talking, did not alarm the seals, they easily detected any movement on the surface and would turn away to another breathing hole. In other words, I could talk, but not move my feet when on the ice. I promised I would try to remain still.

Another hunter with us was a young man, brash and opinionated. I suffered his long dissertations about the engineering skills needed to maintain a snowmobile and which, of course, he possessed. I did not mind his criticism of my clothing and boots. He was far more experienced than I in such matters and I knew there was much he could teach me. I therefore contained my irritation when he pointed out a tear in the hood of my parka and said that the Inuit knew how to look after their clothing and equipment. As photography was my aim, I could not afford the luxury of wearing dark sunglasses to counter the light reflected off the snow and ice, so I ignored his curt chastisement for my refusal to wear them. He was even critical of the photographic equipment I carried. I must confess that I did not enjoy the company of this brash young man, but age had taught me to keep my thoughts to myself. I was glad I was going to be travelling with the older Pijamini, but silently wished it was Geosah who was taking me out.

The day was sunny but cold. I sat on a sledge behind the snowmobile ridden by Pijamini as we moved out into the bay and south-eastward along the Barrow Strait. On route, we stopped to test and set the sights of the rifles. The first breathing hole was found about ten miles away from the community and about six miles out to sea. The two hunters had been standing up on their snowmobiles scanning the surface of the ice as we moved into the area. I could see nothing but the distant undulations of what was obviously land in one direction and the endlessly flat featureless sea ice elsewhere.

Pijamini motioned me to get ready and I stepped off the sledge. He got down on his hands and knees to examine the hole. If there was a thin covering of ice, the seal was probably elsewhere. If the hole was clear of ice and maybe had some loose snow in the water, it was probably in use. The hole, which measured some six to eight inches in diameter, was assessed to determine whether it ran askew or vertically and from which direction the seal was likely to rise. He then took up his position, stooped above it. His thick fur gloves were on and the rifle cradled in his arms. I stood a few yards away with my camera. The other young hunter made a noisy departure from the scene. This was not carelessness, but a deliberate ploy to bluff any seal into believing that whatever predator had approached the hole had now left. Pijamini and I remained motionless. For a while, time seemed to stand still. Suddenly, before I could raise my camera, Pijamini had pulled his hand out of his glove, swung the rifle down and shot into the hole. He then quickly poked a grapple into the hole to secure the seal before the dead creature sank uselessly out of reach under the ice. The hole was enlarged so the unfortunate animal could be pulled out onto the ice and quickly skinned before the flesh froze.

This first kill had taken only a few minutes. I knew there were other hunting parties on the ice. If they were as quick and successful as Pijamini then a general slaughter would have occurred before the day was out. We moved off, looking for other breathing holes. It turned out that this first, quick kill was the only kill of the day. None of the other parties were successful.

The brash young man was right about my boots. They were great for mountaineering and would have been fine for trekking over the ice, but the insulation under the soles was not enough to protect me for long periods of standing rock still on the ice. My reserves of body heat had been sapped. As the day wore on, I got colder and colder until I could stand still no longer and began to fidget. Pijamini glared over the top of his glasses.

'You cold?' he asked.

I nodded.

'Walk that way,' he said, pointing out to sea.

I didn't know whether he was suggesting I walked so as to get warm, or whether he just wanted me out of the way so I didn't make a noise and spoil his hunting. I was past caring and I set off walking in the direction he had indicated, which was out to sea. I would have walked to the North Pole if it would have got me warm again. Without regard for bears, whose prints were clearly visible around the breathing holes, or any other hazards that might await me, I trudged off towards a distant and featureless horizon, wondering whether I would ever feel my feet again. I must buy myself a good pair of Canadian Mukluks I thought.

I was surprised how quickly warmth returned with the exercise. First my hands and then my feet. They tingled as the circulation returned and I began to enjoy myself as a rosy glow embraced me. I increased my stride and held my head high. Perhaps my brain had become chilled, as I still gave no thought to where I was going or how I would eventually rejoin Pijamini. I had only the vaguest notion of the direction to head to get back to Resolute Bay. I suppose I didn't think too much about it until another hunter and his wife pulled up alongside me on their snowmobile.

'Where are you going?' he asked.

'Just walking to get warm,' I replied, and told him that Pijamini had sent me off into the distance.

He grinned, but already I could see Pijamini coming towards us. The wife of this other hunter asked whether I was now warm.

'If our hands are cold, we put them into the sea water if we can find a hole,' she ventured. It wasn't such a daft idea. Seawater freezes at about $-2°C$ and the air temperature was around $-25°C$, so if there was any unfrozen water it was going to be about $20°$ warmer.

'My hands are now warm,' I said, pulling off one of my gloves and holding out my hand to her. She pulled off her gloves and took my hand in hers. They were so much warmer than my own. I looked at her gloves. They were nothing special – certainly not as good as mine. She must have had a wonderful circulation. Perhaps the answer is to eat seal meat – if you can catch any!

It was getting late and I think everyone wanted to get back. I would happily have walked the ten miles or so back to Resolute, but my brain had now thawed and I knew it would be dangerous to walk alone without a rifle. Reluctantly, I climbed back onto the sledge and began to think about a hot meal and a drink.

Terry's warm nourishing food did much to restore my well being, but I was still disappointed that I had got chilled and maybe 'not measured up' to the Inuit's tolerance of the cold. The brash young man had been particularly patronising and that hadn't helped my injured pride. I was not my garrulous self. Pijamini finished his meal and got up to leave the room. I glanced up at him. Perhaps I looked as miserable as I felt but as he passed behind he put a hand on my shoulder and let it slide across my back as he walked out of the room. It was a gesture of respect and friendship and restored my spirits completely. I didn't see Pijamini again.

A day or two later, I had achieved all I needed to do and left to return home. The young man who had so irritated me was assigned to drive me to the airport to catch my flight. He went to lift my heavy rucksack into the back of the vehicle. It was loaded with heavy photographic equipment and the weight of it took him by surprise.

'Hey, man! What have you got in here? Rocks?'

'No. I'm taking a chunk of sea ice back as a souvenir,' I lied.

He gave me a funny look as he climbed into the driver's seat. I said nothing further as he drove the four miles, and periodically he looked across at me with a worried expression. I kept my eyes straight ahead and thought, with smug satisfaction, of the stories he was going to tell about this crazy Englishman taking a lump of ice back to England. I hoped no-one was going to believe him. It would be a satisfactory retaliation.

Perhaps the development of Nunavut will mollify the young Inuit men so that they become as genial and friendly as their elders and the women that were so very kind to me.

My return flight to England was by way of Yellowknife and Edmonton. At Yellowknife, I had to change planes. I was proudly wearing the wolf skin hat I had purchased in Iqaluit. Made from the ruff of the animal's neck, it was delightfully warm, thick and very hairy. At the check-in desk, as the receptionist was dealing with my transfer, the door behind her opened and the crew of the aircraft emerged.

The captain took one look at me and said, 'Jeese! We've got to get that man a haircut.'

# Chapter 5

# CANADA'S MACKENZIE RIVER DELTA

*The trek from Inuvik to Aklavik that didn't happen.*

Canada's North West Territories lie to the west of Nunavut. The terrain is a vast expanse of tundra and boreal forest. Myriad rivers criss-cross the land connecting the multitude of lakes scattered throughout the whole region. It is a veritable wilderness, inhabited by a rich wildlife but few people. To the south are the Provinces of British Columbia, Alberta and Saskatchewan. To the west is the Yukon Territory with the northern reaches of the Rocky Mountains. The northern limits include many of the islands of that great archipelago that sits between the mainland of North America and the Arctic Ocean, through which the North West Passage picks its way between the Atlantic Ocean and the Bering Straits. The northern coast of this part of Canada is the land of the Inuvialuit and Gwich'in people, cousins of the Inuit of Nunavut.

Of the lakes across the vast wilderness, the two greatest are the Great Bear Lake and the Great Slave Lake. Many rivers feed the Great Slave Lake, but it is the Mackenzie along the eastern edge of the Rockies that drains it. It is the longest river in Canada stretching 2,650 miles (4,241 kilometres).

Some 160 miles (250 kilometres) before the Mackenzie River discharges into that part of the Arctic Ocean known as the Beaufort Sea, the river spreads into a complex delta of lakes and channels forming a multitude of little islands. It is around 50 miles (80 kilometres) wide. About 65 miles (100 kilometres) from the open sea, on the western bank, is the hamlet of Aklavik. The name means, 'A place where grizzly bears live'. It used to be the administrative centre for the region but it is prone to flooding when the Mackenzie River wakes up after its winter's sleep of ice. The hamlet was without room for development so, in 1957, a new town was built on the eastern bank. That town is named Inuvik – 'The place where people live'. There is a resident population of 3,500 people, predominantly Kabloona.[1] Inuvik is still growing. There is a developing summer tourist trade, but the economy depends mostly on governmental operations and the development of the oil and gas that has been found in the regions.

Inuvik is at the end of the 'all weather' Dempster Highway, a highway that connects it through the Yukon to the south. From Inuvik, in the winter when the Mackenzie freezes over, the highway is extended by a winter ice road to Aklavik and yet another community on the coast of the Beaufort Sea. This third community is called Tuktoyaktuk – a word that means, 'Looks like caribou.' Locally, the familiar name of Tuk[2] is used. Around Tuk are the remarkable pingos – gigantic frost heaves, the larger of which rise from the flat tundra like cones, for all the world like miniature replicas of Mt Fuji. The geological formation of these pingos is intriguing. There is permafrost beneath the whole of the region but where there are lakes the water in the lakes acts as an insulating blanket to the subsoil beneath. This volume of subsoil under the lake may be saturated but not permanently frozen like the permafrost that surrounds it. If the lake dries up, or the water is otherwise drained away, the insulation is lost and the saturated soil freezes. As it freezes, the water content expands, but the surrounding permafrost prevents expansion laterally or downwards. There is only one way for the freezing soil to go. Outside Tuk, are the two largest in the world, the Ibyuk and the Split pingos. Both are over 1,000 years old. The Ibyuk rises to a height of 160 feet (50 metres)[3] and the Split is not much smaller. Pingos occur wherever the essential ingredients are to be found, and traces of their remains can even be observed in Europe, but it is

---

[1] Non-Inuit from the south
[2] Pronounced like 'Tuck'
[3] The Canadian Encyclopedia (Edmonton: Hortig Publishers, 1985)

around Tuk and on the Tuktoyaktuk peninsula that they are most commonly seen.

In the summer, Aklavik and Tuk are only accessible by air or by river craft. The winter road to Aklavik and Tuk generally follows the same channels used by the river craft and the 190 miles (300 kilometres) of frozen channels are swept by a network of snow clearance vehicles.

I was drawn to the Mackenzie Delta by a number of factors. Of the venues that I had visited, the map showed there was too big a gap between two of my earlier Arctic trips, Resolute Bay in Nunavut and Kotzebue in Alaska. A visit to the Mackenzie region would fill that gap. I was intrigued by the pingos that surrounded Tuk and, more pressingly, I was propelled by the yawning lacuna in my Arctic experiences at least to try a winter trek through an Arctic wilderness. I had to give credit to myself for having past my seventieth birthday and the winter ice road between Aklavik and Inuvik seemed a suitable route. Aklavik might be the place where grizzly bears live, but in the winter they would be in hibernation. It was too far inland for Polar bears and although wolves roam the area all year round, those who really knew about these much-maligned animals assured me they would keep out of my way and present no danger to me. I hoped they were right. The Russian stories of wolf attacks and the tale of Little Red Riding Hood lingered in my subconscious. Enquiries from the Royal Canadian Mounted Police suggested that the walk would be feasible if I was prepared for the weather. As there were oil camps throughout the area, the ice road carried quite a bit of traffic. There were emergency ways out if it all went wrong. I was adventurous, but not suicidal. I may have left this adventure somewhat late in life, but felt reassured that this would be the right venue for a man who was 'past his sell-by date'. March seemed to be the ideal date as the temperatures were beginning to rise. The bears come out at the end of March and the road closes in mid-April. If I left it too late, the bears could be a problem and the ice on the river would be thinning. I could not regain the fitness of my youth but I had a year to work out in the gym and get myself physically as ready as possible.

## THE WARM ARTIC

On Sunday the second of March I arrived in Inuvik and settled into the Polar Bed and Breakfast. David, who ran the establishment, couldn't have been more helpful and raised not an eyebrow when he learnt of my plans. Another person, Hal, was in residence as a guest of the establishment. Hal was a quiet man, a consultant in environmental matters. His home was in Yellowknife on the Great Slave Lake, the administrative centre for the whole of the North West Territories. Whatever his opinions were on the viability of my plans, he kept them to himself.

On Monday I bought my provisions and packed the sledge. I thought I had been careful to keep the load down and pack only what I considered essential, but my sledge did seem awfully full and heavy.

The next day I bid farewell to Dave and Hal, joking that I might be back by the next night, and set off quite happily for my big adventure. My splendid whiskers, which I had grown for the occasion, quickly frosted up from my breath. The temperature was a reasonable $-26°C$. At first I made good speed. The river was wide and the banks quite picturesque. The trees were heavily laden with snow and periodically I would pass little fishing and hunting cabins. Most were deserted, but some had smoke from their chimneys. As I drew away from the town, the number of cabins dwindled until there were none. I was on my own and it was exciting to be trekking into a wilderness. With the sun behind me, I cast a long shadow onto the ice in front. It felt good to be on my way and I knew I wasn't going to be totally alone because of the expected traffic. Private vehicles would be going to either Aklavik or Tuktoyaktuk. Commercial heavy trucks would be going to the oil prospecting camps. What was considered a reasonable amount of traffic in this region was perhaps one vehicle every 15 or 20 minutes during the day time. The cars that did pass me usually hooted their horns and the passengers waved wildly. I waved back happily.

After a couple of hours, fatigue started to set in. The sledge was too heavy for me and I was beginning to recognise this. If I walked on the part of the road that was cleared ice, the sledge slid along quite easily, but I couldn't get any traction with my feet.

Above: The little wooden church with its Coptic Crosses set in the woods in northern Finland, close to the Russian border.

Left: The aurora borealis seen over Finland. The displays are best seen at a distance of 2,000 to 3,000 miles from the North magnetic pole.

This range of mountains stretch down the eastern coast of Greenland for many hundreds of miles and contain the ice cap. Although late summer only snow, ice and rocks are to be seen.

On the rocky ground sit the sturdy and compact houses favoured by the Inuit hunters around the coast of Greenland.

Above: In July between Saqqaq and Qeqertarsuaq broken sea ice pushes past eventually making its way into the Atlantic Ocean.

Left: One of the most awe-inspiring sights of the Arctic is nature's sculptures in ice carved from the glaciers from Greenland's ice cap.

The mountains of Spitsbergen are covered in glaciers that make convenient but sometimes hazardous routes for trekking inland.

One of the colourful Finnish holiday homes set on the shores of Lake Inari. This one had obviously been closed for the winter.

Beside the freshwater lake outside our base camp at Brucebyen grow the delightful little flowers known as Reindeer Roses. Nunataks rise through the glacier in the background.

Behind the wooden houses overlooking the harbour in Murmansk stands a gigantic statue in memorial to the Russian sailors who defended the territory against the Germans in World War II.

A car makes the 75 mile drive across the frozen Mackenzie Delta from Aklavik to Inuvik. This Canadian road is safe for vehicle traffic, including heavy lorries, between December and April.

Ice is always a hazard to ships and this little coastal supply ship is struggling through the pack outside Saqqaq in Western Greenland.

The remote Arctic town of Provideniya in Russia's Chukotka. Although grim to Western eyes a rich family life with love and laughter was to be found amongst its citizens.

A blaze of colourful flowers that are so frequently found during the summer in the Arctic. This roadside display was photographed outside Provideniya in remote Russia.

Scattered throughout Northern Finland are wilderness shelters where a traveller can rest or take shelter from storms. Simple but cosy, they are well insulated and heated with wood burning stoves.

The author's campsite beside the ice road on the attempted trek from Canada's Inuvik to Aklavik.

When I moved back onto the snow cover I could walk easily but the sledge dragged. My leg muscles began to ache and my speed fell to an average of less than two miles per hour. That would have been acceptable if I could have kept it up for five hours, or better still six, but I was flagging. After four hours I was really having trouble keeping up any sort of a pace and after four and a half I finally gave up for the day having covered eight miles. It was then only 3.00 p.m.

I set up camp on a bend in the river. Looking about me it was all very attractive. I was beginning to realise that this trek was going to be very demanding, but when I tried to make myself a hot meal I found my problems were only just starting. To my horror, I discovered that neither of my two stoves worked, though they had been well tested before I packed them. I tried to get a campfire going but on the edge of the tree line, fuel was not plentiful and I had to put on snow-shoes to cross the deep snow on the bank and get to it. What I did manage to get burnt badly, producing lots of smoke and very little heat. The campfire was not a success. I had no alternative but to repair one of the stoves. That was chilly work. I couldn't handle the small parts with gloves on so was obliged to work with bare hands and my fingers became very cold and painful. I succeeded, however, and with the blessed warmth from my stove made a big pan of noodle soup, filled my thermos flask with hot water and prepared a hot water bottle.

I fell into my bed. My down sleeping bag had a sheepskin and reindeer skin underneath; on top there was another reindeer skin and my down jacket. The combination was warm and cosy and I fell into a deep sleep. I slept through to 9.30 – alas, it was 9.30 p.m. Although the tent had chilled dramatically, I was still deliciously warm. The problem was I couldn't get back to sleep. I tossed and turned in my sleeping bag and was surprised at the brilliant static discharges generated by my clothing against the nylon of the sleeping bag in the very dry air. There were flashes of light whenever I moved suddenly – pretty to watch, but not conducive to sleep. Eventually, nature required that I relieve myself. I went outside and was blessed with another spectacle. Ice crystals were suspended in the dry air and they danced like a billion tiny fireflies in the light of my torch, yet when I switched the torch off, the air appeared clear. Fascinating – but I dared not linger or I would start to get cold. I got back in the tent and wriggled into my bedding. It was still warm and I looked around the tent. The dome of the roof was covered in ice crystals and some of them were forming into thin icicles like the collapsed remains of old cobwebs. In the light of my torch the tent sparkled and glistened like some magic grotto. It was really very beautiful, but if I was going to succeed with this trek it was more sleep I needed, and there were still many hours before dawn. I had a few sips of warm water from my thermos, but sleep continued to evade me.

Lying awake at night is a great stimulus to thinking. Was my sleeplessness due to jet lag, I wondered? Only two days before I had been seven time-zones away in England. I considered all the careful plans I had made to ensure the success of my trip. The reindeer and sheep skins that were enabling me to withstand the cold night weighed 4.2 kilos. They were heavy but without them I would have felt the cold badly and to this day I believe they were justified; the other extras I had brought, just in case of contingencies, were more questionable. I had anticipated a seven day trek but, to be safe, I was carrying 21 days of supplies. This – particularly the extra fuel – was very heavy, probably an extra 15 kilos more than my immediate needs. I wanted to be sure of capturing a good photographic record of my travels so I had a full wildlife and travel photographic outfit complete with tripod. What did I want to do, I asked myself, make a strenuous trek of 70 miles or take pictures? I could have got by with a basic camera body, one versatile lens and film that weighed only 1.5 kilos rather than the 8 kilos of photographic gear I was trying to haul. I also carried more than enough clothing and other gear to take care of accidental loss or emergencies. On the other hand if I hadn't been carrying that extra stove I had managed to repair, it would have been the end of the expedition then and there and a far more difficult night for me. Overall, what I had done was to make the classic and fundamental mistake of carrying so much optional equipment that I had created my own major obstacle of excessive weight. Not only did the weight exhaust me, but the sheer quantity of equipment and stores made finding anything in the sledge an unnecessarily difficult chore. I pondered on what I should do. Carry on and hope to get myself better organised, or turn back and admit defeat after just one night away? I could jettison the excess provisions, gear and clothing that had cost me a considerable amount of money, but I knew that wouldn't guarantee me success. If I admitted defeat now there might still be alternative activities that might prove equally satisfying.

If only I could get some more sleep. I might be able to think clearly in the morning.

By 2.00 a.m I was beginning to get chilled on my head. I took more sips of warm water from my thermos and that seemed to help. Inside the tent the icicles that were now forming sparkled by the light of my torch. By 3.30 my reservoir of warm water was finished and I realised I would have to generate heat or I was going to be in trouble. The thought of trying to get that stove working again in the dark was too intimidating. Activity was the best way but as I had now been awake for nearly seven hours my second day's progress was going to be even worse, starting on an empty stomach and without a drink. I tried the water in the now cold hot water bottle, but that was disgusting. The temperature by my little thermometer was −40°C, its minimum reading. The actual temperature could have been even lower. I had no way of telling. What could I salvage? To continue to Aklavik was obviously beyond me. Perhaps pressing on to the first river junction would have been less of a defeat than returning to Inuvik from here, but that would have entailed a further two nights camping out in these conditions and clearly I couldn't cope with many nights like this. I realised that if I broke camp I would lose the only shelter I had. It was decision time, but there was only one sensible course of action.

I packed up and dragged the sledge back to the road. I looked wistfully to the north and hesitated before turning south and heading back to Inuvik with my tail between my legs. My decision to turn back was psychologically devastating after two years of planning but I knew it was correct. I reckoned I was averaging less that one mile per hour and it looked as though it was going to take me seven or eight hours to get back. I needed a lift, but at that time of the morning I was the only person moving. I didn't really need my torch to see the road so I turned it off and at once became conscious of the night sky above me. There was no moon to dim the brilliance of the stars and the effect was spectacular. The background was the inky black dome of the heavens. Set against this the sky was studded with every star in the cosmos, each one shining like a diamond. The Milky Way was abundantly clear and draped across this jewelled sky was the most beautiful aurora. It was highly animated and hung in shimmering curtains. The hues shifted from thin white to greens and flashes of yellow. It was like being inside a gigantic Fabergé egg where Fabergé had created his finest work on the inside. That display alone made all my hardships worthwhile. My dejection lifted.

Away to the north-east, I could see the glow of the sun well below the horizon. Soon I would experience a slow dramatic sunrise. I was so engrossed with my thought I did not notice the sound of a truck as it approached from behind me. By the time I turned around it was passing and too late to flash a torch both to warn the driver of my presence and try to hitch a lift. It was one of the gigantic trailer-trucks used by the oil prospecting companies to shift their equipment and keep them supplied. Damn! I thought. I've missed a chance for a lift back to civilization. Having passed me, the sound of the truck's engine altered. The driver was trying to slow down or stop by changing into lower and lower gears. On the ice, use of the brakes can cause these vehicles to jack-knife. It stopped quite a bit ahead of me, slowly turned in the width of the river, approached and stopped. I went to the driver's window.

'Are you going to Inuvik?' I asked.

What a dumb question? Where else could he have been going in that direction? It also made me sound more like a casual hitch-hiker than someone in need of rescue.

He said nothing but climbed down and helped me load my sledge and rucksack onto the back of his trailer. Still without a word, he opened the door of the passenger side of his cab and cleared away some empty drink cans and other rubbish for me. I climbed into the blissful warmth of the cabin. The trucker was a gruff, monosyllabic individual. He didn't seem pleased with life. He gingerly got the rig going on the ice, then turned south. When he finally spoke, he made his feeling clear.

'People get killed out here. I didn't see you until I was passing. Man, you could'a used a flashlight.'

I was already humbled, but now I felt really small. I mumbled some apology and thought of nothing else but getting some hot food and perhaps a hot bath eventually. Did I really walk all this way? I thought, as we trundled through the night. The driver didn't speak again until we were approaching Inuvik.

'Whereabout in Inuvik do you want to go to?' he asked.

I told him where the Polar Bed and Breakfast was and he nodded. He eventually stopped as close to the place as he was permitted to.

'You seem to have gone out of your way for me. Thank you,' I said.

'Yeh – Some,' was his laconic response.

He left me on the roadside and drove off. It was the ignominious end of a dream.

Back in Inuvik, I sat in a small cafe drinking hot sweet coffee until Dave got in and opened the Polar Bed and Breakfast.

'When I said I might come back today, I didn't mean it,' I ventured.

David gave me a gentle look and let me have my old room. He made no sign of reproach for my over-ambitious adventure.

My fingers were still very sore from the experience of mending the stove but it was when I went to have a hot bath that I noticed three of my finger tips had turned black. I obviously had frost bite. On a previous occasion[4] my feet had been frost bitten; the nerve endings in my toes had been damaged and it was seven weeks before they recovered. I needed to get these fingers seen to and trooped off to the large hospital at the far end of town. Up

---

[4] See Chapter 4

here they had plenty of experience of frost bite. A doctor and physiotherapist who examined my fingers considered it was not serious, but I would lose the skin of my fingertips and probably a couple of finger nails as well and they prescribed an anti inflammatory drug. It was going to be inconvenient, but nothing to worry about. As someone else later commented, I had got myself 'an Arctic suntan'.

Later that day, Hal found me in the library. He just put his hand on my shoulder and said, 'I saw your sledge when I got up.'

Those were the only words that he spoke, but his simple gesture said so much more and recognized the disappointment that I felt.

Was it worth it?

I had tried to grasp a dream rather than let it float away. Too many ambitions in my life had been unfulfilled by neglect. I had experienced again the awesomeness of a winter Arctic night. I had witnessed that display from the heavens of an aurora borealis that must surely have beaten all others. Yes! Not to have had a go would have been worse than failure. My sanity may have been in question and my pride wounded, but that was a small price to pay for 'having a go!'

I now had to salvage what I could from the visit, by working from benign accommodation. Perhaps I could do more photography than I would have been able to achieve on the trek. I could now be sure of exploring this town in some depth and the opportunity to visit Tuktoyaktuk and its pingos was now assured. I could still get to Aklavik by air, or even by road. I decided Tuk should be my next objective.

Tuk was once the harvesting site for tuktu, the caribou. In the past, thousands of Inuvialuit were scattered along the coast from Herschel Island to Cape Bathurst. During the winter, from December to March, they gathered at the Kittigazuit, 16 miles from Tuk, at the mouth of the East Channel of the Mackenzie River Delta. When there was a need for a suitable harbour for the communities to be re-supplied, Tuk was chosen as the site because of the natural shelter from winds and waves. Numerous pingos surround Tuk and the two largest have been used by the Inuvialuit for centuries as markers for navigation. A Bay trading post was established in 1937. The new community was situated on one of the nicest harbours in the western Arctic.

In the northern reaches of this planet, distances are such that travel by air has become informal and simple. The local travel agent had had no trouble in getting me a flight to Tuk at a very reasonable price. It was scheduled to depart Inuvik at 9.30 a.m. I decided I had better be there promptly and arrived at the airport at 8.00 a.m. The doors of the terminal were unlocked. In the background I could see a cleaner pottering about, but he was the only living soul apart from myself. The check-in desks were dark and deserted. I checked my ticket to make sure I had got the right day. I had booked for Monday and it was Monday. I settled down to wait. It was then that I noticed a sign on the front of the check-in desk, which read:

*NOTICE*
PROPER WINTER CLOTHING
<u>MUST</u> BE WORN ON ALL
AKLAK AIR FLIGHTS BY
CREW AND PASSENGERS.
THIS INCLUDES A WARM
WINTER JACKET,
MITTENS/GLOVES, WARM
HAT AND PROPER BOOTS.
PLEASE NOTE PASSENGERS
MAY BE REFUSED BOARDING
IF NOT WEARING APPROPRIATE CLOTHING.
Thank you, Management of Aklak Air

I was pleased that my own attire could be classified as 'appropriate' but wondered how many passengers plan to fly over remote Arctic winter territories in small aircraft in 'inappropriate clothing', psychologically safe in the assumption that nothing can go wrong. I had had a professional life of flying aircraft and have no fear of air travel – only a great respect for it.

At a quarter to nine, a party of men carrying their hold-alls arrived and went through the terminal to an aircraft sitting just outside and climbed aboard. It was the only aircraft to be seen. Was it mine? I wondered, and should I be joining them? As soon as they were aboard, two pilots sauntered over to the machine, climbed in, started the engines and were away. It was still before 9.00 a.m. so I presumed it wasn't my flight.

At nine o'clock a young woman came into the terminal and opened up the check-in desk. I went over. She looked down at some papers on her desk, then up at me and beamed.

'Good morning. Are you Norman Price?'

This seemed to give a whole new meaning to the concept of friendly and personalised travel. I felt flattered.

I was still the only passenger in the terminal and, after checking in my bag, I retreated to a seat to await boarding. The same young lady called me after a few minutes.

'Mr. Price, would you like a cup of coffee?'

She invited me into her little office behind the check-in desk where the ubiquitous Canadian coffee percolator was steaming away. Also in the room was an airline handy man cum baggage handler and another chap. I guessed – correctly – that he was the pilot, or one of the pilots.

'What are you doing up at Tuk?' he asked.

I told him I was anxious to see as much of the North as I could and was particularly interested in photographing pingos and anything of the oil exploration that was possible.

'Oh, you should be able to see them as we come into Tuk,' he advised.

That pleased me. We chatted on other topics until I finished my coffee and then, not wanting to outstay my welcome, I retreated to a seat outside the office.

At 9.25 a.m. there was still no call to board the aircraft. At 9.28 a young man turned up and checked in. The young woman then suggested that I go through Door No. 1 and board the aircraft. By this time an eight seat Beechcraft 99 turboprop aircraft was standing just outside. The only other passenger and I climbed in and chose our seats. The pilot with whom I had just had coffee followed us in, shut the door, gave us a safety briefing and climbed into the cockpit.

It was only a 30 minute flight up to Tuk. The skies were clear and sunny and I amused myself following our progress with the aviation maps I had brought with me. I noticed that although the lakes were iced up and snow covered, their features were still clear and easy to read. The stunted trees that are found around Inuvik quickly thinned out and eventually vanished as we flew north, away from the tree line towards the Beaufort Sea.

Shortly before we arrived at Tuk, an oil exploration site came into view and it was at a convenient angle to photograph. As the aircraft flew a wide circuit of the hamlet of Tuk the two largest pingos stood out clearly behind the town. It was another aerial photo opportunity that I did not miss. My experience as a pilot of many years told me that, for an aircraft as small as the one we were flying in, it was an unnecessarily wide circuit. Once on the ground, I asked the pilots whether they had done this especially for me. 'No problem,' one replied. 'I knew you wanted the photographs.' I was grateful, and wondered where else in the world a passenger would receive such personal treatment.

I checked into the Tuk Hotel Inn. Of wood construction, it was a long straggle of rooms and corridors. An Inuvialuit couple owned it. The wife, Norma, seemed to be the manageress. As I was guided pretty well to the end of the building and taken to my room, I noticed that the place seemed virtually empty of residents.

The room looked fine to me, but Norma said, 'It gets a bit chilly down here. You had better have extra blankets and this electric fire.'

I thanked her, but wondered why, if they were not crowded, she gave me a room that was at the chilly end of the building and not one that was better heated and thus save on the extra electrical heating. However, I kept my thoughts to myself and moved in. Aside from the coolness of the room, it was perfectly comfortable and suited my needs admirably.

I met Norma's husband at lunch time. He was a Natural Resources Officer called Paul. I asked him about getting to the giant pingos, and he said if I was going to be going there I had better go right away because the wind was forecast 'to be getting up.' His daughter offered to drive me to the end of the road where I could get a good view and take some photographs.

'I'm doing nothing. I'd be happy to take you,' she said and brought the car around for me.

The rambling town seemed to consist of little wooden houses and the occasional hall, scattered at random with large empty spaces between them. The few roads meandered around the edges of these spaces. There was time for me to explore the town on foot later. On its edge was the old – and now otiose – radar station that had been part of the Cold War DEW Line[5] system. It was a three-mile drive to the end of the road which ran along a rough surface into a barren wilderness bereft of trees or visible vegetation. Any vegetation there was must have been stunted and buried under the compacted snow that lay over the whole. It was like gazing out over a desert – a very cold one.

I got my photographs of the two large pingos, the Ibyuk and Split. I wasn't as close as I would have liked to have been, but it would suffice. Later, perhaps, I could hire a skidoo or something and get right up to them but, for the first afternoon, I was satisfied. It was calm when I had left Inuvik that morning and I was not aware of any particular wind when I arrived in Tuk, but now, whilst taking my photographs, I was conscious of a cold, cutting blast that chilled my hands and stung my ears. Then I remembered the forecast.

On the way back to the hotel, I saw a large circular dome-shaped hill in the middle of town. It had a base of about 180 yards (40 metres) in diameter and was probably about 30 feet (9 metres) high. Nothing was built on it and I realised that it was a small pingo – right here in the middle of the town – and very close to the hotel. I had read that the original people had used the pingos' frozen interiors for food storage throughout the summer, by the simple expedient of digging into their icy cores and hollowing out places to use as food caches. The Maoris used the volcanic thermal pools of New Zealand to cook their food, so why should not the Inuit employ pingos to store their food in the summer?

When we got back to the hotel I saw on a notice board that there was drum dancing that night in the Kitti Hall at 7.00 p.m. I

---

[5] Distant Early Warning Line

knew of drum dancing, but had never seen it and this was a great opportunity to attend something cultural.

'Where's the Kitti Hall?' I asked Norma.

'Oh, it's the blue building just across the lake next to the school.'

It was then it dawned on me that the large spaces between the houses were frozen lakes covered in snow. I trotted off to the Kitti Hall to make sure it was the right place before returning to the hotel. Walking was getting distinctly uncomfortable as the wind was indeed starting to pick up. There were still three or four hours to go before the drum dancing started but long before that the temperature sunk to around $-33°C$ and, if that wasn't cold enough, the wind had got up to 50 miles per hour (80 km/hr). By my reckoning that made a wind chill of $-57°C$. The blustery wind was driving the fine dry snow before it. The snow also streamed off the roofs of the buildings so that the view from a window resembled a badly tuned television picture covered with horizontal streaks. Vehicles were steadily being buried. I could dimly make out a street light about 30 yards away but the visibility was really only about 20 yards. The horizontal streaks of snow blown in front of the light just outside the hotel produced an eerie effect. The power lines thrashed and whipped in the wind. Outside the only human movement was a RCMP patrol vehicle carefully picking its way between the buildings, making sure everyone was indoors.

I asked Paul if he or other local men still worked in these conditions.

'Nope, we all stay indoors when it's like this.'

And that's just what we did. I was very disappointed because the expectation of the drum dance meeting in the community hall that night had excited me, but I just didn't want to risk walking the 500 yards to see it. Even if I found the Kitti Hall in these conditions, I didn't think I would find my way back again. I wouldn't survive spending a night outside in this wind without shelter. Paul reckoned I had made the right decision and, anyway, the drum dancing would probably be cancelled. That was small consolation for me, but the weather dictates what happens in the Arctic.

The conditions persisted for the whole of the next day. A young Inuvialuit who worked at the hotel came in that morning with a great blue weal across his face.

'See what I got this morning just walking 100 yards!' he said.

It was quite an impressive cold burn.

One benefit of being incarcerated in the hotel by the storm was the sense of comradeship with fellow detainees. Paul was one of those and we quickly developed a rapport. He was a big man with a broad, friendly face. I felt he was a man who could be trusted. Aside from the pleasure of his company, I learned from his experience and work in the region.

He told me that when the local hunters and trappers were 'harvesting' the regional resources, it was his duty to ensure there was no wastage.

I loved that word 'harvesting'. Tactful enquiry confirmed that it meant what I had thought: hunting and trapping.

'In the past,' he continued, 'people were not wasteful, but now they don't seem to care.'

Caribou are their favourite food. Seals are of no interest to them. When the sea ice begins to break up, the beluga whales come into Kugmallit Bay at the mouth of the Mackenzie River to feed and give birth to their young.

'My job,' he said, 'is to see that the harvesting is done in accordance with the regulations.'

One had first to harpoon a beluga so that a float marker would keep track of the whale and prevent it from sinking when it died. Only after it was harpooned could it be shot with a rifle. Belugas are not an endangered species, but the young and their mothers were protected by law.

'How do you tell a mother from the other adults?' I asked.

'The young keep close to their mothers, so you don't harvest a whale next to a young one,' he answered.

I wondered whether the older and more experienced male belugas hadn't worked this out for themselves and learned to stick close to the young when the hunters were about.

Paul's work frequently took him out into the 'field'. Sometimes he was away for a day and sometimes for a week. Having suffered the rigours of a camp in very cold conditions, I was particularly interested to learn how he coped with camping in winter. Mostly, he told me, he slept in cabins which had small stoves or heaters. In the past, there were many cabins scattered along the coast and around the area. (My aviation maps indicated quite a few and their position.) Nowadays, less use was being made of cabins. Rarely did he stay in a tent but, like me, he too used caribou skins with his sleeping bag and a blanket. He also employed the modern foam insulating mattresses. My experience with one of these was that it had frozen solid in a roll and trying to unroll it was like stretching out a high tensile spring. Paul told me that when he extracted himself from his sleeping bag, there would be a shower of ice on him from his frozen breath. I too had experienced that but, unlike him, I found it particularly difficult to cope with. As mentioned earlier, Paul was a big man, but he did not look 'super fit'. Although older, I thought I was probably fitter, but then I compared his unblemished hands with my own fingers discoloured by frostbite. Whatever the merits of our physiques, there was no doubt he was a tougher, more experienced and more robust individual than my humbled self, and I quietly admired him.

We drifted off into talk about family life where his views coincided with mine – that it was up to the parents to teach their children right from wrong and discipline them when they went astray. As to restrictions on parents' liberty to restrain and discipline their young, he was very robust. He would do what he thought was right to maintain standards. Hard drugs were in the area and causing family problems. That was very sad. The community was small but educational standards were high, with the result that the young were increasingly being educated to a standard that could not be utilised in the community and were frequently drifting away to 'the south' in search of better opportunities. Good, perhaps, for the young students, but not so good for the future of the community. I remembered similar comments from residents of Resolute Bay.

I later talked to a couple of hotel guests, both government men. I was impressed to note they carried combined cell and satellite phones. One of them even had a Global Positioning System built into his unit. I suppose when you work in remote regions such instruments are worth their weight in gold. Although they were not particularly expensive, I dithered over whether to purchase such an item. I concluded it was only the magpie in me that was attracted to these shiny, eye-catching objects.

One of these residents was an immigrant Canadian from northern India, a road engineer, and it was part of his work to maintain the winter ice roads. He seemed to think it would take about 30 hours to clear and re-open the road after the storm. There were, apparently, quite a number of sections on the 200 or so miles of ice road, each dealt with by a different crew.

I reflected on the resources needed for so small a collection of communities, albeit supported by the Canadian Government, and recalled how the British motorway system had collapsed after a winter's snowfall one night. How would Britain have coped if the weather now afflicting us in Tuk were to strike the UK? It didn't bear thinking about.

'How do you know what weight restrictions to put on vehicles using the ice roads?' I asked.

'We check the ice thickness with ground penetrating radar and calculate the load from that,' he replied.

The other government officer was a native born Canadian, a Kabloona, who lived and worked in Inuvik, but although I sat and talked to him for some while, I learned nothing about him personally or his work other than the fact that he covered quite a large territory. He had both a combined cell phone/satellite phone and a satellite GPS navigation unit. Considering the time he spent travelling wilderness roads, that bit of kit must have been a godsend. The cell phone would have no coverage outside the communities, but the satellite phone would always have been able to get through if he was in trouble.

From my conversations with these authoritative and knowledgeable people I had learned that the 'tag' system for harvesting polar bears had put a control on the numbers killed and the bear population was now stable. I was also advised that wolves had never been known to attack man, and their hunting of the caribou made the herds strong by culling the weak and diseased. I learned that the grizzly bears move right up to the coast and will even hunt seal in much the same way as a polar bear. Apparently, they come out of hibernation in late April but the sea ice doesn't break up until July and, when the snow clears, there are still berries on the bushes for the bears to feed on. I was told the last time anyone was killed by a bear was some 25 years ago. An oil worker had come in for a meal and was attacked when he went back out. The bear struck him across his head, killing him instantly. His body was eaten. As to the climate, there was a general consensus that it was changing and the weather becoming less predictable and that this might well be a result of global warming. There was a greater incidence of wind and snow from the east causing rough waters and preventing the local hunters harvesting the whales, their open boats being not suitable for such conditions. I was also told that the old local knowledge about how to stay healthy on natural foods was being lost; it was too easy to buy imported vegetables and other provisions.

By 3.00 p.m. boredom had set in and I had to get some fresh air and exercise so I ventured outside. The storm was not at its worst, but it was still impressive. Mindful of what had happened to the young Inuvialuit that morning, I didn't go far. It wasn't too bad with my back to the wind although I had to place my feet firmly and carefully on the ground to stop myself being blown over. My body was quite warm in my protective clothing. I only went as far as the nearby pingo in town before I felt I should go no further. It was when I tried to return and had to walk into the wind that I had quite a struggle to stand up. I tried to keep my face covered with my fur-covered mittens with just a peek-hole between my hands but this made navigation extraordinarily difficult. The forecast was for it to clear that evening; it did ease off a bit, but not significantly. I had come north looking for an Arctic experience, and I was getting one.

I can only admire the fortitude of the people and animals forced to spend their time out in the conditions we were then experiencing. I had often asked how the huskies coped with the cold and the wind. The answer had always been the same:

'They're fine. They are so well insulated by their fur that they prefer to be outside. They feel overheated indoors and don't like it.'

I had seen them up in Resolute Bay and Iqualuit tethered in chains outside in the bitter cold. They can, however, curl up into a tight ball and snuggle their faces under their tails. When their curled bodies are also covered by blowing snow they are then protected from the wind and seem to survive without too much trouble.

As the storm raged outside the Tuk Hotel, a particularly strong gust of wind caused the outside door to burst open and a husky came into the communal room in which we were sitting and looked about. One of the local chaps got up from his seat to shut the door but he also took hold of the dog by the scruff of its neck and dragged it away. I shall never forget the look on that dog's face. If ever an animal was pleading to be allowed to share the shelter of the building and not be thrust outside into the storm, that dog was pleading as hard as it could.

The next morning conditions were still fairly poor. The forecast, however, was for the very severe weather to return. What purpose was being served by my sitting in the hotel in these conditions? I couldn't really go out exploring and I didn't know how long this was going to go on for. During that morning there was a short lull from foul to simply poor weather. The wind had dropped a bit and the morning flight had managed to get in to Tuk. The two government workers who had driven here over the ice road decided to fly out whilst they could. I reckoned that was a good idea, so I quickly threw everything into my rucksack and joined them at the airport. The weather was below take off limits so we waited at the airport for four hours until there was a sufficient improvement in conditions to be able to leave. We got airborne in a hop, skip and a jump in a little twin Otter turbo prop and after a 30 minute flight we got back to Inuvik. It was a bit windy there, but nothing like the conditions in Tuk. Just in case that weather came south, I decided to cancel my planned flight to Aklavik. The last thing I wanted was get stuck in Aklavik and miss my flight back to England. To console me, one of the government officers suggested that there wasn't anything worth seeing in Aklavik in the winter. Nothing would be moving. Events were later to prove him wrong.

Nothing makes the Gods of the Arctic smile more than hearing that someone has made fixed plans. They just don't work up here. Plans have to be flexible. The Inuit have a word most suitable for plans and ideas: ImMaHa – perhaps.

Inuvik had only a light wind with a temperature of −25°C. After Tuk, it felt very mild. I went off to explore more of Inuvik. It may have had a population of only 3,500 people, but it had all the facilities of a city. There were the usual government offices, a very large police station, the post office, two or three remarkably large schools – obviously the children's education was well provided for – and a commendably well stocked public library, complete with seven or eight computers all connected to the internet by broadband. There were a couple of research centres, one specialising in the aurora, and I had already discovered there was a big, well equipped hospital. The town had three reasonably large hotels and a very good selection of shops and supermarkets catering adequately for the needs of Arctic people.

The visitors' centre was closed for the winter. I was surprised that the giant greenhouse was also closed. With 24 hours of light in the summer, the growth would have been terrific but, unlike the Russians in Pyramiden on Spitsbergen,[6] they did not artificially light it in the winter and get year round crops. Perhaps there wasn't the same need in Inuvik. Supplies were frequently flown in to the Canadian north, whereas the Russians in Pyramiden were very much more isolated and needed to be as independent as possible.

Inuvik is famous for its igloo church – its design is round and the roof a dome. The dedication is to 'Our Lady of Victory'. It took two years of voluntary labour to build and was completed in 1960. I didn't think it was as exotic as St Jude's in Iqualuit where more use had been made of local ethnic art, but 'Our Lady of Victory' was interesting nonetheless. Inside, the cross, above the

---

[6] Chapter 2

altar was mounted on a support in the shape of a little igloo. It is a Roman Catholic Church and the priest was happy for me to attend the service standing at the back to observe. I noticed that few of the worshippers wore hats or gloves as they left the church, despite the cold windy conditions. I doubt that any congregation from Europe would have been so stoic!

What Inuvik didn't have was a theatre or cinema. Most homes had television and I suppose videos and DVDs provided much of the entertainment. To give the children some experience of live theatre, the local schools invited small repertory companies to come and perform plays. One day a three man theatre company, based in Toronto, moved into the Polar Bed and Breakfast. The oldest of the three, Jerry, owned the company and he employed a younger man and a girl. They first went to Aklavik to perform, then returned to play at the largest of the schools in Inuvik.

'Come along,' Jerry invited, 'the show starts at five o'clock.'

I was intrigued so, paid my five dollars' entrance fee and sat down to see what happened. The venue was the school gym. A simple set consisting of wooden frames and painted canvas was erected. In front were several rows of benches for the audience. There were no curtains or other means of closing the stage off from the auditorium. Children and mothers trickled in, some Inuit, some Kabloona. I think I was the only man present. There was a growing hub-hub of excitement amongst the children as they gathered and no one could accuse the youngsters of being over-disciplined or inhibited. I was a little disconcerted at the way mothers let their children run onto the stage area before the start of the performance. Only when they were about to cause serious damage did a controlling hand offer restraint. With the start of the performance, things settled down a bit. The play told how virtue and industry could reap rewards while slothfulness and misbehaviour would bring only sorrow. It was targeted at children of about eight to ten years of age so I did not exactly find it gripping. My real interest was in observing the culture and behaviour of the audience. The fact that the school had commissioned the players and that Jerry made a profession out of providing the north with an insight into live theatre was itself interesting. The freedom granted to the children was for me an education. Some sat enthralled. Others collected in small groups, ignoring the performance and talking amongst themselves; only when they became too noisy were they hushed. A few children decided to tear around the back of the hall totally oblivious of the play. Jerry and his players didn't flinch but ploughed enthusiastically through the script. As theatrical artists, they were made of stern stuff and I mentally congratulated them. By the end of the evening, I felt that my five dollars had been well spent. Later, I met the little group back at the Polar Bed and Breakfast.

'I enjoyed your play,' I lied. They were very animated and pleased that I had gone to see it.

Mary was the wife of the man who ran the Polar Bed and Breakfast boarding house whence I was now accommodated. A keen and capable photographer, she twice offered to take me on excursions over the weekend, the weather now being stable and clear.

On Saturday we drove on the ice road to Aklavik, travelling over the route I had intended to walk. That made the outing of particular interest to me. Aklavik is situated on the Peel River, not far from the foot of the Richardson Mountains. It is the most westerly community in the North West Territories, with a population of approximately 735 people.

It has always been, and still is, a meeting place and home for both Gwich'in and Inuvialuit people. Many of the inhabitants still follow the traditional way of life – hunting, fishing and trapping. It is also the home to the Aklavik Fur Factory, which produces designer fur coats, hats and mukluks. Aklavik was a trapping, trading and transport centre for the Mackenzie Delta until the establishment of Inuvik, which was built to take over this function. Many of the residents of Aklavik refused to relocate and are now proud to call their home 'the town that wouldn't die'.

Before I came here and saw for myself, I had great difficulty in visualising what a winter ice road looked like. In fact, it is very simple. The whole road is on the frozen river. When the river freezes sufficiently to carry the loads, roadworking machinery and snowploughs simply make a path down onto the (now solid) river and clear a track along the channels, removing irregularities formed as the river freezes and making a surface suitable for vehicles. For the most part it is as wide as an English main road. The ice road to Tuk is about 130 miles along the north flowing river channels, out into the Beaufort Sea, then along the coast and into the harbour of the hamlet. The road to Aklavik is across the river, so it has to weave its way erratically along interconnecting channels to avoid the islands and cross the main river. Whilst the smaller channels are relatively narrow (typically 200 yards or so wide) and the banks are lined with trees, they offer a windbreak and shelter. Had I been able to pull the sledge, it would have been a fantastic trip, provided the weather had stayed fine (and my stoves hadn't given me trouble). At the point where the ice-road crossed the main river channel it was very wide, flat, featureless and like being on an ice cap. Maybe it was only five or six miles, but if the weather I had experienced in Tuktoyaktuk had hit me here when I was pulling the sledge on foot, I really don't think I would have survived the crossing. To complicate the matter, the cleared surface, for some reason, did not run in a straight line. There would not have been any kind of windbreak and, in anything but clear air, it would be difficult to see the river banks for guidance. If there was blowing snow, the cleared surface would quickly be obliterated and any attempt to move would be foolhardy as one would soon go off into the deep snow of the uncleared area. A traveller would have had to sit out the storm. When it had abated, however, there would have been no sign of where the road had been and, even with satellite navigation, it would have been very difficult to find one's way to the next channel without wandering into deep snow. I could see myself lost in a wind-swept emptiness virtually unable to move – a sobering thought.

But this day was fine and clear, and I was in a warm car. I only had to get out of the vehicle for a few moments to take photographs, however, to realise how cold it was outside. Unprotected fingers, necessary in photography, start to freeze very quickly and hurt – and my fingers were painful enough already.

The day was not without its excitement. Just as we got to

Aklavik, the vehicle threw the belt-drive for the power steering and the generator. It might have been heavy work driving back without power steering but it would be no more than tiring and inconvenient. With the loss of the generator however, the battery would eventually have failed on the 70 mile night drive back over the ice road. With the battery depleted, the lights and the engine would also fail and we would be stuck somewhere in the delta until rescued.

It was a Saturday and there was a wedding in the village hall that everyone was attending. We needed a mechanic but it transpired that the village mechanic was the groom. The Inuit are very friendly and helpful folk around here, but we could foresee difficulties in asking the groom to abandon his guests and fix our car! The options open to us were limited; we could either stay in the hamlet until the groom got back from his honeymoon, or fix the car ourselves.

I spent nearly an hour (with my jacket off) lying on the snow under the car trying to force the belt over the various drive wheels and idlers. Mary had no tools in the vehicle and my attempts to use brute force were proving quite fruitless. It was particularly cold work, the temperature being about $-25°C$. My already injured fingers were not coping and I had to keep popping into the wedding reception to try and warm up. Fortunately, the wedding party were very hospitable and even seemed to welcome our intrusion but we needed practical help.

The children were the first to offer physical help and they eagerly gathered around. Their idea of assistance and mine, however, were distinctly different and after a while my patience became sorely tried. Only the realisation that infanticide would complicate the situation held me in check until they got bored and drifted away. The next offer of assistance came from a young man. He was in his early twenties. This was more promising, I thought. At least he might be able to help me compress the spring-tensioner sufficiently for me to force the belt over the various wheels.

'What's the problem?' he asked.

I told him. To my concern, he gazed intently at a part of the engine that was in no way related to the breakdown.

'Perhaps you are out of gas,' he suggested.

He was being absurd. The Inuit have a slow manner of speech that I find attractive, but this man's speech was not only slow but slightly slurred. I then noticed that his hands were unsteady and he was having difficulty considering the situation. I didn't feel he could provide the help I needed and suggested that he return to the wedding reception and continue to indulge in the festivities. I was relieved when he followed my suggestion without protest.

I was not enjoying this. I would never succeed without tools but, as I began to despair, a couple of Inuit known to Mary turned up. They were more mature and oozed confidence. I was pleased to note that they had steady eyes, firm hands and clear speech. They collected some tools and took over – much to my relief. Mary and I went back into the reception where we were warmly welcomed and very glad to share in the celebrations.

We arrived after the formal part of the wedding was over and the affair was becoming very casual. The venue was a large hall, and the guests were seated around the walls, much like dancers at a school social. There was a table laid with mounds of food, including ham and another white meat I later learnt was caribou. There were dispensers for coffee and other drinks. At the head of the hall was some sound equipment: loud speakers and amplifiers. In front of that was 'Top Table', or perhaps I should say the *only* dining table. Seated at its centre were the bride and groom. Whereas the bride I had seen in Greenland had worn national costume, this happy couple were dressed in formal western style. Neither could be called a youngster. The bride still wore her gown with grace and style, but the groom appeared to have lost his jacket and tie, and his collar was askew. He was a big man with a broad face. Beside them was a bridesmaid dressed in pink, a colour that did not really suit her. The table was festooned with balloons and ribbons and, to my eye, the decoration seemed rather overdone, but I was an uninvited guest and only too happy to be in the warmth of the hall and observe the proceedings. Mary knew some of the other guests and I was introduced to them. They were all Gwich'in as far as I could tell. What struck me as strange was that most, if not all, of those present sat 'stony faced' and silent. How dull! This isn't going to be very exciting, I thought. The silence lasted some little while and then there were roars of laughter. What broke the silence and induced the laughter I couldn't tell but from then on it was a jolly affair.

Then we watched a very nice little ceremony. The groom stood up. Beside him were heaps of wedding gifts. He took each gift in turn, held it up for all to see and, speaking into a microphone, announced who the donor was and thanked him or her. I thought the idea charming and very practical. A pair of running shoes or trainers was displayed and everyone roared with laughter. I presume there was something symbolic about the gift, or perhaps it was one of those private jokes known only to those in the local community.

Shortly afterwards a further traditional bit of fun took place. First the bride came forward, turned her back on the assembled guests and threw her bouquet over her shoulder towards where some women had gathered. The women folk scrambled forward and it was a matronly woman who secured the prize. She beamed. Then it was the groom's turn. He brought a chair to the front of the table and on this he sat his bride. She obviously knew what was coming next, because she was clearly embarrassed. Young 'bucks' – and some that were not so young – gathered where the ladies had stood to catch the bouquet. Kneeling before his bride, the groom reached up her skirt and withdrew her garter, then, with his back to the young bucks, he threw the garter over his shoulder. There was a mad scramble by the men until an elderly chap secured the prize. He must have been a great hunter. I wonder if his relationship with the matronly woman who had claimed the bouquet blossomed.

Half an hour later, Frank, one of the local Inuit men, came in and told us the car was fixed. By this time a very young girl had picked up the microphone and, if I remember correctly, was singing the nursery song 'Ba, Ba, Black Sheep' at the top of her voice. The microphone was doing nothing to improve her rendition. I shall always remember Frank and his companion with enormous gratitude. They had mended the car just in time for us to escape this musical interlude. Mary said she hadn't been really worried that we would be stranded. The locals might keep you waiting but they never let you down if you're in trouble.

By the time we finally left Aklavik, the sun was going down and the little hamlet was bathed in an evening glow with the misty Richardson Mountains in the background. The return to Inuvik was mercifully uneventful and we enjoyed the wonderful sunset as we drove back along the ice-road. We were not however, treated to an aurora display such as I had enjoyed on my failed trek.

On the following day, Sunday, Mary took me south, down the gravel Dempster highway, to see Tsiigehtchic,[7] and Fort Macpherson – which she insisted on calling 'Fort Macphoo'. The Dempster highway is an extension of the Trans-Canada highway and runs 460 miles from Inuvik to Dawson City in the Yukon. From there it connects with the Trans-Canada highway and runs all the way to St John's in Newfoundland, a total road distance of nearly 6,000 miles, roughly the straight line distance from London to South Africa. It seemed a humble little road as we drove out of town, wide enough for two way traffic and with a gravel surface. It was hard to visualise the enormous distances that lay ahead of us, but we were going to be travelling only about 120 miles. We filled the fuel tank; the nearest gas station would be in Fort Macpherson, but that would be closed by the time we got there and we wanted to be sure of having enough fuel to return. After passing the airport the road took us away from the river and we moved into a flat and rather uninteresting snow-covered landscape. Either side of the highway were stunted fir trees that stretched away to the horizon. They were mature trees and yet few, if any, were more than ten feet tall. We really were on the edge of the tree line. There were sometimes patches where there were no trees at all and the flatness of these areas indicated that they were, in fact, lakes. I tried to imagine what it would have been like to traverse this landscape before the building of the highway. I had read that in 1904 the Northwest Mounted Police began to dispatch patrols to this and other parts of the High North to keep the law in the new frontier. They had to travel by

---

[7] Pronounced 'Sig-ger-chick'. Most local maps use its old name of Red River

dog sledge and they patrolled the north to protect Canadian interests by providing a federal presence, and to bring mail and dispatches. They learnt the ways of the Inuit people and provided assistance when it was needed. What I was looking at was precisely the sort of terrain over which they travelled and it looked very hard and devoid of shelter. It was some seven years after the start of the dog sledge patrols that tragedy struck the NWMP. An expedition consisting of a police inspector and three constables perished near Fort Macpherson. Like so many other tragedies, it might have been avoided. Their guide was not a native to the area. He came from Dawson, but he insisted he knew the route. He lost the way and they fell into trouble. The only weapon they carried was a high powered rifle, but a shot gun would have been more useful in a survival situation as they would have been able to take small game which might have provided enough food to keep them alive until they managed to get to Fort Macpherson. They were not adequately prepared for the conditions and it was this that cost them their lives. The search party for 'The Lost Patrol', as they were known, was led by Corporal W.J.D. Dempster. He found their frozen bodies just 26 miles from where they had set off. They were buried on the banks of the Peel River and there is a monument to their memory at Fort Macpherson. The highway over which Mary and I now travelled was named 'The Dempster Highway' in his honour.

Our journey became more interesting when we got to the river crossing at Tsiigehtchic. Here was the confluence of the Red River and the Mackenzie. The Red River got its name from the colouration caused by the amount of iron oxide it carries. Suddenly, the featureless landscape became picturesque. There were high banks on the inside fork of the two rivers and here, sitting above the two streams, was a little hamlet with its church looking down the length of the combined rivers flowing away to the north. It was fascinating and very photogenic. The road approached the river crossing from a height of about 100 feet and then dropped down to the river level. It seemed odd that the ferry boat – and it was a reasonably large ferry boat designed to carry vehicles in the summer – should be parked on the top of this high bank. A moment's consideration gave the answer. This was now winter when the rivers were fast asleep in their strait jackets of ice. They would start to awake from the south first and as they thawed would begin to press northward. The ice to the north would resist that pressure until, weakened by the increasing warmth of its own thaw, it would crumble and the river would become dynamic with rushing water sweeping along large blocks of ice. Any boat moored in that stream would break free and be swept away downstream, so the labour of somehow hoisting a large vessel to the top of a hill made good sense – but I couldn't even guess how it was achieved.

Tsiigehtchic is a permanent settlement, first established as an Oblate Father Catholic Mission in 1868. In the early 1870s, a Hudson Bay Company trading post was established. I had been told that most of the 170 inhabitants were Gwich'in[8] and still followed a traditional lifestyle of hunting, fishing and trapping, many spending extended periods of the year living 'out on the land', just as they had always done. The place was almost deserted so perhaps they were doing just that. Mary and I took some time to drive around. The houses were small but well cared for and it all seemed very neat and tidy, but without life and people there wasn't much to hold our interest.

We pressed on to Fort Macpherson, but the light was getting very low for photography. This is a much bigger town than Tsiigehtchic and has a relatively large Kabloona population as well as Inuit. There was the usual co-operative store, now closed because of Sunday, and an interesting church. They had obviously had the last service of the day because it was closed. I reflected on the legend of Albert Johnson, known as the Mad Trapper of Rat River. It is a story of courage and incredible tenacity in the face of hardship in unrelenting terrain and extreme weather conditions, the tale of a manhunt that took 40 days and ended after a 150 mile foot chase and a shootout in which Johnson, the Mad Trapper, died in a flurry of shots on the snow covered barrens of the Yukon's Eagle River, far from Fort Macpherson. He had covered

---

[8] Their official name is Gwichya Gwich'in

the incredible distance without provisions or a dog team and tested the Mounties to their limits.

Albert Johnson was a petty criminal. In 1931 he set up a small eight by ten foot cabin on the banks of the Rat River, near the Mackenzie River delta. In December of that year one of the local trappers complained to the local RCMP detachment in Aklavik that someone was tampering with his traps, tripping them and hanging them on the trees. He accused Johnson. Two constables of considerable northern experience trekked out to Johnson's cabin to ask him about the allegations. Johnson refused to talk to them; he simply ignored them. One constable approached and looked in at the window, at which point Johnson placed a sack over the window. The officers returned to Aklavik to get a search warrant.

They returned two days later with two additional RCMP officers and a civilian deputy. Johnson again refused to talk. Eventually, an officer decided to enforce the warrant and force the door. Johnson shot him through the wood. A brief firefight broke out and the team managed to return the wounded officer to Aklavik, where he eventually recovered. A large posse was formed, carrying dynamite to blast Johnson out of the cabin. The explosion collapsed the building and the men rushed in, only to have Johnson open fire from a foxhole he had dug under the building. No one was hit but, after a 15 hour standoff in temperatures of $-40°C$, the posse decided to go back to Aklavik for further instructions.

By the time they returned to the hut, having been delayed by blizzards, Johnson had left. They gave chase and eventually caught up with him and surrounded him at the bottom of a cliff. Johnson fought his way out, shooting one constable through the heart. The troops remained in position, but that night Johnson scaled the cliff to escape once again.

Local Inuit and Gwich'in, who were better able to move in the back country, joined the posse. Johnson left for the Yukon, but the RCMP had blocked the only two passes over the local Richardson Mountains. That didn't stop Johnson, who scaled a 7,000 foot peak and, once again, disappeared. This feat was only discovered when an Inuit trapper reported odd tracks on the far side of the mountains.

In February he was found. The pilot of a chartered aircraft discovered the trick Johnson had used to elude his followers. Johnson had been camouflaging his own tracks by following those of the caribou in the middle of the river, leaving the trail at night to make camp. The posse were given directions and found Johnson only a few hundred yards in front of them. He attempted to run for the bank, but didn't have his snowshoes on and couldn't make it. A firefight broke out in which one RCMP officer was seriously wounded. Johnson was eventually brought down after being hit nine times.[9]

A search of his body revealed that he had over two thousand dollars in bills in his pockets, as well as some gold, a pocket compass, a razor, a knife, fish hooks, nails, a dead squirrel and a dead bird.[10] Albert Johnson's ability to traverse the Arctic with such scant resources is staggering. He seemed to manage on far less than 'The Lost Patrol' who had perished.

Mary and I drove a little further south to another river crossing, but it was getting dark and we turned back to Inuvik. I had been watching the fuel gauge with some concern as we were not carrying any extra cans; it indicated nearly half empty and I presumed we would burn the same amount of fuel on the return journey. There would be precious little in the tank by the time we got back. Periodically we stopped and looked at the sky hoping for a sight of the aurora, but there was only a very weak display just before we got back to Inuvik. It was not worth photographing.

Everyone had been extraordinarily friendly to me in the north, but when I got back to my accommodation early one afternoon, I found a youngish 'native' man sitting in an armchair watching television. Whether he was an Inuit or a 'First Canadian'[11] I could not tell. I said 'hello' and was completely ignored. Perhaps he was

---

[9] Albert Johnson now lies buried in Aklavik
[10] http://www.yukonterritorycanada.ca/madtrapper.html
[11] i.e. A person of another indigenous tribe

absorbed in the programme, so I left him alone. That evening I met him face to face in the kitchen. 'Hello' I repeated. He walked passed me without acknowledging my existence. I'm not suggesting that he was under some obligation to be friendly but his behaviour was so uncharacteristic of the Inuit and so contrary to my experiences of the people of the north that I was a little shocked. He went out of the building and I never saw him again.

Later that night, when I was clearing up the kitchen after having cooked myself a meal, I heard a booming, 'Hello, I'm Roy, nice to meet you.'

I turned and found an unusually tall Inuit smiling at me. After the 'silent treatment' I had received from the other man, I was delighted to be greeted with such open friendship. What a difference!

'Let me put down my things and it would be nice to sit and talk with you,' Roy said.

Talk we did – until 1.00 a.m. He was a journalist and community elder from Holman on Victoria Island. He told me about their society, beliefs and history. He felt that all circumpolar people are of the same stock. He said he had attended many of the circumpolar conferences attended by people from all around the Arctic. He observed that the culture was the same – as indicated by the design of clothing and stitching – and this, he felt, was evidence that the people were the same. Roy also taught me little technical things. For instance, he explained the qualities of the seal skin and caribou. Caribou was just as warm as seal skin, but harder wearing, though seal skin was better for boots if you were likely to come into contact with sea water. Seal skin will tolerate the sea water whereas caribou will be ruined. I learned the Inuktitut word 'NaKaaTak', which means a sighting instrument. They use it for the sights of a rifle, the Pole Star and anything else that gives directions. If they went fishing in a lake, they would look to see if any large stone had been disturbed or placed in an unnatural position. If they found such a stone, it would probably be a NaKaaTak and they would know it had been put there by a previous fisherman. A second such stone would be nearby and these two markers would line up to point to a good place to catch fish.

I wish I had been able to make copious notes as he talked. Some of his conversation confirmed what I had already learned but some of it contradicted what others had assured me was fact. Perhaps none of it was true. I don't know, but it was a fascinating evening. Roy had come to Inuvik to sell the pelt of a wolf he had shot on Victoria Island. He showed me a picture: it was big; I judged it was nearly six feet from its nose to the tip of its tail. I later learned that he got Canadian $450 for the pelt. After taking into account the cost of his return airfare from Holman to Inuvik, there wasn't much profit in it for him. Perhaps his visit was combined with some other business. He was hearty in his condemnation of the 'Greenpeace' movement.

'Do-gooders who don't know what they are doing. Their work is an assault on the economy of the Inuit people,' he complained. I was sorry not to see more of Roy. He was a really likeable and interesting chap.

I spent many evenings down on the twin lakes, or on the river itself, trying to capture displays of the aurora. I never again saw anything as breathtaking as the one I had seen returning from my aborted trek. One night, however, the combination of full moon and a faint trace of dark red sunset caught my eye towards the north. The air was still and the light from the moon very bright. I had no difficulty in picking out details of distant trees and bushes and it would not have been difficult to read by the moonlight. The stars stood out as crisp points of light. The constellation of Orion was just above the horizon and the dog-star, Sirius, so low on the horizon that it was shining through the branches of the trees. Venus shone like a beacon and there was another planet – Jupiter or Saturn, I could not decide which – that also shone brightly. Through all this a broad band of the aurora stretched from one horizon to the other. It was not many-coloured, nor of any complicated or interesting pattern. It didn't move or thrash about. It was just the combination of all these features that made it worthy of comment.

The Beaufort Delta Region Career Fair was to take place in the

Midnight Sun Recreational Complex. Considerable effort was obviously being made to offer career opportunities to the youngsters. There were stands for the Wildlife Service, various industries (including the oil industries) and some tribal opportunities. I was most interested to speak to a First Nation or Inuk Army Sergeant from Fort Smith. He was there to encourage enlistment by the aboriginal people. He was everything you would expect of a smart soldier. He wasn't busy so I asked him how the free-thinking Inuit of the north responded to military discipline.

'They find it hard at first, but there is a special entry for northern aboriginal recruits to ease them into the cultural shock of army life. We understand their problems and help them through.'

Apparently there is a reasonably large number of Inuit now in the Canadian Armed Forces and, once they were recruited and trained, any racialism was well controlled.

The only wild creatures I found in the delta were the mammoth ravens that gathered in the towns. Catching sight of a wolf on the skyline, or seeing a herd of passing caribou would have been an exciting distraction from the apparent emptiness of the region, but I had no such luck and the ravens were my only wildlife experience on this particular sojourn. The northern variety of these birds really is enormous; they dwarf the ravens at the Tower of London. They seem to populate all parts of the Arctic. Certainly they have been present in the Arctic regions that I have been fortunate enough to visit. Where they roost or how they avoid the worst of the elements I have never learnt, but they are supreme scavengers and have the good sense to live close to human habitations where the pickings are easy. Inuvik was no exception. I commented on their seeming freedom of the city to one of the residents.

'They're protected,' he said. 'Wily creatures. They live to a great age and have a mean sense of humour,' he added.

After a pause, he went on to say that he had watched ravens stealing food from the sledge dogs that are normally kept out of doors on tethers. When the dogs are fed, three or four of the birds group together and warily approach from one direction. In defence of his food, the dog naturally attacks the birds. The birds back off just enough to be safely beyond his reach and, whilst the dog is suitably distracted, another bird swoops in from a different direction and steals the food. Most wild creatures would be content to escape with their booty and quit the crime scene, but not these ravens. When the dog's food is snatched, the villain pulls back just beyond the limit of the tethered dog and there, joined by its colleagues from the diversionary assault group, they share their ill-gotten gains under the nose of the frustrated canine.

'They certainly know how to add spice to their meals,' he commented.

I also asked about the tracks I had seen in the snow. Were they dog, or wolf?

'Oh, they are probably dog, but occasionally the wolves do come into town and kill a few dogs.'

Not long before I left Canada's North West Territories for home, I wandered into the craft shop of the Inuvialuit Corporation to look for souvenirs and purchased a little memento of my visit. The Inuvialuit lady who was looking after the shop observed that I was not from these parts.

'No,' I said. 'I'm from England.'

'I have a sister living in Cornwall,' she responded. 'She is married to an English guy.'

I mused over this for a moment or two. Outside there was deep snow and the temperature was about −30°C. The cool, short Arctic summer was still three months away. I thought of the lovely coves and headlands of Cornwall, tucked away in the southwest corner of England. It could be a little damp at times, but it did have a very mild climate.

How does she like it? I asked.

'Too cold,' was her reply!

I had been too long in Inuvik. It was time to go home.

# Chapter 6

# ALASKA

*On the shores of the Bering Straits – an old gold mining area and the people who make it their home.*

Seward's Folly turned out to be the least appropriate of the names given to America's 49th State. William Henry Seward (1801–1872), an American lawyer and statesman, had a remarkable professional career, but, for the purpose of this book, we need only consider his most important act when Secretary of State in the cabinet of President Andrew Johnson.

In the 18th century, Alaska was a neglected Arctic and sub-Arctic wilderness with a thinly scattered indigenous collection of Eskimos and Native Americans before it got the attention of Russia. In pursuit of furs – those great riches of 200 years ago – Russia's expansion eastward across Europe and Asia was faster and more dramatic than America's later expansion westward in pursuit of homestead land. Russia assimilated this new European and Asian land into her own territory all the way to the Pacific Ocean and the Bering Strait. The continued pursuit of furs then took her across the strait. However, Russia decided against a political annexation of this land on the American side and decided on a commercial involvement. Russia tried to emulate the British commercial colonial administration which had been so successful with the East India Company and the Hudson's Bay Company. She formed the Russian–American Company to handle settlement and commercial development in Alaska. It was a failure. Although the company spread across Alaska and at times even infiltrated as far down the Pacific coast as California, the scheme was not a success. At no time were there more than 1,000 settlers, and those who did settle were fur trappers. No one was interested in farming the land to provide a stable food supply. Alaska had become a financial burden and Russia no longer wanted to occupy this land across the Bering Strait. Lacking the foresight of William Henry Seward, Russia decided to dispose of the territory she had administered since 1799. Few Americans shared Seward's faith when he negotiated its purchase in 1867 for the princely sum of $7,200,000, or just 2 cents per acre. Despite the opposition from the American general public, Congress appropriated the purchase price the next year. In 1880, not twenty years later, gold was discovered. 'Seward's Icebox', as it was also known, was literally a gold mine. By the 20th Century, oil fields were being developed and it is tempting to speculate what price Russia would have been prepared to pay to repurchase the state at the height of the Cold War.

Alaska is the largest state in America. It has been said that if you wanted to annoy a Texan you could point out that if Alaska were divided in half Texas would become only the third largest state.[1] There are two great mountain ranges, The Alaskan Range, crowned with Mount McKinley at 20,130 feet (6,194 m.) and other great mountains in the south of the state, and the softer Brooks Range in the north. The mighty Yukon River flows through its interior. There are several national parks, including the Denali National Park, that offer this great wilderness and its wildlife some protection against the ravages of man.

The skies were spectacularly clear on my flight to Alaska. I had had a grand view of the inland sea-way flying up from Seattle and now the St Elias and the Chugach mountains stood clear and tall, seeming to reach up as my aircraft descended into Anchorage. It was mid-June and the mountains were still wearing their mantle of snow well down towards sea level. Numerous glaciers stretched to a coast dotted with islands.

This part of Alaska is home to the Inupiat, one of the Eskimo groups. Whilst in Greenland and Canada the term 'Eskimo' is not

---

[1] Alaska, 586,400 sq. miles – Texas, 267,339 sq. miles

## ALASKA

appreciated and they prefer to be called Inuit, here in Alaska I discovered that 'Eskimo' seemed to be their preferred term and I found it more convenient and acceptable to use that name.

I had a day to provision myself for my stay in Alaska, and subsequently Russia.[2] Anchorage is not a large city. It is clean and neatly laid out with ample greenery between the wide streets. As the principal commercial city of such a vast, unspoilt territory, it has well organised shopping for all and particularly for those wishing to explore the State's wilderness and culture. Aside from supplies of dried provisions and a few items of equipment, I needed to consider matters of personal safety. Whilst I did not expect to meet with any polar bears in the summer, I knew that I would be at risk of meeting their equally unpleasant cousins, the brown bear – better known as the grizzly – and possibly the smaller black bear. My maxim is always to listen to the advice of the local folk with experience. After consultation with a hunting outfitter, I rejected the idea of wearing bear-bells[3] for fear of looking and sounding like an English Morris dancer, but I did purchase a small pepper spray. It was designed to resist a mugger's attack but, as bears have sensitive noses and a keen sense of smell, it was recommended for use as a bear deterrent, albeit as a last resort. I was also handed a pamphlet detailing how to conduct myself in 'Bear Country'.[4] It was an eminently sensible publication full of advice on how to avoid contact with bears. What was less reassuring was the advice given if one were unfortunate enough to be attacked. It pointed out that an attacking bear can reach speeds of 35 miles per hour, so it did not advocate running. The advice was:

> If a bear actually makes contact, surrender! Fall to the ground and play dead. Lie flat on your stomach, or curl up in a ball with your hands behind your neck. Typically, a bear will break off its attack once it feels the threat has been eliminated. Remain motionless for as long as possible.

---

[2] Chapter 7
[3] Bells attached to a rucksack to make a noise which alerts a bear to the presence of a human and avoids encounters that surprise the bears
[4] BEAR FACTS The Essentials for Travelling in Bear Country, by Larry Aumiller, Revised 1/92

If you move, and the bear sees or hears you, it may return and renew its attack. In rare instances, particularly with black bears, an attacking bear may perceive a person as food. If the bear continues biting you long after you assume a defensive posture, it likely is a predatory attack. Fight back vigorously.

With a fully grown brown bear measuring nine feet in length and weighing in at 1,100 pounds and even the smaller black bear being five feet in length and weighing 400 pounds in weight, I thought the pamphlet seriously flawed in its failure to define precisely what period of time was meant by 'long after' when in the defensive position and the bear is continuing to bite. I was comforted with the thought that I had tidied up my personal affairs before leaving home and I was sure I could remember the Lord's Prayer. As I was travelling alone, I wondered which would be the most effective – reciting the Lord's Prayer or vigorously fighting back against 1,100 pounds of angry, and probably hungry, bear. I thought it might be difficult to concentrate on both at the same time. It seemed that my best plan was carefully to memorise the advice on avoiding contact in the first place. In retrospect, I seem to have been very successful.

The weather was fine and warm and I had been out most of the day. My shopping attended to, I trudged wearily back towards my bed and breakfast accommodation called 'Alaskan Friends' in the suburban area south of the town. On the way, I stopped to rest in a park. Hot and thirsty, I settled on the bench by a picnic table and was pleased to meet my first Alaskan Eskimo. I didn't see him at first as he was stretched out on the grass on the other side of the table from where I sat. My arrival must have disturbed him from his slumbers as he sat up and came into my view. He was a short, slender man of about my own age (62), and appeared to have been celebrating, or had otherwise gone to great pains to quench any thirst that may have afflicted him – or, it seemed to me – was likely to afflict him for some hours yet. I noticed that he was without shoes and this was the opener for our subsequent conversation. He stirred himself and came and sat on the bench next to me peering around. "Had I had seen his shoes?" he asked.

I assured him that I hadn't seen his shoes but was ready to help him find them. We peered about together looking vaguely in places where shoes might have been left, and in doing so we established our rapport. When eventually the shoes were recovered – I think they were behind some trash can – he told me something about himself. I learned that he had served three years in the US Navy in Vietnam during the conflict but since then had been doing a bit of 'this and that'. I took this to mean living on welfare and making a token, but ineffectual effort, to avoid the demon drink that so plagues the people of the north. He also talked about hunting and something about the animals of the region. It was from him I learned that the pelt from a wolverine[5] made the best lining to the hood of a parka. As we talked – or rather as I listened and he talked – a family of Afro-Americans set up a barbecue nearby and the aroma of their cooking drifted our way. We were both very hungry. I tried to ignore the tantalising smell of food, but my new friend's eyes kept turning in the direction of the feast. He made no other gesture towards them. Eventually, the man who was cooking at the family barbecue, picked up a large sausage, wrapped it in an equally large bun, garnished it with pickle, brought it over and offered it to my Eskimo friend. This was gratefully accepted and immediately devoured. We carried on talking and, within a few minutes, another offering was made and accepted. I was intrigued by this spontaneous generosity and at the first opportunity I asked the family whether they knew my Eskimo friend personally.

'No,' they replied. 'He just looked hungry.'

Eventually, some other Eskimo joined my little clique. One was from Point Hope on the eastern extremity of land where the Brooks Range reaches down to the Chukchi Sea, north of the Bering Strait. When I mentioned that I was heading for Kotzebue the next day, he said he knew the area well. This young man gave me the name of his uncle who was a local pastor there (a useful contact if I was in need) and told me about the fishing camps on

---

[5] A heavy, short-legged animal somewhat bear-like in appearance with long dark brown fur, the largest member of the weasel family

the beach which he thought I would find of interest. I eventually left my new-found friends in the park and continued my travels, comforted and reassured that – aside from the bears – Alaska was a very friendly place.

The next day I flew north to Kotzebue, an important Eskimo town sitting on the northern tip of the Baldwin Peninsula. This neck of land reaches into Kotzebue Sound, some 26 miles above the Arctic Circle. It has a population of about 3,000 people, mostly Eskimo, and was a great trading centre. Furs, 'oogruk' (seal) skins, hides, rifles and ammunition were traded and, except for a period during the Cold War, the Yupik Eskimo people from the Russian side of the Bering Strait took part in the trade. Whalers, missionaries, gold prospectors and other traders from the outside world participated in the life of the town and surrounding villages and have made their contribution in one way or another. It now has a reasonably large airport, a good hospital, shops and an excellent museum. The NANA[6] Museum of the Arctic is designed to be educational and records and promotes Eskimo culture. Originally, the town was called Oikiqtagruk in the Inupiaq language, but the name was changed to honour Captain Otto von Kotzebue[7] of the Russian navy who sailed into the sound in 1816 on a round-the-world voyage looking for the Northwest Passage.

Despite its importance, Kotzebue is a very small town. It was much as I expected it to be. There were small wooden houses so typical of the Arctic, utilitarian and well insulated. There were also the occasional nicely decorated buildings resembling log cabins. The larger government buildings had freezing systems built into their foundations. These consisted of rods with fins driven deep into the ground by the foundations. The object was to dissipate any heat caused by the building and its weight in order to prevent melting of the permafrost and thus stop subsidence. Everyone was friendly and helpful but the aesthetic appeal of the town was diminished because the people suffered from the

---

[6] Northwest Arctic Native Association
[7] The grandson of the German dramatist and politician August von Kotzebue

common Arctic syndrome of 'let's not throw it out, it might yet be useful'. Around each home lay broken sledges and snowmobiles, packing cases, defunct household machinery and all manner of clutter in various states of disrepair. I found that people going about their business in the town were always ready to stop for a chat and be helpful. One man preparing dried seal meat on the road side offered me a piece to try. It had a strong flavour and was a bit oily but otherwise very pleasant. I was more impressed by his generosity, however, than the experience of eating the meat.

The fishing camps on the beach that my friends in Anchorage had told me about were full of activity. The beach was reasonably steep but not very wide. A long line of beach huts and fish drying racks appeared to stretch for ever southwards from the town along the seaward side of the peninsula. Families seemed to live there for the whole summer, catching fish and seals and preparing their harvest for storage during the long cold winters. I noticed groups of men in deep discussion, no doubt about important matters, but it was the women who seemed to be doing the practical things. One woman, using an Ulu – a metal knife with a large, half-moon shaped blade – was carefully stripping clean the skin of a bearded seal. Another two women were plaiting seal gut and hanging it to dry. A little girl played at their feet. These two women greeted me in English but between themselves they spoke in their own Inupiat language. I could not, of course, understand what they were chatting about, but I doubt the substance was significantly different from the chatter that might be heard between two women hanging out the washing in England. Behind the huts were groups of huskies sitting out the summer, waiting for their winter of work. The dogs spend a very idle time during the ice-free months and these looked bored and dejected. I could imagine how different they would be in the winter when they had a job to do. They would be alert, sleek and raring to get out on a hunt.

The beach didn't seem to be a good place for me to camp, so I decided to move out of town to a small lake about four miles away. I picked up all my heavy gear and started trudging down a road that led south. It was the only road out of town. I hadn't gone far when a pick-up truck driven by an Eskimo lady stopped and offered me a lift.

'Where do you want to go to?' she asked.

I told her I wanted to get to the lake and was happy to climb onto the back of the truck.

The lake was not big, maybe half a mile in diameter. The ground was rolling and covered with willow bushes and deep moss. The low hills the other side of the lake still had snow in patches. It was certainly very peaceful. The Alaskans joke that the mosquito is their national bird and I had been worried that I might get plagued by them. Maybe it was too cool this far north, despite the summer, and I was happily spared this menace. I just set up a basher[8] over a slight hollow in the tundra. This would be adequate unless I got prolonged heavy rain. An advantage of this kind of shelter is that its ends are open and that gave me the magic of being able to remain sheltered and hidden, yet still able to watch the early morning life on the lake. Being mid-June on the Arctic Circle, there were 24 hours of light, but at midnight the sun was low on the horizon. As morning approached, the air was still and a mist formed on the waters of the lake. Its glassy smooth surface was slowly stirred by the movement of a muskrat going about his business; then some ducks arrived, followed by a few divers, and life began to stir. As I lay in my sleeping bag, hidden from the wildlife by the basher, I could watch this gentle scene beyond my feet. It was certainly a tranquil spot and had the rain held off, I would have found it all too easy to let the summer slip idly away. Unfortunately, the rain did not hold off. In such a confined space I would find it difficult to stay dry and comfortable. In any event, I had come north to meet people and I felt I had to move on. I had enjoyed some successful encounters by the fishing camp and I collected all the material I needed; now it was time for me to move on to Nome.

I was not so fortunate getting a lift back to town. I had been a little hasty buying all my provisions in Anchorage for the whole of my stay, but I wasn't sure what would be available in Nome. The

---

[8] A rudimentary shelter using a tarpaulin rather than a tent

result was that I was carrying an excessive amount of food and kit for three weeks. The four miles back to the airport was not a journey I remember with much pleasure. When I dumped all my gear on the baggage scales at the airport I found I had been carrying a total of 58 pounds in the two bags to be checked in and another 12 pounds in my hand baggage. I had staggered the four miles along the road carrying a total of 70 pounds!

At the airport a large and noisy group of Taiwanese tourists waited to join the flight. On my first encounter with the Eskimo, I would readily have mistaken them for Chinese – such is their Mongolian origin. Now that I had had some experience of mixing with them I could see the differences. The physical distinctions were subtle but, in my experience, Eskimo tended to be laconic and quiet, even when having fun. I was pleased that the Taiwanese were enjoying themselves, but by comparison they were loud and raucous. A few Eskimo waiting to join the flight sat quietly and patiently amongst the hubbub of the tourists. When the plane arrived, I noticed it disgorged another large number of Taiwanese into the little town. Clearly Taiwanese tourism was an important industry.

A peninsula of land jutting into the Bering Straits towards Russia honours William Henry Seward with his name. On the south of the Seward Peninsula is Norton Sound, and on the south western corner is the town of Nome, with a population of about 4,000 persons. This was my next destination. One English television presenter described Nome as 'a wacky little town full of friendly drunks'.[9] Like so many other northern towns, it does have its population of drunks and they are indeed friendly but it is a pleasant, comfortable, and well-equipped little town. There is a sizeable king crab fishing fleet and processing factory that supplements the tourism industry and today Nome is probably best known to the outside world for being at the end of the Iditarod Run – the all Alaskan championship dog sledge run. The town has a history of gold. Coinciding with the end of the great gold

---

[9] Michael Palin, presenter of the BBC Television series 'Full Circle', documenting a journey around the rim of the Pacific Ocean

rush in the Yukon on the Klondike River, 'Three Lucky Swedes' discovered gold on a site known as Anvil Creek in 1898. News reached the waning gold fields of the Klondike that winter and by 1899 a town called Anvil City had sprung up with the Klondike miners continuing their search for gold in this new territory. The news eventually reached the outside world and, when the ice of Norton Sound melted in the spring of 1900, the stampede was on. That year, the US Census listed one-third of all 'whites'[10] recorded in Alaska as living in the town and although the recorded population was 12,480, its estimated population at the height of the gold rush was as great as 20,000. It had become the largest city in Alaska and by 1911 had mined $60 million from the beaches, hills and streams. In its early days, before supplies of timber reached the area, it was a vast tent city stretching 30 miles between what are now known as Cape Rodney and Cape Nome.

How the city changed its name from Anvil City to Nome is an amusing story:

> In the 1850s an officer on a British ship off the coast of Alaska noted on a manuscript map that a nearby prominent point was not identified. He wrote '? Name' next to the point. When the map was recopied, another draftsman thought that the ? was a C and that the a in 'Name' was an o, and thus the map-maker in the British Admiralty christened the point 'Cape Nome.'
>
> For fear of confusion with a village called Anvik on the lower Yukon River, the United States Post Office Department would not accept the town's given name of Anvil City and insisted on the name of Nome. The city merchants reluctantly agreed that their town was to be so called – not after a famous explorer, hero or politician, but after a 50-year-old spelling mistake by the British Admiralty.[11]

Nome's gold rush was short lived, but even as Nome celebrates its centenary, it is still a gold town. More than 40 of the great dredgers still litter the tundra about the area and, until recently, some of them were still working. Descendants of some of those

---

[10] 'Whites' seems to be the officially accepted term for those who are Kabloona or non-Eskimo
[11] Cole, Terrence, *Nome, City of the Golden Beaches* (Anchorage: Alaska Geographic Society, 1984)

early gold miners live in the town and every summer the beaches are being worked by a dedicated band of visitors. Everywhere there is evidence of its gold history. Sadly, a number of serious fires and some violent storms have destroyed a great deal of Nome's gold rush architecture but what does remain has a touch of the Victorian detail that was so characteristic of the gold rush period.

There have been some other notable events in Nome's history. In 1926 Roald Amundsen landed in his airship, The Norge, after his epic flight over the North Pole from Spitsbergen, and the story behind the Iditarod Run is representative of the frontier spirit of the area. In 1925, Nome suffered a serious outbreak of diphtheria that quickly spread. The only serum available to fight the epidemic had to come from Nenana, a town near Fairbanks, and the fastest way to get it to Nome was by dog sledge. Twenty dog teams in relays raced the medicine 675 miles in just 127½ hours. In March of each year, the Iditarod Run celebrates that humanitarian dash to bring in the serum. The race now has its starting point in Anchorage and covers a distance of some 1,049 miles (1,678 km) over the old Iditarod dog sled mail route first blazed in 1910 from Knik (just outside Anchorage). The 'mushers' and their dogs endure a gruelling journey of two to three weeks across difficult and desolate terrain. The name Iditarod is derived from an Athabascan Indian word: Haiditarod, 'the distant place'. The route for the race passes through the hunting grounds of the Athabascan Indians and that name became 'Iditarod' when gold miners founded a town at the Indian hunting camp.[12]

Even today, there are remarkably few roads in Alaska. Distances are too great for a population of so few, so the Alaskans have taken to the air. It is not unusual to pass an isolated home and see in a carport a small aircraft such as a Piper Cub fitted with enormous tundra tyres (or skis in the winter) standing next to a four-wheel all-terrain vehicle. One would be forgiven for believing that there are more aircraft per head of population in Alaska than

---

[12] But some sources state that Haiditarod is an Ingalik Indian word, and others that Iditarod is a Shageluk Indian word for 'clear water'

there are cars per head of population in most other countries. Certainly they are used like cars and taxis and their proliferation and frequent use makes them a remarkably cheap form of transport. The advent of the Second World War gave Nome an efficient airport that handles the scheduled jet traffic of Alaskan Airways and others. Such is the importance of air traffic in the region that this little town of so few even has a second airfield for its private aircraft.

Kotzebue and Nome are two of the many towns and communities that do not have a highway system, either between them or connecting them with the rest of Alaska. Whilst Kotzebue's only road out of town stretched a mere four miles south down the Baldwin peninsula, Nome was better off and could boast three roads measuring nearly 100 miles in each direction. In the summer, this was a convenient way to reach the outer settlements, but one had to remember that fuel for the vehicle could be purchased only in Nome. I hired a suitable vehicle and made the pilgrimage as far down each road as time and road conditions permitted, luxuriating in the vastness of the tundra, its clusters of wildflowers and the fields of cotton grass, the clean smell of the air, the low gravel hills, and its near emptiness except for the the various isolated communities.

On my second day, meandering at a leisurely pace in a northwesterly direction, I spotted one of Nome's 40 dredgers sitting abandoned on the tundra. I stopped my car and picked my way on foot through the low willow bushes to get a better look at it. The dredger was on the bank of a small river, looking very dilapidated and weather beaten. It obviously hadn't been used for some years. My curiosity satisfied, I decided to make my way back to the road by following the course of the river. Rounding a bend, I stumbled into a small gold working camp. There was a sluice, an engine driven water pump, shovels and various other bits of machinery used for extracting gold from the gravel. These were obviously in good working order but the site was abandoned. Curiosity overcame good manners and I investigated. I am ashamed to say that as my only knowledge of gold mining had been gleaned from bad films about the Wild West, I feared that an outraged gold miner might appear at any moment and suspect me of disturbing his claim – or worse. Curiosity prevailed until I spotted a gold-pan sitting on the bank with a fair handful of the precious metal glistening in the base. This haul of gold must have been worth several hundred dollars. At this my courage failed. I backed away quickly and fled the area rather than risk confrontation with the owner.

The following day, on my return journey, I approached the spot where I had found the abandoned working, and noticed a pick-up truck parked on the roadside. I reasoned that the gold miner had probably returned. Curiosity overcame my misgivings and I made a noisy direct approach to avoid any suggestion that I was sneaking up. A nervous young dog of indifferent breed barked at me. Next, a boy of about ten or twelve years stepped onto the bank and then a man's head appeared. I sauntered directly towards them and found a small family at work. The woman was an Eskimo but the man greeted me with a central European accent. The child was obviously theirs. They welcomed me into their working and happily chatted as they went about their business. The man was digging out a bank and feeding it into the sluice, whilst the woman was scooping out gravel from the shallow river and panning it by hand. The boy seemed to be totally unproductive. The man said he was from Czechoslovakia and had 'run away' to America in 1976. Apparently, he leased the site from the concession holder for a fee of 10% of his own takings. He estimated that he made between $100 and $500 per day but owing to the severity of the climate, it was a short working year. We chatted for a while and I enjoyed a cup of tea with them. I was flattered by an invitation to stay in their mining camp just a mile or so up the road if I felt inclined. To my eternal regret, I did not accept. That family must face many problems and insecurities working alone in the Arctic but, whatever their difficulties, their life on the tundra seemed very tranquil and I could not but envy them a little.

Just before I left, I asked the man whether he was anxious about bears, working, as he was, on a river flowing through low willow bushes.

'That's why we have the dog,' he said. 'His barking gives warning if anything approaches. In the fall, the bears' bellies are full and they are content with life, but in the spring, they are hungry, bad tempered and totally unpredictable.'

Returning to my car through the willows, I was convinced there was a bear behind every bush.

I spent that night camped on a beach outside Nome and awoke the next morning to the sound of the surf pounding on the shore. There was a thick mist and it was cold, but when you choose to live rough in the Arctic, life is rough, and to maintain good health, you still have to keep yourself clean. I couldn't put off having a bath any longer. There were the waters of the Bering straits pounding through Norton Sound onto the beach at my feet. I sprinted into the surf clutching my bit of soap and emerged – not long afterwards – considerably cleaner, very chilled and feeling very, very smug. Several mugs of hot coffee took care of the chill and I returned to Nome to refuel my vehicle and continue my explorations of this land and its people.

I had the luxury of time: three weeks to keep my eyes open and take what opportunity was available to meet and talk with people and find out about their lives. Back through Nome, I called on the offices of the local social workers. It seemed to me that there was an easy going relationship between the Eskimo and the white Americans, but was this really the case? According to the social workers it was, although intermarriage between the two groups was uncommon. A division of the community that was sometimes a source of tension was that between rural and urban Eskimo. Those living a rural life tended to regard their urban brethren as having abandoned their culture, while those living an urban life held the rural Eskimo in low esteem. Strong within their culture is an open house policy – particularly among relatives. Visitors would expect to be accommodated and fed by the host family. The rural groups still led a subsistence life style and no doubt they worked hard to provide for themselves. The urban Eskimo sought employment and earned an income. Their freedom to fish or hunt for extra provisions was seriously limited by their obligations to their employers. When rural relatives chose to visit a town such as

Nome, they tended to take advantage of the natural hospitality of their urban relatives, and this could cause their hosts serious financial hardship, particularly if the stay was extended.

In the police station in Nome, I met an Eskimo police officer. He was genial and ready to chat. In Greenland[13] I had learned that serious crime, and particularly violent crime, was low by European standards, but in Canada,[14] the RCMP in Iqaluit had told me that violent crime was a serious problem. I asked this officer about crime in the area.

'We haven't had a killing for over three years,' he said. 'There's some pilfering but not much.'

Apparently, one of the summer beach miners had had some possessions taken that same day.

'What about drugs?' I asked.

'Well, that side is dealt with by a special unit, but there might be some marijuana misuse as an alcohol substitute, but not serious drug taking.'

Realising that I was English, he told me he had been on a vacation to England, and had enjoyed himself. The only real difficulty had come when he visited Soho in London. Because of his strong Mongolian features, the many Chinese that live and work there assumed he too was Chinese and kept addressing him in their language.

'Hey! I'm not Chinese,' he told them. 'I'm an Eskimo. I don't understand you.'

But they were not convinced. London and Soho have so many foreign visitors in the summer that the English sometimes feel their own language is in the minority, but I don't suppose the Chinese of Soho found many Eskimo, Alaskan or otherwise, wandering amongst them. It would have been amusing to hear (and understand) the comments of the Chinese after this Eskimo police officer had left.

Some 30 miles or so on the next long road out of Nome my travels took me past Salmon Lake. This was a beauty spot. There

---

[13] Chapter 3
[14] Chapter 4

was a small picnic ground with tables, which made life more convenient for someone like myself, living simply. Heavy banks of snow still lingered in patches and a mist floated over the water. Low hills clustered with wild flowers surrounded the site. It was an ideal spot to stop and see what fortune had to offer. After I had set up my simple camp, a lone cyclist arrived and pitched a tent. He was heavily laden with photographic gear, the sort that only a professional wildlife photographer would use. He was a German named Andreas, hoping to increase his collection of bird photographs. I cooked a meal sufficient for two and asked him to join me. He provided bread and biscuits and with this simple fare we cemented a friendship that has now stood the test of several years.

Once again, it would have been easy to let the days slip away, lazing in a peaceful setting, watching the moods of the lake as it responded to the light and the weather, but next day I continued northwards towards Pilgrim Springs. The road was a gravel surface and ran through tundra covered with rich vegetation which alternated between areas of low willow bushes and fields of wildflowers. On each side were high hills. There were very few other vehicles on the road. A cow moose ambled in front of me and, but for the patches of snow, the scene reminded me of Kenya's rift valley. Pilgrim Springs was a bit of a disappointment. There was obviously some thermal activity in the area and for the first time in Alaska I saw reasonably tall trees, rather than stunted bushes. I could not work up an interest to explore this spot, however. I preferred Salmon Lake. Not finding anything else to hold my attention, I turned back. About half way through my return journey I noticed a car parked on the roadside and a group of six Eskimo ladies busy about something off the road. I stopped and ambled over to see what they were doing. They were gathering a form of wild rhubarb, much as English people gather blackberries in September. The ladies chattered away with me and between themselves, but this time they talked in English. The similarity with a party of English blackberry pickers was remarkable and struck me as incongruous.

When eventually one of the ladies called to the others, 'Come on now, ladies, it's time to go home for tea,' I could scarcely believe my ears. They waved to me, got in their car and drove away, leaving me wondering whether I had imagined the whole incident.

I continued back towards Salmon Lake, keeping my eyes peeled for the unusual and, just before the lake, I saw movement in the willow bushes. I stopped and watched. With a mixture of fear and excitement, I observed what looked like the thick fur ruff of a grizzly or black bear. I reached for my camera. The fur moved slowly amongst the bushes. Keeping a careful measure of my distance between what I was watching and a safe escape, I tried to get a better view. The fur rose up and revealed a baseball cap followed by an arm that waved a plastic bag in greeting. What I had been watching was an Eskimo man wearing a parka with a fur hood, bent double as he gathered tender young willow leaves. I can't say whether I was disappointed or relieved but I picked my way over to him. His wife was nearby and this was a regular weekend activity for them. I said I was going back to camp at the lake and asked if he and his wife would care to have tea or some other refreshment, with me when they had finished. By the time I had settled back at the lake and got my stove working, the couple arrived, and at the same time Andreas returned from a photographic trip. We sipped our tea and Andreas and I listened to stories of their life in the region. For some years the man had worked for an airline but he now advised a local university on the skills of reindeer herding. The Eskimo have always hunted the caribou – and still do – but a scheme had been set up many years ago to introduce herds of domesticated reindeer and the European Saami had come over to teach them this husbandry. The reindeer and the caribou are virtually identical animals, but one is a domesticated version of the other. Consequently, its meat is sweeter and has less sinew. He assured us that hunting was a way of survival and not a sport. They never took more than their needs. The young willow leaves they had been gathering were a natural way to supplement their vitamin intake but nowadays, he admitted, they also supplemented their diet with provisions bought from supermarkets. I found their leisurely, laconic form of speech attractive and was sorry when they took their leave, but before they left, I asked the man whether he worried about bears when he was moving unarmed through the willows.

'No,' he said, 'I just take my chances like everyone else.'

I looked into his placid eyes but for the life of me I could not be sure whether he was stating his philosophy for the wilderness or simply pulling my leg.

Andreas and I spent another day at the lake, doing our own separate things before we loaded his bicycle and equipment into my vehicle and made our way back to Nome. We refreshed our provisions, then set out eastwards along the third road out of Nome. I left him camped at Safety Lagoon, where he could find an abundance of birds to photograph, while I continued my explorations north-eastwards. About 34 miles out of Nome is the ghost town of Solomon and the relics of the old railway built during the mining era. In the evening light these rusting remnants of the gold rush still conjure the atmosphere of those turbulent days. Standing amongst them it is easy to feel the ghosts of the past about you.

In the Skookum pass, the mountains were higher and their grandeur added to the beauty of the area. All along the side of the mountains could be seen the man-made scarring where the miners had built an aqueduct to divert water for their panning. The aqueduct had long since gone, but the scars remained – yet another reminder of Nome's golden history.

I ambled my way north-east at a very leisurely pace enjoying the scenery, and I must confess the lack of traffic lulled me into becoming rather slovenly about watching my rear view mirrors. Not long before I got to Council I saw that another vehicle was patiently following me. I immediately pulled over to let it pass and the vehicle overtook. The driver and passenger, both women, waved in a friendly way but I was embarrassed to think that I had inconvenienced them. Less than a mile further on, the road terminated at a river crossing. Across the river was the village of Council. It seemed that cars had to be parked on one side of the river, and those wanting to visit must make their own way across the river. I caught up with the two ladies from the other car and apologised profusely for my negligence.

# ALASKA

'Oh, we could see that you were enjoying the view and we didn't want to hurry you.' they responded.

I wondered whether English drivers would be so tolerant. As we stood on the river bank, I saw an old Jeep picking its way across the shallow river. Obviously the driver knew where the gravel bottom was at its most shallow and the vehicle never went over the depth of its axles.

'Do you want a lift over to the town?' they asked. It seemed an opportunity not to be missed and I climbed into the back of the Jeep. I also took careful note of the route taken by the driver so that I could wade back when it was time for me to leave. When we got to the other side, the ladies invited me to call for coffee when I had finished exploring. I accepted gratefully.

The small community was attractive and carefully maintained. The buildings were all well painted and the grounds tended. Altogether there was an air of simple affluence about it, without ostentation. It didn't take me long to explore to my satisfaction; then I found the home to which the ladies had invited me, into which I was welcomed. As well as the two ladies, there was an older couple whom I judged to be the parents and home owners. It was spotlessly clean and tastefully but simply decorated. After introductions, I was offered coffee, but they said they were about to eat and invited me to join them. Such wonderful hospitality I couldn't refuse. Aside from the simple fact that I wanted to learn something about them, I presumed that I was a bit of a curiosity. The man was a retired school teacher and I learned that Council was both a holiday and retirement retreat. The lack of a bridge over the river was a deliberate attempt to exclude visitors. Supper was a generous dish of macaroni cheese and it really suited my palate. The only remarkable thing about our conversation was the older woman's opening gambit. The year was 1995 and the British Royal family had been shaken by the breakdown in the marriage of Prince Charles and Princess Diana.

'What do you think of your prince running off with a married woman?' she asked.

I was a little taken aback by this opening salvo. I realised that this part of the United States is noted for its right wing, rather puritanical views so I did not take offence. I cannot recall exactly how I answered, but I was not going to make disparaging remarks about any member of the Royal Family. I diverted the subject to more neutral ground. They were a very genial family and altogether it was an interesting afternoon which I remember with pleasure. I couldn't have upset them too much because when I took my leave, the man offered to give me a lift back over the river to my car, saving me from wading across knee deep (or deeper if I took the wrong route!).

I drove back towards Nome, taking my time and carefully monitoring my rear view mirrors. At what looked like a suitable spot, I set up camp on the banks of the Solomon River. After an unsuccessful attempt at gold panning from waters that had once made men rich, I settled into my tent and drifted off to sleep. I awoke to the sound of a pickup truck's engine and a toot on its horn. This vehicle was on the track some 100 feet away. I looked up towards the road and there stood a burly man beside the vehicle. He beckoned me urgently to join him at his truck above the riverbank. I climbed up, wondering what it was all about.

'I've just seen a she-bear with a couple of cubs not two miles up the river coming this way. She's going to be very defensive and mean. I'd get the hell out of that tent and into your vehicle if I were you,' he warned.

It sounded like good advice, particularly as I could see that his truck was marked: 'Osborn River Service-Fishing***Sightseeing-Day Trips or Drop-Off & Pick-Ups-You Name it – We Do It $$'.

The slogans might not have been composed by the leading advertising agencies of London or New York, but to me they indicated that John Osborn was a man who knew this part of the Alaskan wilderness and its ways. If he thought I was in danger I wasn't going to question his judgement, but I'd got something in my tent that I wanted to talk to him about and asked if he would come back to my camp with me.

'No sir,' he replied. 'With a she-bear and cubs coming this way and getting closer, I'm not moving away from my truck.' I was now infected with the urgency of the situation; I hurriedly broke camp and moved into my own vehicle. John Osborn headed towards Nome and I tried to get some sleep on the back seat of my car. If the she-bear and her cubs passed my way I didn't see them and they didn't pester me.

I slept badly that night and by morning I was feeling in need of exercise, so I decided to climb one of the higher hills overlooking the river valley. I chose the highest one that was marked on my map at just over 1,000 feet, with an interesting rock formation on the top. I plodded steadily upwards, taking in my surroundings. What is so attractive about the tundra are the wildflowers that grow in clusters in secluded spots – some brightly coloured and some in pastel shades. I'm no botanist, but I'm sure I have seen the same species in Greenland. A penetrating drizzle seemed to work its way through each chink in my clothing, but the cloud base was high enough not to obscure the panoramic view from the summit. Picking my way back down, I was surprised by the sight of a small bird. It was on the ground to my left, cheeping pathetically, and shuffling up the hill away from me trailing a damaged wing that hung limply by its side. I turned towards it wondering whether I could administer some first aid to the pathetic creature, but it shuffled further away. In the end, rather than distress the injured bird any more, I decided to leave it alone and continue on my way. The pathetic cheeping grew louder and I stopped. The bird stopped and we looked at each other. I then followed my original track. Next there was a flurry of wings and the bird landed in front of me. To my amusement, it repeated its convincing performance of the 'broken wing shuffle'. It was clearly trying to lead me away from its nest. The bird grew quite agitated when I ignored its sham, so I struck a compromise and found another route down the mountain that took me away from where I guessed its nest might be. After five hours of walking and climbing I got back to my camp sodden and ready for a hot meal and a rest.

John Osborn woke me up again. This time he was on his way back to Council and stopped when he saw my vehicle.

'Just thought I had better check to see whether you got ate last night.'

It is so comforting to know that people care.

There seemed to be two sorts of weather on the Seward Peninsula in the summer – dry and sunny, or overcast, windy and wet. The dry, sunny weather brought out the mosquitoes and clouds of dust on the roads. The dull, wet weather got rid of the dust and mosquitoes, but replaced it with mud and a distinct chill. I couldn't make up my mind which I preferred, but this year, according to the residents of Nome, it was predominantly wet.

Near Safety Lagoon is the Nook fishing camp. Some of the little houses seemed to have been built from the mounds of driftwood that line the shores of most Arctic beaches. One home was even built in the shape of a tepee but with the addition of a stovepipe poking out through the side. Almost all had fish drying racks. I noticed smoke rising slowly from the racks by one of the houses and wandered over to investigate.

A small fire was smouldering upwind from a drying rack covered with fish, the breeze gently taking the smoke through the fish. As I took in the scene, the owner came out to attend the fire and showed himself ready to chat with me.

'Why the fire?' I asked.

'When the weather is damp like this, the fish are likely to go bad before they dry out. The smoking preserves them, and anyway,' he added, 'the smoke gives the fish a good flavour.' After a pause, he went on. 'Last year it was wet like this and my neighbour spent too much time playing cards with his kids and didn't bother to smoke his fish and it all went bad. In the winter I had to give him half of my catch so he had something to eat.'

I was interested that he showed no resentment of his neighbour's slothfulness and would no doubt bail him out again if he got into trouble.

I asked about his life of hunting and fishing. In the winter he went off Cape Nome, where the current was strong, to hunt seal and king crabs. The king crabs have a body diameter of about nine inches. He would cut a hole in the ice about two feet across and drop bait on a line. If the king crab takes the bait it hangs on and will not let go. He would just haul it out of the water – as easy as that. He described the hunting of the seal in the same way as I had seen the Canadian Inuit hunt.[15] The ice, he told me, was normally two or three feet thick off Cape Nome and thicker up near the town of Wales.

Back in Nome, I checked in my hired vehicle and put up in June's Bed and Breakfast. June was the daughter of one of the early successful Swedish gold miners. Her son was at that time a pilot with one of the Bush Airlines that offer such a wonderful service around Alaska. I spent about ten days living at June's whilst I explored the town. I met some of the crab fishermen and visited the canning factory where the king crabs were being prepared for the Japanese market. In the town, near to a bust of Roald Amundsen commemorating the 1926 landing of his airship, The Norge, is the sign marking the end of the Iditarod Run. There I met Billy, one of Nome's drunks. He seemed to make a small living out of waiting by the sign and offering to take the photographs of tourists standing before it, using their own cameras. I thought him a most likeable man. He had a kindly face, soft eyes and a soft manner of speech. Like the man I had encountered in Anchorage, Billy had also served in the US Navy during the Vietnam conflict. He had been a medical orderly and, if he was telling the truth, had served with distinction. Sadly, drink got to him; he went absent without leave too often and was discharged. From then on his life degenerated to an existence on 'Skid Row' – a sad waste of a good man.

I was in Nome on the 4th of July and the whole town was a-buzz with the excitement of Independence Day. There were to be general festivities, parades, competitions and races. For such a small town the celebrations were very well organised and everyone joined in the fun. There was a cross-country race, fancy dress parades for the children and a slow-speed bicycle race. They even had a race for unicycles. The National Guard put on a show and the Fire Department gave a display of its only appliance. American Independence Day is not something that the 'Brits' generally celebrate – for obvious reasons – but I had been living with these friendly folk for some weeks and found myself fired up with the

---

[15] Chapter 4

spirit of the occasion. When it came to the Old Timer's Race, my landlady's son pointed out that I qualified as I had passed my 60th birthday. I decided to enter. There were about eight of us: two white Americans, five Eskimo and me. At first they set out a course of only about 30 yards, but some of the old timers were a bit offended by this and demanded 100 yards. The race organisers were reluctant; they didn't want any cardiac seizures on this fun day, but they relented. At the sound of the starter's gun I was away in the only footwear I possess, some heavy leather trekking boots. I gave the race everything I had, but a fellow Old Timer stayed shoulder to shoulder with me and we crossed the finishing line in a dead heat. The first prize of $10 was shared between us. I didn't think it appropriate for a Brit to win a prize on American Independence Day so I donated my winnings to the mayor's favourite charity, the Fire Department. To have taken part and shared in the fun was sufficient reward for me.

I decided it was time to try my hand at panning the golden sand on the sea front. To the eye it is a dirty grey-brown in colour but, judging by the little cluster of people working the beach, the gold was still there. First I tried to learn something about the process of extracting alluvial gold. The library and information centre had sufficient information for my needs. In simple terms, the gold is originally forced up into the gravel hills by volcanic activity. In the Nome area it was mostly a 'powder' gold, or very fine dust, but large nuggets worth several thousand dollars have occasionally been found. As the hills are eroded by the weather the gold is carried down with the gravel in the rivers. Being the heaviest element, the gold works its way downwards to the rock or clay base where it slowly accumulates under the lighter gravel and sand. The process of extracting the gold is to dig down to the area above the clay, or bedrock, scoop up the mixture of gold, sand and gravel and agitate it in flowing water. The gold obligingly sinks to the bottom and is collected whilst the gravel and sand are washed away. The mighty dredgers of the tundra can work down to 70 or 80 feet and shift 350 cubic yards an hour. The excavated mixture is agitated under high pressure water in a massive washing trommel to remove the large rocks which are rejected on a conveyor belt[16] while the 'fines'[17] drop into a sluice box where the sand is washed away leaving the gold in the ribbed collecting trays. If you're using a shovel and hand pan the process is the same but, of course, you can't dig so deep and can only handle very small amounts. In short, dig down to a base, pick out the rocks and carefully wash out the sand, leaving the gold to collect in the bottom of the pan.

Armed with this information, I sheepishly picked a site on the beach near enough to the other miners to watch what they were doing, but far enough from them to avoid being accused of trespassing on their pitch. These miners were living rough on the beach and were mostly young men of fearsome appearance: unshaved, unkempt and wearing rough working clothes. Had I met men of their appearance in the back streets of any major city, I would have feared for my personal safety. Self-consciously, I dug down a little and then washed my shovel full of sand in water flowing across the beach. Nothing! After several more attempts, none more successful, I saw the nearest miner come across.

'You're doing it all wrong,' he said. 'Whatever gold you've got in there, you're chucking it away. Look, I'll teach you.'

He took my gold pan and showed me the subtle technique that kept the sand in gentle motion so that it slowly lapped over the lip with the water and, to my delight, left glistening flakes of very fine gold to manifest themselves in the bottom of the pan. Easier to say than to do, but I eventually got the hang of it.

'There you go,' my tutor said. 'You're getting it.'

This was no way to get rich quickly, but I was not in a mood to be reasonable. As I watched the steady accumulation of the shining element I was struck with a serious bout of gold fever. Looking back, I must have behaved much as Toad did when he first saw a motorcar.[18] The next day I returned to feed my craving for the precious metal. The weather turned particularly nasty. There were strong winds and driving rain and it was *very* cold. My

---

[16] A man is normally posted at the end of the conveyor belt to ensure that gold nuggets the size of large rocks are not thrown out with the rubbish
[17] The mixture of fine sand and gravel that contains the gold
[18] The episode occurs in Chapter 2 of Kenneth Grahame's *The Wind in the Willows*

fellow miners had the good sense to retire to the shelter of the Nugget Inn and while away the day over a pint or two of good Alaskan beer. I alone worked on the beach, leaning into the wind, oblivious to the icy trickle of rain down my neck. The daily tourist bus full of Taiwanese arrived. An item of their one-day itinerary in the town was to see the miners working on the golden sands of Nome. I was the only one there. I carefully avoided the eye of the unfortunate tour guide who tried to explain what I was doing whilst the throng of tourists leant avidly out of the windows of the bus taking photographs of my efforts. I don't for a minute think I fooled the guide into believing I was an experienced beach miner, but I had saved him the embarrassment of an empty beach and, judging by the excited chatter of those in his charge, his band of tourists were satisfied.

Perhaps, in return for the great kindness I had received from so many people in this area, I had done a small service for at least one resident of Nome.

## Chapter 7

# RUSSIA'S CHUKOTKA

*A visit to 'the furthest corner' of Russia and the warmth of living within the community.*

When God made the world, he left the Devil to make Chukotka. This is how it was put to me by Stanislav Mitrofanov, a Russian who was born in the region and had always lived there. One might question the geological accuracy of the utterance, but there is no denying its graphic powers.

Russia's Chukotka was part of the land called Beringia when it was attached to Alaska. The Bering Strait now divides the two continents by a relatively narrow waterway, at one point only 56 miles across, but even the hardy Alaskans admit that both Chukotka's terrain and climate are more taxing than anything found in their own land. It is mountainous, but not dramatically so. There is nothing on Chukotka as high as Mount McKinley in the Alaskan range but, seen from the air, Chukotka's high ground seems to stretch endlessly into the distance, a veritable barrier to easy travel even if the climate were benign and – it is not. The warm Kuroshio ocean current, also known as the Japan Current, that ameliorates the Alaskan climate manages to avoid Chukotka. Instead, the cold Oyashio current casts its foggy influence and adds additional bleakness to the effects of the Arctic Ocean and the vast land mass of continental Asia. Whilst the snow will generally have melted in Alaska by late June, in Chukotka the snow clings on into July and in some places will even stay on the lower hills all year round.

Even with the coming of the Western Russians, the area

remains isolated. Situated in the shelter of a large fjord on the south-west extreme of the Chukotka peninsula is the town of Provideniya. Today's population, including military personnel, is less than 5,000 persons. It is nearer to America's capital city, Washington, than to its own capital, Moscow. Two hundred and fifty miles across the Bering Strait is Nome, but the nearest Russian town of similar size is Anadyr, four hundred miles to the west. To get to the nearest large Russian city one would have to travel 1,200 miles to either Magadan or Petropavlovsk-Kamchatskiy.

Whilst many people refer to this part of Russia as Siberia, the Russians will maintain that it is not correct to do so. They point out that Siberia stretches across the plains between the Ural Mountains, running roughly north/south at about longitude 60° east to Verkhojanski Hrebet[1] mountains, just east of the River Lena that meanders south to north around longitude 125° east. From the Verkhojanski Hrebet to the Pacific Ocean – a distance of nearly 3,000 miles – is what the Russians call 'The Far East'. The extreme easterly point of mainland Russia, Cape Dezhinevo, even stretches 10° longitude into the western hemisphere and the Russian island of Big Diomede in the Bering Strait is even deeper into the west at 169° – only 2 miles away from America's Little Diomede island.

Many years ago, when my flying took me frequently across the Atlantic, I would spend my free time enjoying the sights and culture of New York City. I often stood enthralled by two of the exhibits in the Natural Science Museum. They depicted Big Diomede and Little Diomede Islands in the Bering Strait and their bird life. They were anything but scenes of soft beauty and would never have found their way onto the front covers of tourist brochures. They depicted a barren rocky landscape under a dark, heavy overcast. A troubled sea was pounding the cliffs that fell to their shores. A varied collection of sea birds swooped or clung to the rock faces. It was grim. I was bewitched. An urge to visit that area one day was burnt into my psyche. That urge smouldered

---

[1] Verkhojanski Spine

within me and when, some twenty five years later, I planned my visit to Alaska, I could not resist the opportunity to cross the Bering Strait and see something of the Russian scenes that had gripped me.

The Russian land across the Bering Strait from Alaska is the territory of the Yupik Eskimosy, the cousins of the other Eskimo that populated the lands all the way across North America to Greenland. In the past they were steadily pushed back by the more aggressive Chukchi until now they inhabit – at least, in any number – only the extreme east of the Chukotka peninsula. Like all their brethren, they prefer to hunt and fish and now have taken up reindeer herding. Some also farm foxes for their fur. Although the communities of the Chukchi and Yupik are small and scattered over this vast area, it would be wrong to dismiss these people as lacking art and culture. The Yupik at Uelen on Cape Dezhinevo are renowned for producing the most exquisite art in ivory carved from the tusks of the walrus. The themes of their elegant work are, as one would expect, predominantly Arctic, but there is no doubting their artistic skills.

Getting information on this part of Russia was depressingly difficult, particularly from Europe. Not even the best libraries in London have much to offer on the subject but, after purchasing some US Air Force aviation maps of the area and pursuing a great deal of research, I found the key to getting across the Strait and satisfying my long-held desire. The entry town in this furthest corner of Russia is Provideniya. From Nome in Alaska there was a small 'bush airline'[2] that included an informal schedule to Provideniya. It was not until I got to Nome that I found those who had made the trip across the Bering Strait and, although they were keen to help, it was difficult to get a picture of what to expect.

'You'll kiss the ground when you return,' is the discouraging comment Alaskans tend to make.

'How did you manage to get a visa without an invitation from my office?'

---

[2] Bering Air

'How did you know about Provideniya?'
'Why have you come here?'
'Why do you want to come here?'

These were some of the questions asked of me the morning after my arrival in Provideniya, when I had been hastily summoned before the deputy mayor. On arrival, I had cleared customs and immigration with the greatest of ease and thought I was home and dry. Now I found myself the subject of interrogation.

I was in the town's administrative building. The room was Spartan furnished only with a conference table and a few chairs, some of which were drawn up to the table and some scattered along one wall. At the head of the table sat the deputy mayor, a man in his early forties, smartly dressed in a lounge suit. His countenance was stiff and formal. Opposite me was a uniformed middle-aged woman who had been introduced as the police officer responsible for visitor registration. I could not help but notice that she was impeccably groomed. Her demeanour was stern but her eyes were not unkind. She did not speak at any time during the interview. Next to her was the interpreter, an attractive girl in her late twenties. She too was well dressed but less formal. Her eyes were bright; she spoke excellent English and was delightfully animated. I would have enjoyed the situation more had I not realised that if I gave the wrong answers I risked ignominious deportation or, worse, a prolonged stay in some penal institution. On my side of the table was Stanislav Mitrofanov looking slightly worried and following the questions and answers most earnestly. Stanislav was my host. The trouble had started when he took my visa and passport to the police to register my arrival and it was noticed that the visa was not of the type normally issued to Americans. Apparently, I was the first Englishman ever to plan a stay in the town and my visa, issued in London by the Russian embassy, was not what they were accustomed to.

Maintaining what I hoped was an expression of injured innocence, I answered the questions as best I could and explained that I had applied via Intourist, the Russian State Tourist office, in London, for the visa which had been duly approved and issued by the Russian Embassy. The visa gave me leave to visit Provideniya,

Lavrentiya and Uelen. Surely I had done all that was expected of me.

'You see,' explained the deputy mayor, 'these people in London do not understand the law as we apply it in Provideniya. Your visa should have been applied for after a letter of invitation had been authorised by my office against payment of a fee.'

All was now clear to me. I explained that I prided myself on meticulously abiding by the laws of all the countries I visited and had no intention of evading any fees that might need to be paid. I was happy to pay such a fee immediately.

'No! That would not be appropriate,' said the deputy mayor. 'You are clearly innocent and I shall instruct the police officer to accept your registration for the normal fee, but on condition that you do not leave the town of Provideniya.'

Stanislav looked relieved. So was I, and I smiled my thanks to the deputy mayor, who smiled back and nodded. I smiled at the police officer and she beamed a big smile back to me. I fell into an all too brief discussion over the exact meaning of an English word that had been used during my interrogation with that attractive interpreter, then reluctantly took my leave of her and walked out of the building with Stanislav. That afternoon Stanislav dealt with my registration and I saw no change out of US $100.00. The deputy mayor got his fee after all.

I owed a great deal to Stanislav. In Nome, before I departed Alaska, I had chanced to meet an Alaskan business colleague of his and he had promised to get a message to Stanislav in order that I should have a contact. The arrangement had not been confirmed and I thought the offer would turn out to be so much 'hot air'. After my arrival in Provideniya I asked someone, who appeared to be an airport official, how I might find Stanislav.

'That's him, waiting for you in that car,' she said, pointing out of the window.

The Gods were looking after me. I had done my humble best to learn some Russian but it was less than adequate for anything other than survival. My only assets were equipment to enable me to live rough, a will to deal with whatever contingency arose and a mistaken belief that, as I was carrying about US $3,000 in currency notes, I would be able to negotiate my way through most difficulties. Stanislav offered rental of an apartment that lay empty in the town, or accommodation and full board in his home with his family. I had gone to Chukotka to meet the people and what better way was there than to live with a family? I jumped at the offer. This made the survival equipment unnecessary; rather than having to look after myself, I was going to be looked after and would see something of Russian family life. To me, that was worth much more than a visit to Uelen. The importance of this chance arrangement became all the more obvious when I tried to convert some of my $3,000 into Russian roubles. The bank in Provideniya was not authorised to change foreign currency. The nearest bank was probably in Magadan, more than 1,200 miles away. To get there I would have to buy a local return flight, but I would have to pay the air fare with Russian roubles. The perfect 'Catch 22'! In any event, I didn't have a visa for Magadan. The local traders and shop keepers would not accept payment for any goods in foreign currency. In short, I was sitting on $3,000 and effectively destitute. I still offer prayers of gratitude to Stanislav and his wife Yadvega for solving this problem for me. They were more than ready to accept US currency in settlement of my board and lodging.

Provideniya is not the sort of town one wants to judge too hastily. The drive from the airport through the military town of Ureliki and around Komsomolskaya Bay (formerly called Emma Bay) revealed hills bare of noticeable vegetation. The sea mist that had kept the airport closed for some days before my arrival had lifted to a low cloud and that added to the gloom and dullness of the town. It had been some while since the gravel roads had been re-graded and they had many pot holes. Most of the buildings were in need of maintenance; Virtually all required redecoration. The infrastructure was crumbling. Heavy cranes loomed menacingly over the docks. Unfamiliar to English eyes was a massive coal-burning power station that emitted a powerful roar and belched black smoke into the sky from its towering stack. As Stanislav drove me through the town I looked about me and kept a smile on my face that I hoped would be interpreted as pleasure. I wondered what I had let myself in for. The one visual relief to the eye was a delightfully decorated wooden building that turned out to be a bar.

Stanislav and Yadvega welcomed me into their home and introduced me to their two sons, Adik who was nine and Yan who was four. A young Alsatian dog called Tooman[3] presented himself in friendship. Stanislav spoke very good English. Yadvega spoke about as much English as my very limited Russian. It would seem Russian is a language very tolerant of a limited vocabulary and shocking abuse of grammar as, much to my surprise, our combination of languages was sufficient for free and easy conversation. I later learnt that, although my linguistic endeavours were abysmally devoid of correct grammar, I was intelligible to the Russians. What was more important, however, was the fact that I tried to speak their language and did not presume, as so many other visitors did, that they should speak English. This did much to establish respect and a rapport.

The family apartment was set on the ground floor of an archetypal Russian concrete building. A classical Russian wooden building would have had some 'romantic' appeal for me and fitted better into the image of Russia I had from books and plays, but the few wooden buildings that were in the town, although visually attractive, were in poor structural and decorative condition. The front door of my host's apartment was off the building's stair-well and led into an entrance hall. There were two spacious bedrooms, a living room, and kitchen with dinette, bathroom and separate lavatory. Only the kitchen and dinette were decorated with colourful tiles, trinkets and lacquered utensils. The apartment was comfortable and warm. The windows had thick double-glazing with some three or four inches of air space between the panes. In this household, the nicely decorated kitchen was the room for social intercourse and seemed to be reasonably well equipped. It had the all-important samovar, a stove, a refrigerator and a microwave oven. The only amenity that appeared to be missing was a modern washing machine and drier for laundry. Persistent

---

[3] The word means 'fog' and was given to him on account of his colouring

sea fogs in summer and intense cold in winter would defeat the usefulness of an outside washing line; in any event, there was no private land attached to the apartment that would have been suitable. The bathroom had to double as a laundry and as it was an 'inside room', and consequently poorly ventilated, the condensation seriously affected its decoration.

I was offered one of the bedrooms. It was spacious and the bed was comfortable, but as the door had a defective latch I sometimes found I was sharing the bed with Tooman. I was intrigued that Stanislav, a trained civil engineer, showed me how to wedge a curtain in the door jamb to prevent it swinging open when I, a simple 'do-it-your-self man', could have fixed it easily with a screwdriver. However, it was not my place to interfere. I was there to be a good guest, observe, and try and melt into this family. My hosts made me feel very much at home. My reservations about the grim appearance of the town were beginning to wane.

Both Stanislav and Yadvega were in their mid-thirties and both worked. Yadvega had a lovely face, broad and smiling. She was a telecommunications engineer working shifts at the telephone exchange. She usually dressed well and I never saw her 'slopping' about the home, careless of her appearance. Stanislav was tall and slim. He always dressed casually in jeans. Although he had trained as a civil engineer, he appeared to be very busy with numerous business contacts and always had meetings to attend. Exactly what his work was, I never discovered. Their food was tasty and nutritious and their helpings often more than I could manage. I could see why Yadvega was fighting a losing battle to stay trim.

I was generally left to my own devices to explore the town and observe the life around me. If I had dressed as John Bull and carried a Union Jack as I walked about I could not have been more obviously a stranger, an object of curiosity, a novelty. The towns-folk were too polite to stare, or even to turn their heads to observe me. They would continue their activities, whatever they might be, but their eyes would follow me for a while. In the early days of my stay in the town, even officers in police patrol cars kept their faces forwards, but followed me with their eyes. Within a week, I could see that the police had lost interest in my presence and generally ignored my wanderings about the town. Good humoured groups of young men might greet me in fractured English, and I would try to respond in Russian with a grin. The day after my interrogation, I saw the deputy mayor in the street. I smiled at him and waved, and he responded with a pleasant smile and nod of the head. I also came across the police officer who had attended my interrogation and in response to my smile she beamed back at me. It was as if my entry had never been at risk. I was not so naïve, however as to think that I was beyond risk of deportation or arrest if I did something to destroy their trust in me as a curious but harmless visitor.

One day, when I stood in front of the administrative building trying to compose a photograph of Lenin's statue against an austere background, two men walked by and said, 'Don't bother photographing him. We're going to take him down and throw him into the harbour!'

They were hardly politically repressed. Stanislav had some very firm ideas about the nepotism, rather than outright corruption, which afflicted the town, and he was outspoken about the administrative inefficiency, at both local and central level. Provideniya's remoteness made it very dependent on supplies of necessaries coming in regularly. I was told how, one year, the stocks of coal that fed the power station were down to three weeks' supply and winter was approaching fast. Without that power station, electricity and central heating to all the buildings would be lost. A coal ship managed to get in just before the sea froze for the winter. It would have been a terrible winter for them if that supply had failed. Sometimes the inefficiency appeared in more comic forms – at least to an outsider. On one occasion they needed potatoes and other important food supplies. Stocks were nearly depleted and the township had been agitating for fresh supplies for months. When the next supply ship finally docked, instead of potatoes and important food, it offloaded sufficient toilet rolls to supply the town for three years!

It seemed that the news of my arrival in Provideniya had spread far and wide in this tight-knit community. I had not been there more than a few days when I met a Yupik woman. Her name was Elina and she claimed to be part of a local Yupik dance group. I'm not sure whether I found her, or she found me, but it was the sort of contact I was hoping to make. I wanted to get some photographs of the Yupik people and she was prepared to pose wearing various styles of their local costumes. We met up for the photo shoot later that day. I was delighted. Elina was a large woman of middle years. She was not a relaxed model and over-dramatised her poses, but the shoot went well enough and she put on a variety of dresses from her own Yupik tribe and the costume of the Chukchi. I was amused to note that there was some inconsistency in the costumes in that her boots were more typical of Western Russia than the ethnic boots of the region and her gloves could have been bought in a branch of Marks and Spencer. When we had finished, the question of a modelling fee was solved by her producing various pieces of local art to sell – she would be pleased to accept US dollars. This suited me well but in a fit of misguided generosity, I deliberately paid more than the goods were worth, reckoning that it was still an infinitesimal fraction of what I would have been expected to pay in England for a model. This was a mistake. It wasn't difficult for Elina to find out where I was living and, as it seemed she now considered me a new and bountiful source of income in US dollars, she started to make a nuisance of herself. Two days later I finished up cowering behind Yadvega, whilst she came to my defence. I can only guess what passed between the two women, but eventually Elina retreated, never to be seen by me again.

'Crazy woman!' Yadvega snorted.

Elina had told her that she had a sick aunt living in California and wanted some dollars to send to her. I found the concept of a Yupik Eskimo woman from Russia's Far East sending aid to California mildly amusing. I reflected, however, that even this part of Russia was a socialist state and everyone was provided for, albeit to a basic standard. Life in California may be very glossy when one is successful and earning, it is very different if one is sick and out of work, so I am not sure that the concept of aid from Russia to the USA was really quite so strange. But I had yet another reason to be grateful to Yadvega.

Most of the shops in town were difficult to see, being tucked away in buildings that could be mistaken for apartment blocks and not generally having display windows. The few I did find were quite well stocked with a variety of goods, a high proportion of which were imported from countries all over the world. The two 'provision' shops, or grocery stores were more obvious; the larger of them sold vodka. I stood outside until it opened at 4.00 p.m. As opening time approached a small crowd gathered, waiting patiently. Most of them were men. When it opened, I followed the crowd in and saw there was a general rush to buy the half litre bottles of vodka kept on a top shelf. Within the space of a few minutes, the 15 or 20 bottles on display had gone, been replaced, cleared and restocked again before the rush subsided. The town could well have a drink problem if this rate of sale was the norm. Stanislav and Yadvega themselves were very moderate drinkers; I saw no drunks in the street and certainly never felt at personal risk. However, for such a small town, there seemed to be a large and attentive police force, and this might have been the reason why there was no public drunkenness. An exception occurred one afternoon in the form of two sailors off a ship from Vladivostok. Although the behaviour of those who are intoxicated is always unpredictable, I judged that these two came under the classification of cheerful drunks. They waved a bottle of vodka and invited me to join them as they headed out of town. The temptation to do so was strong, even if only to experience another aspect of Russian life, but caution held me back. I had nothing to contribute to the binge and, although I was sober, reasonably fit and co-ordinated and they were unsteady on their feet, there were two of them and only one of me. I could not be sure their genial mood would last. I had no intention of being rude to them. In my homeland, I would have simply walked away. Instead, I tried to exchange some light banter but they were insistent that I join them. When they finally accepted that I was going to be a very poor drinking companion they insisted that I kiss them farewell. It seems that kissing between men in Russia is a perfectly normal social act, but I was far too British to comply. I'm afraid that as an ambassador for the average Englishman I was a great disappointment to them. As they weaved their erratic way down the road, I considered that whatever vodka there was in their bottle would go further between two than three. I would have loved to have learned more about their lives. It was an opportunity lost.

I occasionally had the privilege of joining Stanislav and Yadvega on social outings to visit their friends. It was kind of them to include me because my poor Russian tended to stall the conversation. The best way to deal with any awkwardness was to get involved with the children in their various games and leave the adults to converse more freely, though I continued to observe the social scene. I noted that little social gatherings in the Far East of Russia were really no different from social gatherings in England. There would be lively conversation with much laughter and leg-pulling. In the families I mixed with, there was very little hard drinking. Those I met really seemed to be very happy with their lot. I was amused to note it was generally the ladies who dominated the conservation.

In front of the administrative building is a small square, and on the other side of the statue of Lenin, above a high bank, was a building marked 'Dom Moleetva' – The House of Prayer. I would have liked to find something like an Orthodox Russian Church, complete with domed roof and icons, but it was a simple wooden structure, more like a school outbuilding than a place of worship. I found it was indeed a house of prayer – run by an American Baptist minister. He had been there two and a half years and gathered a respectably large congregation. As I was later to find out for myself, foreign church missionary organisations were active in Chukotka. This mission may have been the only church in the town but it was not the only example of religious activity. The minister passed on some useful local knowledge and seemed very happy with his work.

'How do you find this community as a whole?' I asked, and went on to say that, although there were obviously problem areas, I thought the people were delightful.

His reaction was almost passionate.

'I'm so pleased you think that,' he responded. 'There is so much good amongst these people and yet most visitors can only see the crumbling buildings in need for repair. If only these visitors would open their eyes and see the good that is all about.' I was relieved to hear him say that, as I was beginning to think my growing affection for this scruffy little town and its people was unbalanced. I should have attended one of his services. I'm sure I would have been welcomed and it might have given me a further insight into these people.

The children were a delight and quite unrestrained in their approaches to me. The schools were on holiday and youngsters of all ages played in the town. I felt like the Pied Piper of Hamlin as flocks of them followed me about. Some would take my hand and even offer me simple gifts. A couple of young lads with bicycles stopped to chat and pulled some unwrapped biscuits from their pockets and offered them to me. I was torn between offending them and my concern at the questionable hygiene, but I took the offering and munched biscuits with them. Fortunately, a life of travel has granted me a degree of immunity from dubious food. To avoid confusing their affectionate attention with 'cupboard love' I deliberately refrained from offering gifts in return and, for fear of misunderstanding by watching adults, I always tried to avoid any form of physical contact. One young girl in particular attached herself to me with gusto. She was perhaps six or seven years of age and always wore a distinctive deerstalker hat. Her name was Zyeninhan. She asked whether I was American.

'No, I am English,' I replied. Thereafter she took it upon herself to answer this question for the other children.

'He is English,' she would state with authority.

I wondered whether Zyeninhan even knew where England was. Another little girl of about the same age latched on to part of my photographic kit. I carry a small Lastolite reflector to 'bounce' light into shadows and thus reduce unwanted contrast. The reflector will unfold from its packed size to a reasonably large circular disk with reflective fabric surfaces on it. With a little practice it is easy to twist it so that it folds for storage into a very small disk, a fraction of its unfolded size. Of all the children who tried to fold my reflector, only this little girl was able to manage it, and from then on she was the Queen of the reflector. Whenever a new child joined my little group they were put to the test. Then, with glowing pride, she would demonstrate how she alone could manage it.

Only the very young toddlers were supervised by an adult. Those from about five years of age and above were given a freedom that would be considered reprehensible in England and most other Western countries; a sad reflection on the West that our society needs us to be so protective of its young. Here the older children kept a watchful eye on the younger ones. There were virtually no private cars to cause traffic hazards and the scourge of paedophilia seemed unknown. Violent crime was confined to quarrels in private, usually under the influence of alcohol. Tactful enquiries about the freedom of the children revealed a simple philosophy: the winters are most severe and the children have then to be constrained indoors. Every year, two or three people are caught out by inexperience or bad luck and freeze to death, perhaps by misjudging the thickness of the ice when taking a short cut over the bay, or perhaps, uncoordinated and confused by drink, they wander into a deep snow drift and are unable to extract themselves. There are many ways for the unlucky, the inexperienced, the careless, and particularly the drunk to lose their lives in the Arctic. Winter temperatures are not abnormally low – only about $-25°C$ – but the region suffers from squalls and blizzards which make outdoor activity unbearable. When the sky clears and the wind drops, the temperature will often plunge to $-40°C$ or even $-50°C$; it is greeted with relief and people take advantage to go outside for fresh air and exercise. In a climate such as this, the summer is when children can enjoy what freedom and exercise is available. I observed that this did not interfere with their duty to assist in domestic chores, nor did it weaken their obedience to their parents when a command was issued.

There seemed to be ample fun and affection displayed within the families of people with whom I came into contact. At first I could not be sure that I was not witnessing behaviour influenced by the presence of a stranger, but the longer I stayed with the family in the town, the more I sensed that my novelty had faded and I was being accepted as one of their number. Confirmation came to me one day when the dog Tooman committed some transgression and Stanislav gave him a sound telling off and sent him to his bed. Instead of obeying, Tooman came to me and put his head on my lap. Thoughtlessly, I gently stroked him. Stanislav angrily admonished me for interfering with his disciplining of the dog. I apologised and reflected that he would not have spoken to me in those terms if he still considered me a guest to be treated deferentially. I had, I reasoned, become one of his family. The infrastructure of the town may have been crumbling but it could boast a very rich and satisfying family life with fun and laughter that many other communities would envy. I was beginning to realise that I was very happy living in Provideniya.

Touching physical evidence of family affection was to be found in the austere burial ground overlooking the entrance to the harbour. Little gifts of food, drink or toys often adorned the graves of children. Many grave sites were provided with tables and benches for families to partake of a simple meal on significant anniversaries. The grave yard was barren and bleak, yet love for the lost ones was evident from these simple displays. I found it haunting.

Some while after my arrival, I was sitting alone in the apartment when the phone rang. I answered it and an American voice said in English, 'Tell Stanislav we'll arrive at three o'clock.' It was a pilot called Dick Page phoning from Nome. At that time, Dick worked for a small Alaskan air operation called Lake Clark Air Inc. who were flying a service for The Samaritan Purse charity. They were bringing in two American doctors, a husband and wife team, and supplies of medicines and medical equipment provided by the charity to support the local hospitals in Provideniya and Anadyr some 400 miles to the west. I passed on the message to Stanislav when he came back and he set off to the airport to meet them. The party arrived, laden with presents and goods for the family. The two doctors moved off to another apartment and Dick settled in with Stanislav and Yadvega. I kept my bedroom, Dick moved into our host's bedroom and Stanislav and Yadvega moved with the children into the living room. The plan was to drop off the medical supplies in Provideniya, then fly on to deliver the rest in Anadyr. It wasn't to work out so easily however, and to get the aircraft to Anadyr and back became something of a farce. Anadyr and Provideniya are in different administrative areas and each of the airports was controlled by the military. Clearances were needed for the flight. The next day, when Dick and his doctors were at the airport ready to leave, the military pointed out that no flight clearance had been received from Moscow. They dispatched a telex to Moscow requesting clearance but, unfortunately, there is an 11 hour time difference between Provideniya and Moscow, so it arrived when the offices were closed. In other countries, one would have expected 24 hour coverage by personnel qualified to attend to such matters but that did not seem to be the case in Russia. The person in charge in Moscow did not have a suitable deputy. It seemed that principals who had acquired deputies found that the deputies tried to oust them, so principals felt more secure in their position if they did not have deputies; thus, it was not until the person in authority arrived for work the next morning and had attended to his mail that he dealt with the telex. In effect, his reply said, 'The clearance has already been sent to you.' By this time, it was night in Provideniya and, as the airport was operational only during the day, no one was there to receive it. It was not until the following morning that the military in Provideniya replied to Moscow saying, 'Well we haven't received it.' It was now night in Moscow. The next morning, Moscow insisted that it had been sent and that it ought to be in Provideniya. By the time Provideniya had persuaded Moscow to send another clearance and had it safely in the hands of the military authorities, nearly a week had elapsed. I was amazed at Dick's phlegmatic patience whilst this display of bureaucratic bungling was sorted out. On the plus side Dick and I had a chance to get to know each other and we became good friends. He, like myself, had a great affection for this little community, whatever its administrative failings.

Periodically, during the summer months, *The Explorer*, an adventure tourist cruise ship would come into port and the quiet tempo of life in the town would be disrupted. The tourists, a mixture of 'Western' nationalities – American, German, English, French, etc. – would come ashore for three or four hours. They moved about singly or in groups to take in this little Russian town on the Bering Strait. The townspeople responded with excitement and all the shops opened; guided tours were conducted of the bakery, the museum and the cultural hall, where a concert was put on for their entertainment. I mingled with the groups, unsure whether I was being mistaken for a tourist or a resident of the town. I was interested to see how the tourists behaved. With only three or four hours ashore, they didn't have time to sit and melt into the community as I had done. They could only gather a 'first impression'. It is difficult to make a safe judgement about what others are thinking but I did notice that many of the tourists tended to have their heads together, eyeing the failing infrastructure of the buildings, rather than looking into the faces of those who were so earnestly showing them their town and desperately trying to make them welcome.

The show at the cultural centre was worthy of comment. Provideniya was reputed to have a very good music school. In the anti-room to the auditorium where the show was to take place a very young band played. I have suffered many a school concert in England, but this band of youngsters was really very good. The earnest dedication of their conductor, probably their music teacher, was touching as she swung her baton and beamed at the visitors. Inside the hall the main attractions were the accordion soloists. The very high standard of music was impressive, and certainly the tourists responded with enthusiastic applause. What really pleased me was the way they were introduced. The musicians were naturally nervous as they came in and sat down centre stage, but the woman introducing them, another music teacher, stood with her hand on their shoulder maintaining a physical contact as she made the introductions. Having done so, she looked carefully into the soloist's eyes for a few moments willing encouragement and then stepped back and let her hand slide across and then off the musician's shoulder as she retired from the stage. Such a display of affection and encouragement could not be misinterpreted. I find it very sad that in Europe, such physical contact between teacher and pupil would now be considered inappropriate and probably the subject of complaint.

The one who stole the show for me was an eight or nine year old girl called Zhenya. Little Zhenya and her mother, Svetlana, appeared in Russian national costume and conducted the ceremony of welcoming visitors with salt and bread. With a clear and remarkably powerful voice for one so young Zhenya, speaking in Russian, described the symbolism and history of the ceremony. Her words were translated into English by a school boy standing at the edge of the stage. Whatever first impression of the town the tourists may have held, there was no mistaking their appreciation of Zhenya. The applause when she finished was thunderous.

Immediately after the performance, I approached Svetlana and Zhenya and asked if they would pose for photographs whilst still in their costumes. They agreed and were very patient. When photographing people, I have learned the value of keeping up a line of chatter. Professional photographic models know their trade and will keep their eyes alive and remain animated. Those who have not had a model's training lose their alertness and become flat and self-conscious if the photographer doesn't keep their attention by talking to them. This presents a problem when a photographer can barely speak their language, but I did my best. It must have been my linguistic ineptitude that kept their eyes alight with amusement and barely concealed smiles on their lips.

It would have been most inappropriate to offer them a modelling fee so I ran back to my lodgings where I knew I had a few suitable gifts I had brought with me from America. I selected some hand cream for Svetlana and some coloured cottons and needles for Zhenya and hurried back to the cultural centre. The tourists were by now all heading back to their ship and I was met by a caretaker lady. She was an elderly woman, a little portly and dressed in black. Her face had the expression of a Rottweiler guard dog uncertain of an intruder.

'Yes?' was all she said.

I explained I was looking for Svetlana and Zhenya and wanted to say 'thank you' to them. She kept her eyes on me and talked into a telephone. Her speech on the phone was too quick for me to understand all that was said but I recognised the word 'photographer'. She hung up, turned to me and her face broke into a beautiful smile.

'They'll be down in a minute. Please wait.'

It never ceases to amaze me how easy it is to be misled by appearances unless you are very familiar with the local culture. I had thought the door keeper was a hard, severe woman, but that smile painted a totally different image. Eventually Svetlana and Zhenya came down from the dressing room and I thanked them again for being so patient with me and offered them my little gifts. Svetlana accepted the gifts but was quite embarrassed and her cheeks went a little pink. Zhenya's eyes turned to her mother and back to me as she accepted the coloured cottons. To avoid further embarrassment to them, I hastily withdrew.

Two days later, I was meandering between the apartment blocks trying to photograph the artistic designs of the window frames and the clusters of flowers or pot grown vegetables that most residents seem to have on the sills, when Zhenya stepped in front of me. I didn't recognise her at first as she was now with a friend and dressed in the everyday woollens and anorak that almost all the children wore. I was pleased to stop and talk with this little girl who had so captivated me. I noticed that she carried a toy plastic camera. I handed her my camera so that she could take some real photographs of her friend. We sat on a rock and talked for a bit and when I stood up to leave, she took my hand and told me to shut my eyes. I did as I was bid, and felt something being pressed into my hand. It was the watch off her wrist and she wanted me to have it as a present. No previous travel experience of mine could have prepared me for such a gift, delivered in this fashion, from one so young. The effect was devastating. I could not, of course, accept the watch. I wanted to hug her but dared not, so I returned it as kindly as I knew how and retreated out of the town onto some high rocks overlooking the harbour. There I sat for some while trying to get my emotions and thoughts into order. I didn't meet Zhenya again, but I sometimes look at her picture and wonder how she is getting on. By now she will be a young woman. I worry that the troubles that seem to befall Russia and her people all too often may be making her young life difficult.

My activities were not confined to the town. In my explorations, I wandered into the tundra or the surrounding hills and mountains, sometimes with a companion and sometimes alone. I frequently climbed to an abandoned military lookout post, high on the hills that back onto Provideniya. From there, straight ahead of me, I had an excellent view down the main fjord that leads into the Gulf of Anadyr and the Bering Sea, with Plover Point jutting into the fjord and forming a perfect shelter from storms. Over to my left, I had an equally excellent view of what was once called Emma Bay, now renamed Komsomolskya Bay, with the military town of Ureliki across the water and the airfield. I reflected on the history of the area which I had learned from the little museum in the town. The involvement of the Western Russians in this region goes back to 1660 AD when it was first mentioned by a trading expedition. Later, in 1728, Vitus Bering, a Dutch navigator in the service of the Tsar Peter II, was sent into the area to discover whether mainland Russia was attached to mainland America, and in the process discovered the Diomede Islands for the white man. In the course of his expedition he used this fjord, now known as Provideniya Bay, for shelter. Various places around the area still carry the names of some of his crew.

The event that led to Provideniya getting its name is almost whimsical. When, in the middle of the mid 19th century, Sir John Franklin's expedition sailed to find the North West Passage and failed to return, numerous further expeditions were dispatched to try to find and rescue any survivors. It was reasoned that Franklin might have successfully navigated the North West Passage but become lost somewhere north of Alaska or in the area of the Bering Strait. Two British ships, The Plover, a brig used for hydrographic survey work, and The Gerald, were dispatched to search this area. In 1848, The Plover, under the command of Captain T. Moore, was badly damaged in a storm and in danger of foundering. The rugged coast prevented beaching and the crew became seriously concerned for their safety. It is said that the ship's chaplain, having conducted prayers for their survival said they were 'in the hands of Providence' and, as he did so, the lookout called that a safe haven was in sight. It proved to be the fjord leading into the bay where the town of Provideniya now stands. With the help of the Yupik Eskimo, the crew were able to overwinter and repair their ship without loss of life, a most unusual achievement in such harsh conditions. The bay became known as Providence Bay, the Russians subsequently adopting the name in their own language: Buhkta Provideniya. Captain Moore called the inner part Emma Bay after his daughter. The town, when it was eventually built, was called Provideniya. Emma Bay retained that name until 1953, when it was renamed Komsomolskya Bay in honour of those who effected a daring rescue of the passengers and crew of a ship being crushed by ice in the North East Passage. The spit of land that stretches a protective finger into Provideniya bay is still known as Plover Point.

The bay remained undeveloped but was used as a naval refuelling base for many years. Not until the 1930s did any rapid development take place. In 1937 new houses were built and the following year a modern sea port was developed. It was needed to cope with the town's increasing importance to the sea traffic from the Pacific Ocean to Russia's northern cities along the Arctic coast all the way to Murmansk on the Kola Peninsula of European Russia. The town is now an industrial community with a trading port, key industries and a commendable collection of facilities including, a hospital, schools, shops, cinema, a cultural centre and even a dairy farm.

The airport where I landed, and which I could see from my observation post, was developed during the Second World War. There was an urgent need to ferry aircraft from the United States to Russia's front with Germany so, in 1942, the Americans built a suitable airfield just outside the town. It is not very grand but it is still operational and, other than a sea passage, is the town's only link to the rest of Russia and the outside world. The runway lies between two hills and the flight in offers a stimulating view for the passengers.

On one of my trips into the hills, I had the companionship of a local photographer named Sasha. As we looked for scenes to photograph, we came across a family picnicking and went over to talk to them. Before I had said anything, one of them addressed me in English. The conversation was unimportant but when we continued on our way I asked Sasha how that man had known I was English.

'Oh, everyone knows who you are and where you come from.'

Fame comes in the most modest forms!

Part of Sasha's income came from selling his pictures as local post cards; he also intended to publish a reference book on the area's wildflowers. Sasha and I planned to wander the hills of the area as long as the light lasted. I was carrying some bread and a water bottle, as I would always do when in an isolated area. Sasha also carried bread, but no water.

'We Russians always know how to find water and can look after ourselves in the wilderness,' he boasted.

The Russians love their country and are proud of their achievements and their stoicism in the face of difficulty and hardship. Their history supports this self-confidence, but I prefer to take precautions – just in case. It was a lovely day in the hills. The sun shone and there was virtually no wind. We were both busy with our cameras gathering lots of material, and the hours ticked by. Every time I took out my water bottle, I offered Sasha a drink.

'No, no. I shall find some natural water,' he replied.

The sun was making me very thirsty and I was puzzled at how long he had managed to go without a drink. Soon I began to notice, however, that he spent more and more of his time looking in crevices in the rocks and less and less time looking through his camera lens. By evening, he still hadn't found any water and eventually admitted defeat.

'Norman, could I have some of your water, please?'

I handed him my water bottle, avoided his eye and busied myself with some photographic tasks whilst he drained the vessel dry.

On another of my solo trips into the mountains looking for interesting subjects to photograph, I noticed a woman, also alone.

She had her eyes to the ground and was obviously collecting something. The Russians love their mushrooms and I thought it was these she hunted. I wanted a photograph of a Russian woman collecting mushrooms so I approached. In my very best Russian I greeted her. She responded demurely.

'Are you collecting mushrooms?' I ventured.

'No,' she replied. 'Not mushrooms, Wildflowers.'

Clearly she had understood me and I was delighted that I had no difficulty understanding her. She showed me her collection.

'Beautiful,' I said. 'May I take some photographs?'

'Certainly,' she replied, and I clicked away.

I felt more confident in my Russian and asked her if her home was in Provideniya.

'No,' was her response. 'I'm a botanist from Fairbanks, Alaska.'

I switched to English.

'You're an American? Well, I'm English. How do you do?'

We laughed together on that lonely mountain top. Perhaps the unexpected should always be expected – particularly in the Arctic.

I was picking my way around the point between Komsomolskya Bay and the main fjord one cold and foggy day when I was approached by a Yupik Eskimosy man and a woman. They were on their way to enjoy a picnic and, spotting me with a camera around my neck, asked me to take their picture. I was happy to oblige. They invited me to join their simple feast which seemed to consist of a bottle of beer, some potatoes they were going to bake on the rocks and an adequate supply of cigarettes. The woman was large with a very round face and marked Mongolian features. As the Eskimo have their roots in Mongolia they all have Mongolian features but on this woman they were more pronounced than I was accustomed to. It turned out that she was not a Yupik but a Buryateya, from the region around Lake Baikal some 2,500 miles away, near the Mongolian boarder. She had come to Chukotka ten years previously. The man was small and wiry with a great shock of black hair. He was a born comedian, boisterous and full of fun. I could not venture into serious conversation. It would have taxed my Russian vocabulary beyond its limits, but there was no need to try as they were too animated and lively to be serious. The Buryateya girl did have one or two words of English and she spoke her Russian in a voice that was intelligible for me. The man's speech, however, was too excited and fast for me to follow. In an endeavour to help me understand what he was trying to say he raised the pitch of his voice and seemed to speak even more quickly. Needless to say, that did not help my comprehension. In the end he was bending over me and shouting in my ear at the top of his voice. This gave me a very painful ear and confirmed my belief that shouting at foreigners does nothing to improve understanding. On the other hand, I had a clear conviction that he was trying to be very friendly and for that I shall remember the occasion with pleasure. I suppose I was with them for about an hour. I helped finish the bottle of beer, but refused their cigarettes and finally left them to their baked potatoes. Sadly, when I got up to go, it was the Buryateya girl who shook my hand and the Yupik man who kissed me.

Many years ago I had listened to an English television commentator saying that the Russians were so badly equipped they were obliged to wrap their feet in rags as they could not afford socks. I was not convinced by this. Back in England I had noticed a Polish farm worker wrapping his feet in wool before donning boots on very cold days and this made me realise that here was a technique worth learning. My stay in Chukotka was the perfect opportunity to find out about this. Stanislav had done his national service attached to a specialist Arctic force and, if anyone could, he could teach me about survival in the cold. He also taught me how to wrap my feet in wool before putting on my boots. The wool was not thick but loosely woven and best if the weave enabled it to stretch in all directions. It took me four or five attempts before Stanislav was satisfied that I had mastered the technique. The folds and wrapping made a firm heel and I can confirm that there is no tendency for the wool to shift or form uncomfortable ridges within the boot – as has been my experience with many pairs of socks. I was so impressed by this that on all my subsequent sojourns into the Arctic, and indeed on any very long trek, I wrap my feet rather than wear socks. When in

Vancouver, Canada, I was purchasing a new pair of winter boots I intrigued the salesman and some of the other customers with the technique. I subsequently learned that the Finns and Saami wrap their feet – and, to my surprise, so do the Maoris of New Zealand when shearing sheep. In England, however, I was given stern advice by one outdoor supplier that it was not to be recommended. Did he really think he knew more about the cold than the Russians, Canadians, Finns and Saami?

Stanislav would take me on trips into the surrounding area, sometimes just to see the locality and sometimes for a picnic. The scenery was wild and dramatic. If only it were covered in lush vegetation and forests, it would be as picturesque as anywhere in the world, but I was happy with the drama of the terrain and felt very much at home in what I saw about me. There were vistas across deep valleys and lakes, snow, even in late July, spreading down almost to sea level. On one trip Stanislav took me as near as he could to New Chaplino,[4] a Yupik community some ten or twenty miles east of Provideniya. He stopped about two miles outside the hamlet and said he dared not go closer without a permit. It seemed that the Yupik minority groups have free and easy access to Provideniya, but those who are not of the minority group did not have access to their communities without special leave and a written licence. I was interested to learn that the Western Russians, although great expansionists, still gave special consideration to the many ethnic groups spread across their land. I was disappointed not to be able to enter the community, but my time to study the people in the town of Provideniya was adequate compensation.

There was one opportunity to learn that I regret not taking advantage of. On a leisurely picnic day on the tundra with the family, Adik, the nine year old boy, after exhausting me with games of baseball and football, asked me to construct for him a toy gun. I hacked a replica out of a piece of firewood with a large sheath knife I always carry. He then insisted that I help him construct a fort overlooking the track we had used to get to the

---

[4] Named after a crew member of one of the exploration ships of Vitus Bering

spot. His object was to guard it against the enemy. We staggered around collecting large stones and rocks and I took the opportunity to teach him the art of dry stone walling, as practised in the north of England and north Wales, but all the time I kept asking myself who, in his young eyes, was the enemy. I never did ask and now I shall never know! I had developed such affection for the family and local community that it was my earnest hope he and the others of Provideniya never have to face a real enemy.

It is a great privilege to be able to live as a member of a family in a foreign land. The guest must be particularly astute to assimilate the culture, quickly learn the rules of the household and be careful not to take advantage of any situation in which he finds himself – nor, of course, outstay his welcome. Not an easy trick to learn. Although each day brought a new experience, I felt I had done all that it was possible for me to do under the circumstances. Dick Page, the Alaskan bush pilot who was ferrying supplies and medical missionaries into Chukotka had finally made it to Anadyr and back and offered me 'a ride home'. It was the catalyst to end this particular adventure, and I accepted his offer.

Shortly before I left, Yadvega prepared a special supper for me. Earlier in my visit, I had said how expensive caviar was in England and they were shocked at the price. On this particular day, Yadvega came in with a three kilo jar of red caviar and said she wanted to be sure that if ever I was offered caviar when I got back to England I would be forced to admit that I had had so much of it in Russia I never wanted to see it again. I am happy to say that she failed. That evening we feasted on red caviar on slices of hard boiled eggs, tasty little fillets of keeta (an Arctic fish akin to the salmon), rice, ham and the excellent local dark bread, with vodka to wash it down. After dinner Stanislav and Yadvega produced a photo album and we turned the pages and talked about their life together. Stanislav told of the day they were married in Khabarovsk, the University City where they met as students. It was winter and flowers were very difficult to obtain but he had managed it. Proudly Yadvega held her bouquet during the service. Afterwards, Yadvega wanted to go and freshen up, so she handed her precious bouquet to Stanislav to hold. Whilst he waited, another bride just about to take part in her wedding spotted the flowers and was so enthralled that she pleaded to be able to hold them at her ceremony.

'Take them,' Stanislav had said in a fit of generosity and passed the flowers to her.

When Yadvega returned and asked for her bouquet, she was not much amused to learn what had happened to them. As Stanislav told the story Yadvega was still having trouble finding it amusing! We talked long into the night and, if I recall correctly, the bottle did not survive the evening.

On the morning of my departure Stanislav and I joined Dick and one of the Russian military pilots for a local flight around the area. The Russian piloted the aircraft from the right hand seat with Dick sitting beside him on the left hand.[5] After clearing the mountains, we flew low along the coast towards the west, taking in the views of the extraordinarily rugged coast. We circled a number of local Yupik communities and I was able to pick out those that had fox farms and some that had the traditional whalebone arches perched by small jetties. It was a stimulating joy-ride of just less than an hour. I presumed the presence of the Russian military pilot might have had the practical purpose of oiling the wheels the next time Dick needed some help from the authorities. I was sorry when it was over.

I helped Dick Page with the refuelling and loading of his small aircraft before the flight back to Nome in Alaska. A very young frontier guard kept watch on our activities. He was grim faced, carried a sub-machine gun and wore a heavy great coat, leather boots and thick gloves. It is true that his duties required him to stand about in the wind – probably for long periods but this day was sunny and relatively warm. There were many bits and pieces that had to be carried and loaded and I began to get quite hot with the physical effort, so I removed my jacket and rolled up my sleeves. With him so warmly dressed and me stripped to a shirt, I could not resist the impulse to tease the young guard as I passed.

I smiled at him and asked, 'Are you cold?'

---

[5] The left hand seat on a dual control aircraft is traditionally the commander's seat

'No,' he replied sharply, then went a little pink and grinned as he realised that I was pulling his leg.

After a fond farewell to Stanislav, I went to board the aircraft. Two police officers and an immigration officer stood expressionless by the door. As I stepped into the machine, I turned to the trio, smiled, gave a mock salute and said, 'Thank you for letting me stay in your country.'

Big grins spread across their faces.

'Have a good trip,' they replied and waved.

After we took off, Dick let me fly the aircraft. I turned onto an easterly heading – back across the international date line and the Bering Strait into yesterday and the West. As I flew I couldn't help dwelling on the thought that if I had not made that simple gesture, my last contact with the Russians would have been of expressionless faces rather than the smiles that I took away with me.

One of the great joys for a traveller is the eventual return to the security and comfort of family and home. The suggestion that I would 'kiss the ground when I got home' was, to me, an unkind slander against Chukotka and its people. I returned with a heart and mind enriched by new experiences and new friends, and the affectionate memory of a scruffy little Russian town.

# Chapter 8

# MURMANSK

*Russia's Arctic city and seaport on the Kola Peninsula.*

At the Western limit of Russia's Arctic coast, some 3,500 miles from Chukotka, is the Kola Peninsula. The land is geologically the eastern extension of the Scandinavia peninsula, but on the Kola Peninsula the mountains of Norway have flattened to lowlands with some rolling hills and numerous lakes. It forms part of Lapland, the home ground of the Saami who inhabit the region across Norway, Sweden and Finland. By tradition, the Saami are reindeer herders who, over the centuries, have managed their herds across the stark and unforgiving tundra. As early as the 11th century, a few western Russians, mostly fishermen and peasants, moved into the region, but for centuries its northern shores remained undeveloped, a 'backwater'. Although situated almost entirely above the Arctic Circle and subject to the savagery of the Arctic winters, there is one feature that gives the land a special quality. The warm Gulf Stream flows across the Scandinavian north coast and the Kola Peninsula and retains sufficient heat to keep the north shore of the Peninsula ice-free all year round. Away from the Kola Peninsula, across the White Sea, at the mouth of river Dvina is the old and well-established city of Arkhangelsk (Archangel).[1] Although this city is to the south of the Arctic Circle, it is cut off from the warmth and protection of the Gulf Stream and the White Sea freezes over from late autumn until early summer, closing the city's port facilities. As

---

[1] Founded in 1584 as Novo-Kholmogory and given its present name in 1613

Russia has warmer, ice-free seaports in the Baltic and Black Sea, this did not pose a problem to the maintenance of supply routes for the country. Russia's troubled relationship with Sweden may have caused their borders to flow backwards and forwards over the centuries, but Arkhangelsk was sufficiently removed to the east to escape the immediate friction from the disputes and the Kola Peninsula's undeveloped tundra remained unaffected, undisturbed and ignored. Arkhangelsk continued to prosper and was the centre for commercial and industrial life in the region. There was no pressing need to develop the Kola Peninsula. The Saami continued their traditional ways and the little fishing villages on the north coast continued in their isolated existence.

It was the advent of the First World War that marked a sudden transformation for the region. Russia's Baltic and Black Sea supply routes were cut off by the central powers. Arkhangelsk was not open to shipping all year round. Her ports on the Pacific coast were too far away to serve Western Russia effectively and it became essential to find a route to maintain supplies during the winter periods. The fact that the Kola Peninsula remains ice-free throughout the winter was brought to the attention of those charged with solving the problem. The little fishing village of Murmansk, situated beside a well-protected natural harbour, became the site of rapid development and in 1915–16, to open the country's lifeline to another ice-free harbour, a railway was built connecting Murmansk with Moscow and Petrograd (now St Petersburg). The little fishing village developed rapidly into a major port.

It is interesting to note that, following the eruption of the Russian Civil War in 1917 and whilst the country was in confusion, White Russians controlled the region. Between 1918 and 1920, British and American troops occupied the Kola Peninsula until the balance of power became clear. Murmansk was established as a northern city and busy seaport.

During the Second World War the city once again became prominent. In an endeavour to keep Russia supplied with essential military and domestic needs and prevent her succumbing to the German onslaught, courageous North Sea convoys operated by the British ran the gauntlet of U-boats and aerial attack. Many ships and men were lost fighting to supply Western Russia. The city of Murmansk also suffered heavy aerial bombardment, resulting in damage and loss of life, but the stoic character of its citizens helped it to survive.

Today Murmansk is a fine industrial seaport city of some 309,000 persons (1970), said to be the largest any country can boast north of the Arctic Circle. It has been a remarkable transformation from a small fishing village to a major university city and harbour in such a short space of time.

The Kola region is now well served with hydro-electric power and has rich mineral deposits, mostly of valuable copper-nickel, very large quantities of apatite[2] and some iron. Whilst the region has become rich, the exploitation of the minerals has been ecologically careless and, sadly, the Saami reindeer herders have suffered from the resulting pollution.

The port has continued to develop with the city and is now a major naval base. It has an important fishing fleet and is the terminus for many ships using the Northeast Passage. Its other important industries include timber and textiles.

It was March when I visited the city. The winter was still very cold and the city and surrounding country was blanketed with deep snow. I had flown in from Finland on a Russian airline calling itself Archangel Airlines and was pleased to note that the aircraft was new and in sparkling clean condition. The two flight attendants were smartly dressed and courteous, but on a flight of short duration a single cup of tea was the only service offered. I noticed that my few travelling companions had boarded in Sweden and were well dressed Russians. The men wore business suits and the ladies ankle length coats of fine quality fur. Uncharitably, the word 'ostentatious' crossed my mind, but they seemed pleasant enough people. I sat quietly on my own, dressed in the more earthy winter clothing I use for rough travel in the Arctic. I spent the flight looking out of the window, tracing the features of the land, noting the sparseness of the trees, which became more

---

[2] Used in the production of superphosphates

stunted as we flew north-east, and wondering why most rivers and lakes were frozen into immobility whilst some seemed to flow and there was open water where the rivers fed into lakes. I reflected that I never look down from an aircraft onto temperate lands and imagine what it is like to live there. However, when I view an Arctic landscape from the air, I imagine myself trekking over the harsh white wilderness, revelling in the clean pure air that has a taste only the Arctic can produce.

The airport of Murmansk is situated on reasonably flat ground some 15 or 20 miles south of the city. It seemed to be efficiently run. I was pleased to be back on Russian soil, but my first difficulty came with the bureaucracy. I was well armed with visas, but currency and immigration forms had to be completed. They were scattered about in a variety of languages on a central table, but none were in English. My ability to read Russian was not up to the technical terms on the Russian forms. There were other copies in Norwegian, Finnish, Swedish and, I think, German. All were beyond my powers of interpretation. There was neither an airline nor airport representative from whom I could seek assistance in the room. My confusion must have been obvious. The richly dressed ladies who had been my fellow passengers gathered about me and did their best to be helpful. I was much impressed by the time and efforts they devoted to trying to sort out my problem; however, they could not find a form that was within my limited linguistic abilities. Their kindness and concern for me made me regret how uncharitably I had labelled them 'ostentatious'. Eventually, they abandoned me and I realised I was going to stay in that arrival hall forever unless I completed some sort of a form. I 'guessed-my-best' on a form that was quite unintelligible to me and approached the uniformed customs/immigration officer in the next room. He was a large man. He took the form, stared at it for a few moments, frowned and then with a sigh asked me in perfectly good English for the details required. With relief, my vision of an eternity in confinement at the airport evaporated. He seemed to correct every entry that I had made and I felt like a young schoolboy who had handed in a deplorable essay to his teacher. In answer to his question, 'What items of value do you have?' I honestly declared my camera equipment and a satellite navigational system. When he grasped what I meant by a satellite navigational system, he looked shocked.

'You cannot have that,' he said sternly. 'This is not permitted.'

Visions of an eternity in close confinement returned. It was duly confiscated and sent off to the bonded warehouse. I explained that I had no need of it in Murmansk, but I would have need of it when I returned to Finland and travelled alone in the forests. I had only brought it with me because there was nowhere else for me to leave it. He softened and smiled when I apologised for having caused problems.

'It's not your fault,' he said. 'You can't be expected to know all the rules of this country. You can have it back when you leave.' And he gave a receipt for the offending instrument.

Relieved, but feeling that I had just passed through an old wash-mangle, I left and headed for the city in a taxi. I did not mention that deep in my rucksack were detailed US Air Force aviation maps of the area.

Rather than a tent or hut in the wilderness, I found myself in the Arktika Hotel. It was neither grand nor palatial, but a perfectly acceptable establishment facing a large square at the top of Lenin Prospect.[3] It was warm and comfortable and suited my simple needs. I had a room on the fifth floor with a view over the town to the surrounding hills. There was a casino and nightclub in the basement of the hotel but these were of no interest to me. The casino may have accounted for the well-built young men in ill-fitting suits standing about in the lobby, unsuccessfully trying not to look like security men. They barely gave me a glance. At the door was a uniformed doorman short in stature but thick set, a man of middle years with kindly eyes and a magnificent spade beard. I could imagine him as a faithful family retainer from a classical Russian fairy tale and, although I did not know his name, I kept thinking he must be called 'Ivan Ivanovich'. He held the door open for me and we exchanged polite nods as I stepped out to explore this Arctic city.

---

[3] 'Prospect' generally translates as 'Avenue'

# THE WARM ARTIC

The gloom of a winter evening was descending rapidly. Snow was thick on the ground but the roads and footpaths were kept well clear. Every hundred yards or so a man or a woman wielded a large snow shovel in an endeavour to keep the city moving. Deciding to leave Lenin Prospect until I had more daylight, I turned towards the railway station where an illuminated Red Star at the top of a pinnacle caught my attention. There was no life or movement at the station to hold my interest but in front of it was a short row of flower stalls. They were brightly lit and glazed over. The stallholders were entombed in their stalls having only a one-foot by one-foot window through which to conduct business with the sparse straggle of customers that passed by. If the stalls were as warm and scented as they appeared to be, the vendors would have enjoyed an exotic environment in which to earn a living. Less comfortably established was a lady sitting on a stool selling roasted Siberian pine nuts from a basket at her feet. Having learned from Russians whom I had met on earlier travels that these nuts were a delicacy, I purchased two scoops, one each of the white and dark nuts and did not regret my purchase. They may not have been as warming and sustaining as hot roasted chestnuts plucked from glowing embers, but their flavour was delicate and sweet.

After a short walk around the vicinity of the hotel to get my bearings, I returned to its cafeteria for a hot meal. As I passed the receptionist, I murmured, 'Good evening.'

In return she hastily wrote out a bill for Roubles 1.50 (about 17 pence). I couldn't make out what this was for so simply handed over the money and went into the cafeteria. It was crowded and lively, filled mostly with young people out to enjoy an evening together. Some were clearly unmarried men and women in their early twenties; other groups consisted of families. There was nothing unusual about them – indeed, it was the ordinariness of the people that struck me. If I was going to find examples of the despairing people of a wrecked society, such as one is led to believe (by the Western media) typify the population of Russia, and particularly Arctic Russia, then I was going to have to search elsewhere. I was happy to relax amongst the throng and chose something to eat from the counter and a litre of good local beer from the bar. Perhaps the food could have been better, but not the beer.

The next morning, I wandered back to the railway station. The day was cold, the skies clear and there was a crisp wind. The city was awake and people were about their business. Now I could see that almost all the women were dressed in long coats that fell to their ankles and that the vast majority of these coats were of fur – some of very good quality fur indeed. I knew that my dress was strange and unconventional in Russia and to local eyes it must be clear I was a foreigner, but I was generally ignored. My Canadian wolf-skin hat was the only item of clothing in keeping with local dress. My vanity allows me to record that it was the smartest fur hat I saw in Murmansk. Of the rest of my clothing, the thick, red, down-filled duvet with its parka hood and my padded, blue salopette leggings were clearly not fashionable, but they drew no comment. The only thing that did receive attention was my boots. I was wearing a pair of Canadian Army winter mukluks. These I had bought after my winter experiences in Canada.[4] They were exceptionally warm, but the all white, rubber insulated soles and white canvas tops were just too conspicuous in a city. Even though the leggings of the boots were hidden within my trouser legs, they still caught the attention of the Russians about me. Being too polite to stare directly, those who passed me in the street did not move their heads, but their eye rolled steadily downwards to take in my white footwear. For the young girls it was just too much and, to my amusement, if I turned quickly I would catch them giggling and pointing at my feet. In England, it would have been the wolf-skin hat which would have excited attention. Here it was nothing out of the ordinary.

The time was just after 9.00 a.m. The army of people with their snow shovels were getting on with their work and the citizens of Murmansk moved around me. I stood looking at the railway station, wondering how to compose my photographs, when I became aware of a powerful smell of stale vodka. Turning

---

[4] See Chapter 4

around, my eyes met those of a tall, slim young woman in her mid-twenties. She wore a simple woollen overcoat and neither hat nor gloves. Her tousled hair was a natural blond, cut short, and her eyes were deep blue. She was a little unsteady on her feet. What really caught my attention was a bruise that discoloured her left eye. She made a brave attempt to give me a winsome smile. I have no idea of her name, but I shall call her Svetlana. She whispered something to me in a soft voice. Her words may have been unintelligible to me but her intentions were as obvious as they were unacceptable. My distinctly foreign clothing must have attracted her to me as a bee to a honey pot and I was amused by an approach so early in the morning. I had learned in my youth, more than fifty years ago, how to evade unwanted soliciting and had no intention of succumbing to her blandishments, but equally I had no intention of being rude. At the same time the photo-journalist in me saw an opportunity and I wondered how I could get some worthwhile photographs of a girl with a black eye without compromising my position. Svetlana had with her a companion, a shorter and much older woman who read my expression immediately. This older woman tried without success to deflect Svetlana but she persisted. I must admit that I admired her persistence. As the little drama developed, one of the army of shovellers looked up from his snow bank behind Svetlana and sauntered over to follow the details of the action more closely. He was an older man, probably about my own age and short in stature. Despite his size, he carried his shovel as a Roman Centurion might have carried his sword into battle. He looked at us one by one as he considered the scenario. By now I could hardly keep a straight face. Svetlana was doing her very best to be enticing and I was trying to stand my ground without being offensive and manoeuvre her into a position for a photograph. Finally, my Roman Centurion had seen and heard enough – he acted decisively. Waving his shovel threateningly he entered the fray and admonished Svetlana for pestering a visitor. He ordered her to be gone – couldn't she see that I wasn't interested? Had Svetlana been sober, she could probably have taken the shovel off my little champion and bounced it on his head. But she wasn't sober and accepted her defeat graciously. Flashing me one more of her winsome smiles she departed with her companion, but not before I had taken a photograph of those glazed and bruised blue eyes.

'Thank you,' I said to the little man. 'I think she may have had too much to drink.'

The Centurion just snorted, gave me a curt nod and the hint of a wry smile and went back to his snow bank. He had not been just an interfering busybody; he had displayed the hospitable inclinations of most ordinary Russian fellows to defend and protect a visitor – and that's what I found impressive.

Slipping back into anonymity and my quiet traveller's role, I turned my camera towards the railway station and took my photographs. It was soon afterwards, out of the corner of my eye, that I saw Svetlana with a satisfied smile on her face sitting in the passenger seat of a car being driven away by some gentleman of less fastidious taste than mine.

With no particular plan in mind, I started to walk around the city to see what it had to offer and what impressions it made on me. Lenin Prospect was the city's main thoroughfare. It was wide and flanked with flowering trees – though these were now stark and leafless. A busy trolleybus service ran its length and despite the clearly efficient public transport system, there were quite a few private cars among the traffic. The buildings were solid and robust but not without grace and varied in design from an ornate theatre to a squat and solid department store. The commercial banks possessed the newest and grandest buildings. Where the shopping in Murmansk most differed from places like Oxford Street or New York's Fifth Avenue was in the absence of window displays. This I found puzzling, for it was sometimes difficult to establish whether one was entering a department store, an office building or an apartment block. Provideniya had also been like that, but Provideniya was a remote community of only three thousand people – hardly a metropolis with a busy shopping centre. I presumed the lack of window displays was not only cultural but also something to do with the climate. It was now mid-March, but the winter showed little inclination to release its grip on the city and there was plenty of snow banked on the sides of the roads by that little army of people with their shovels keeping the pavements and carriage-ways clear.

Many years ago when I had last visited Tokyo in Japan, I discovered that the glossy brilliance of Ginza Street vanished if one turned down a side road. 'How would Russia's Murmansk look down its side streets?' I mused. I turned left and plodded my way up a hill. The buildings were generally much lower than on Lenin Prospect and perhaps the snow clearance had not been so diligent, but the character remained unchanged and the people about me were just as smart. Ladies were shopping for groceries in their long fur coats and carrying their purchases in plastic bags – an odd combination. Away from Lenin Prospect there was the added interest of some traditional wooden buildings which are so much easier on the eye than those of concrete and brick construction and seemed to have emerged from the sets of *Dr. Zhivago*.[5] There were many open areas and, even in these wintry conditions, parents played in the snow with their young children. I watched one father teaching his son how to carve a face in a snow-bank. He was conscious that I was taking their photograph but just glanced sideways and winked at me.

There were many more of those little booths, selling everything from soap to goodness knows what, that are so characteristic of Russian free enterprise. I watched one of them being set up. A woman of uncertain years was going to occupy it. There was no form of heating and the walls were of fabric. She wore the valenki boots of compressed felt and was so well wrapped up it was impossible to assess whether she was stout or slim. Layers of blankets seemed to cocoon her. The space was small – no more than seven feet square. A chair was placed for her to sit on and her produce was stacked around her so that, without moving, she would be able to reach whatever item was called for. When she was satisfied with the arrangements, she sat on her seat while the young men who were helping her fitted the front of the booth.

---

[5] A film based on Boris Pasternak's novel of the same name

An Inuit demonstrating the building of an igloo on the shore of Baffin Island, Canada.

Two friendly fishermen in the Ilulissat Fjord waving to passing visitors on a fishing smack.

Ben with some young Greenlanders being ferried from Ittoqqortoormiit to the campsite on Walrus Bay.

Hunters of Ittoqqortoormiit in Eastern Greenland gather to hunt for seal on the rocks overlooking Walrus Bay.

A whaling boat sells its catch to the public at the quayside in Ilulissat. Whale and seal meat form an important part of the Inuit diet.

Two seal hunting parties meet up on the frozen sea of the North West Passage. Even though it was April, the ice was still 6 feet thick and perfectly safe for travel.

The head of an Inuit completing the last stages of building an igloo on Baffin Island, Canada.

A young mother in Nunavut with her child carried in the hood of her jacket. She did not think that a temperature of -30°C was too cold for children to play outside.

A cheerful Eskimo lady waves in greeting on the shore of Lake Salmon in Alaska. She had been gathering willow leaves as a vitamin supplement.

Above: Eight weeks of supplies are loaded onto the cutter at Longyearbyen to ferry the expedition to its base camp on Spitsbergen.

Left: The author with the husky named Tank. This creature was intended to act as a guard dog to warn of polar bear attack. His lovable character more than made up for his failings as a guard dog!

A Saami reindeer farmer in national costume leads his reindeer and pulk across his farm. His assistant sits in the back.

The author's genial Russian hosts in the remote Arctic town of Provideniya preparing food in their decorative kitchen.

It was easy to stride along the surface of the glaciers. Note the ice carving into the fjord from the snout in the background.

The author takes a dip in the ice off Walrus Bay. It is important to keep the body clean to stay healthy. Swimming in ice is certainly invigorating!

A lighter is unloaded by hand to supply the little town of Saqqaq in Greenland. The women often contribute their physical labour to communal activities.

The young Russian girl named Zhenya wearing her national costume at the cultural hall in Provideniya.

An exceptionally friendly Yupik Russian Eskimo who invited the author to join him and his Buryateya girlfriend for a picnic outside the town of Provideniya.

There she was, entombed for the duration of her spell of duty. I could see no way for her to get up and stretch her limbs, or answer the call of nature. I have no idea how long that woman was to be incarcerated in her little emporium but clearly it wasn't going to be a comfortable day for her. I hope it was a financial success, but I slipped away before the arrival of her first customer. Perhaps that first customer should have been me; it would have been a gesture and only a small investment for me to have bought something simple, like a bar of soap, and given a start to her working day.

I wandered the city for some seven hours, turning wherever my curiosity took me and taking in whatever caught my eye. On one corner, a group of skiers gathered for a ski bus to take them to the nearby hills. In a park children played in the snow, either on toboggans or skis. Couples strolled hand in hand. Individuals were walking their dogs. Interesting wooden buildings rubbed shoulders with modern structures. Only the hotel in which I was staying seemed to be intended for tourists.

I was hoping I would come across a Russian Orthodox church with its gilded domes and ornate wooden structure. If there were any such buildings in the city, I didn't find them. However, overlooking a large park was a modern building that I guessed was a church. I arrived just as the last of the congregation were leaving. A dapper young man looked at me curiously. I asked if it was a church and if I could see inside it. As soon as he realised that I was an interested foreigner, his enthusiasm knew no bounds. I was ushered into a clean and spacious building capable of holding a congregation of several hundred worshipers. It was the New Apostolic Church. The stained glass was modern and the pews were of polished light-coloured wood arranged in a semi-circle around the altar which was set in one corner of the building. I gather that branches of this church can be found all over the world. The literature he gave me, entitled 'Наша Семья' (Our Family), listed branches in England, Canada, the Far East and South America. I wished I had been able to join the congregation during the service that had just finished; even if I had not understood what was being said I would have picked up the atmosphere of those around me. Instead, I basked in the man's enthusiasm and pride as he showed me around his church.

I took my leave feeling warmed and gratified by the experience and plodded off in the general direction of my hotel, knowing only that it was somewhere to the north. It wasn't going to be difficult to find if I kept the railway line to my left because that would lead me to the station. I arrived back as the winter sun slipped behind the hills across the river. I find the colours and light of a winter sunset particularly magical and soothing and I felt very much at peace with the world. Ivan Ivanovich, the hotel doorman, opened the doors for me.

'Have you had a good day taking photographs?' he asked as I came in.

'Yes, very good, thank you,' I replied. As I walked past the reception desk, I said 'Good evening,' and the receptionist hurriedly wrote me out another bill for Roubles 1.50. These little bills were a puzzle to me. At the sterling equivalent of 17 pence, they were not a financial embarrassment, but for the life of me I couldn't understand what they were for. I took the bill back to my room and studied it with the aid of a Russian/English dictionary but to this day it remains an enigma. Personal pride prevented me challenging their validity.

As I stepped into the lift to return to my room, I was conscious that an attractive woman in her early thirties and a child of about ten years had entered just ahead of me.

'Which floor do you want?' she asked.

'Five, please,' She selected the appropriate button. At the fifth floor, the doors opened and I stepped out. As the doors started to close, I saw her select whatever floor it was that she required. It was only as I walked away from the lift that I realised she had been careful to ensure she gave me no clue as to her own room. I was not in the least offended, but I couldn't help smiling at the neat way she had handled her own, and her young daughter's, security.

My fifth floor room overlooked the square that led into Lenin Prospect. The next morning when I awoke, it was snowing heavily. As the large, heavy flakes of snow settled, the army of snow shovellers were already hard at work shifting them but, in addition to their efforts, snow-clearing machinery was in action. I was familiar with the regular snowplough that was busy clearing one corner of the square, but what caught my eye was an extraordinary machine that had mandibles like those of a gigantic beetle. Beside it stood a woman heavily wrapped in thick layers of clothing, clutching a birch broom. She seemed to be using the broom to conduct operations by waving it towards points that needed attention. As the gigantic beetle crawled forward, it ingested the snow onto a conveyor belt. Under the far end of the conveyor belt was a truck that collected the snow as it fell off. As this gigantic beetle worked its way across the square, the truck followed in reverse until it had a full load. It then drove off to dump its load while a new truck slipped in to take its place. It was a very efficient performance. With a system like this in England, many English cities would be able to stay active in blizzard conditions. I grabbed my camera and headed for the scene to capture some photographs. Ivan Ivanovich's eyebrows went up as he opened the door for me. The wind was howling and the snow swirled. I have no idea of the temperature but it must have been below $-10°C$. It was not until I was outside in the swirling mêlée, however, that I realised that I was wearing only trainers, a short-sleeved shirt and a normal pair of trousers without any insulation. I had neither hat nor gloves. No wonder Ivan Ivanovich's eyebrows had gone up as I hurried past him, but I decided to keep going and take my photographs. I must confess to being somewhat chilled when I eventually returned to the warmth after satisfying myself that I had a sufficient record.

'Cold!' I remarked as I came in covered in snow.

Ivan's eyes just twinkled.

I thawed out after a hot breakfast and set off to see what the rest of the day had in store for me. This time I was well dressed against the elements and Ivan nodded in approval as I went out. My intention was to get into the dockland to see if I could see anything of Russia's rusting navy that I was assured was littering the harbour. It was worth a try, but I was not optimistic. Dockyards, and particularly naval dockyards, are usually securely shut away from public access and I had no intention of carrying cameras into a sensitive military area unless it was clearly open to the public. By nosing around the alleyways and back roads I did get to see the rougher end of town but, there was nothing remarkable other than a workers cafe whose billboard indicated that it sold 'Хот-Дог' – literally 'Hot-Dog'.

Where a road crossed over a railway junction at a freight yard, a young woman was clearly in charge. I stood fascinated as this bright, perky soul went about her duties. She was wrapped up in a heavy greatcoat, wore the compressed felt valenki boots that most outdoor workers preferred and a scarf around her head. There appeared to be a permanent smile on her face. I could not be sure, but I think she was singing to herself as she bustled about in charge of her domain. Her sceptre of office was a large broom which she wielded with great authority. Her duties seemed to be to keep the points free of compacted snow and see that the motor traffic was properly controlled over the lines. She danced between the moving freight wagons and monstrous locomotives, clearing the snow and when the line was clear waved cars across. There were traffic lights for the road vehicles, but this did not interfere with the girl's command of her territory. If she thought it was safe for a car to go, she waved traffic over red lights; equally, if she was not satisfied, she prevented cars crossing on a green light. It wouldn't have been my choice of an occupation, but clearly this girl was very happy in her work and had no intention of letting rules and regulations confuse her command. I would have loved to have had an opportunity to sit and chat with such a happy soul doing such a mundane job, and perhaps learn something of her philosophy of life.

In pursuit of a way down to the river or harbour I found myself in the north of the city. The buildings were older and mainly residential. From this position I could see on the top of a hill, a colossal statue of a Russian soldier in World War II uniform overlooking the harbour approaches. It dominated the skyline. On the side of the hill were little wooden cottages with lights in their windows and smoke rising from the chimneys. They seemed comfortably secure in their situation. I tried to find a track that led directly to the statue, but without success. A man was attending to some outside chore in a wooden home at the end of the track that I was following.

'Is there a way up to the statue?' I asked.

'Not possible,' was his reply. 'The snow will be up to your chest.'

He advised me to return to the road and take a number 52 trolley bus. Indeed, the snow did look very deep off the track, so I reluctantly retraced my steps and took the longer route. The thought of climbing the hill in chest deep snow with a howling 50 mile-per-hour wind was too intimidating.

This route was sheltered from the wind but there was nothing remarkable about the suburban area through which it went. Near the top of the hill was a school whose pupils were enjoying an 'open day' of sports activities. I mingled with the crowds, who took no notice of me. The terrain had moderated the wind and the snow had stopped falling, but it was still very cold, yet the events progressed as if it was a fine summer's day. Teachers and parents were in attendance as with any school event.

I moved on to the war memorial at the top of the hill. Situated as it was on the brow, the wind raged unabated around it. The statue was so colossal that I found it was impossible to see properly what it represented from such close proximity. It was like standing next to The Sphinx outside Cairo. Standing anywhere was, in fact, very difficult. The strength of the wind was frightening. It must have been blowing at 60 to 70 miles an hour. Ice covered the paving around the statue and not even my boots could grip the surface. To stop myself being blown away like an autumn leaf, I clutched whatever I could for support. I was correctly clothed for such conditions but the fine particles of ice and snow were driven into my face like a sand blaster and the sub-zero temperature made the wind-chill most uncomfortable. The uncompromising view of the harbour, however, made it all worthwhile. It was, I thought, a classic view and gave me a lasting impression of this Arctic Russian city.

The next morning, I flew back to Finland. Once again I was sorry to be leaving Russia. I always feel at home on her soil and amongst her people. The country is so similar to England, and yet so very different. When I checked out of the hotel, I instinctively said goodbye to the receptionists and one of them hurriedly wrote me out another bill for Roubles 1.50!

At the airport, a young customs officer escorted me to the bonded warehouse to collect my satellite navigator. There was no charge for its detention. As we walked back to the terminal building, I apologised again for having caused everyone so much trouble by bringing it in.

'Don't worry about that,' he said. 'Murmansk is considered a special area and everyone is still playing James Bond. It's all so silly.'

# Chapter 9

# FINNISH LAPLAND

*The woods and lakes in the land of the Saami reindeer herders.*

Tourist brochures will tell you that Finland is the 'Land of 1,000 Lakes'. That is an understatement. There are, according to official statistics,[1] 178,888 lakes with nearly as many islands stretching over this low-lying land between the Gulf of Bothnia and Russia, and north of the Gulf between Sweden and Russia. Norway straddles its northern tip. Deprived of the ameliorating effect of the warm Gulf Stream and screened from prevailing westerly winds by Norway's mountainous spine, it suffers a sharp Northern climate with, on average, half the year below freezing.

As a sovereign state, it has a short history. During the 17th and 18th centuries, Sweden was a thorn in Russia's side and battles were fought over territorial claims to the lands around the Baltic. In the past, what we now call Finland was claimed by Sweden – as were parts of present day Russia. During the reign of one of Russia's more notable Tsars, Peter the Great (1672–1725), Russia became more powerful. With this new power, Sweden was tamed and her territorial claims in the region neutralised. The land that now makes up Finland was absorbed into Russia and by 1809 had become a Grand Duchy of the Russian Empire. The upheaval of the Russian revolution in 1917 brought about many more changes and one being the transformation of Finland into an independent state. At the outbreak of the Second World War, Finland

---

[1] Finnish Tourist Board, 1997–1998

declared its neutrality, but conflict with Russian territorial claims to secure the approaches to Leningrad (now St Petersburg) resulted in the Winter War between the two nations. Although the Finnish forces gave a good account of themselves, they were forced to sue for peace. By June 1941, when Germany attacked Russia, Finland had over 70,000 German troops operating from its northern territory. Finland reiterated its neutrality, claiming they were not allies of the Germans, but Russia bombed Finnish cities so Finland declared war on Russia. Despite the fierce resistance by Finland's courageous little army, Russia took control of its northern land. An armistice was eventually signed in 1944. Finland ceded territory and was obliged to expel the German troops. Germany responded by devastating Finland's northern lands.[2] With her borders re-drawn, Finland lost her only coastal link with the open Barents Sea and the territory's rich deposits of copper-nickel.

When discussing this history over a beer or two with a young Finnish gold prospector on the shores of Lake Inari, my questions about Finland losing the war were met with the sharp retort.

'Finland did not lose the war. It just came second.'

It would seem that the indomitable spirit of its people lives on!

Some 10,000 years ago, following the retreat of the ice cap that covered so much of northern Europe at the end of the ice age, the Scandinavian north was quickly populated. Today's Saami, or Lapps, are probably the descendants of these aboriginal people. The Saami origins are not clear but they are thought to come from central Asia, probably in the last millennium BC and were pushed to their northern limits by the migration of the Finns, Goths and Slavs. Their language is Finno-Ugric and their culture largely nomadic.[3] Without regard to the lines drawn on today's political maps, these people inhabit the northern lands from Norway, across Sweden and Finland and into Russia. Reindeer husbandry and fishing have been their traditional pursuits over the centuries. Norway has the greatest number with about 21,000;

---

[2] Microsoft (R) Encarta – Finland
[3] Microsoft (R) Encarta – Lapland

there are about 11,000 in Sweden, 4,000 in Finland and 2,000 in Russia's Kola Peninsula (figures for 1975).[4] Although there has been considerable intermixing with the other races who followed them into the north and it is hard to distinguish the Saami from their neighbours by personal appearance or occupation, their culture and language remains distinct. In today's enlightened age, those who claim to be Saami enjoy certain privileges of occupation and freedom of movement across frontiers. Retaining their distinctive culture and language, however, does not lie easily with the advantages of being part of a larger nation. Until recently, schools did not teach the Saami children in their native tongue nor include their culture in the curriculum. Happily, the four nations who now host the Saami are tackling the problem of mixing statehood and ethnic minority culture and the Saami are happier with the educational arrangements.

Just three miles south of the Arctic Circle, at the confluence of the Kemijoki and Ounasjoki rivers, is the town of Rovaniemi. It is a charming and friendly little town with good shops and plenty of activity for those who enjoy an outdoor life. It is the business centre for the Province of Lapland, but it has to be stated that tourism is its principal industry and it offers good facilities for summer and winter activities. The town also boasts it is the home of Santa Claus. However, his nearby workshop villa and own post office were a bit too 'touristy' to interest me.

As it was still winter when I arrived in Finland with the intention of travelling alone into the forests, I knew I must prepare myself for the experience. Having clear memories of the discomforts of cold camping in the high Canadian Arctic, when caribou skins had helped me to survive the extreme conditions,[5] I took the opportunity to go into one of the town's many department stores and buy myself two reindeer skins to augment my bedding when I camped in the wilderness. Thus armed with what I

---

[4] Armstrong, Terence, Rogers, George and Rowley, Graham, *The Circumpolar North* (London: Methuen, 1978)
[5] Chapter 4

## THE WARM ARTIC

shall call nature's hot water bottles I turned my attention to the facilities of the town.

For anyone with an interest in the Arctic and its people, the town contains the superb 'Artkium', a multidisciplinary science centre which researches and observes the phenomena of the whole Arctic region. It is built into a small hill overlooking the river junction and has a great glass canopy which is both modern in style and gives it a lightness that distinguishes it from so many other gloomy museums. A building as unusual as this, in such a setting, and surrounded by deep snow deserved a photograph. Being well used to the rigors of the High Arctic, I was not intimidated by the wintry conditions in my endeavour to get the best possible angle. I was, after all, virtually in town. My attitude showed the classic complacency that results in a hard lesson, and I was about to get one. I found a side door that led to part of the building which faced the river and picked a route that would get me into a good position without leaving footprints to disfigure my photographs. In the regions of High Arctic I had already experienced, the snow was compacted by the wind and shallow, and that made walking easy. I foolishly assumed the same would be so here and although I was conscious that the snow was behaving differently underfoot to that which I was used to, I pressed on. After all, the hard crust appeared to be carrying my weight. Just before I reached my chosen position, however, the crust gave way and I dropped into the snow – nearly up to my waist. My first reaction was amusement but when I found it difficult to get out of the hole this changed to irritation. I tried repeatedly to extract myself and then realised I was in trouble. I could barely move. All I seemed to achieve was a deepening and widening of the pit into which I had deposited myself. My irritation then changed to concern as I struggled without success to extract myself from my predicament. Having broken the crust, I could not retrace my steps. I suppose if I had yelled hard, someone might have heard me and come to my rescue but the embarrassment would have been too much to contemplate. I stopped struggling and did then what I should have done in the first place: exchange frantic concern for logical thought. Having made sure I had the photographs I wanted, I concentrated on my situation and slowly developed a technique that allowed some progress through the weak snow crust down towards the frozen river where I could walk normally. Eventually, I extracted myself from the deep snow, exhausted and dispirited, but a much wiser and much more humble man. I lost no time in buying myself a good pair of snowshoes, as I didn't want to repeat that experience anywhere, least of all in the isolated forests around Lake Inari.

I didn't stay more than a day or so in Rovaniemi, as I was in transit to Inari, my base for this Finnish experience. The only direct way from Rovaniemi to Inari is by road and the Finns run a very efficient coach service. Like all Finnish public transport, it subsidises the fares by two thirds for senior citizens. Not only was the fare subsidised for Finnish nationals of more than 65 years of age, but it was also subsidised for foreigners like me. It was a wonderful opportunity to see something of the endless forests of pine and birch trees and lakes that make up so much of this land. On the journey north, I noticed there were remarkably few townships or communities to break the isolation of the travel. Except where the numerous lakes dictated otherwise, the road ran straight and was kept cleared of snow. Occasionally, there were stops for refreshment at the few very small hamlets on route and once even at a reindeer farm. Rather than finding the endless forests and isolation tedious, I felt I was learning from the experience. My only concern was that, with the proximity of so many lakes in an Arctic region, the summer might not be so comfortable. The deciduous trees might be in leaf and the lakes would be idyllic, inviting and picturesque, but there would be millions of midges and insects swarming from the waters when the land and the lakes were released from winter's icy grip. I remembered that when I was choosing my reindeer skins, many of those I had examined had small holes eaten through them, and realised that reindeer also suffer miserably from insect attack. I resolved that if I ever returned in the summer I would be well armed with insect repellent and netting.

The journey had lasted most of the day and I arrived in the late afternoon. Inari has been a Saami trading centre for many years.

It is small and neat and sits on the southern edge of a large lake named Inarijärvi. When in town the Hotel Inari was to become my home. It was a white two-storey wooden building. I stepped off my coach just outside the main entrance. To the side of the hotel were parked ten or twenty snowmobiles but only one car. Beside the door were a couple of strange devices resembling supermarket shopping trolleys on skis. I later learned that that was exactly what they were. Not only did the ski supermarket trolleys take the weight of the shopping, but they helped to steady oneself when on ice. I later saw some of the younger grocery shoppers standing with one foot on a ski and propelling themselves along with the other foot as if they were on a scooter.

I entered the hotel with my possessions to find myself in a general hubbub of noise and chatter. Immediately on my left was a coffee shop and bar. On my right was an open saloon with tables where a variety of people of all ages appeared to be in earnest conversation. Their costumes were colourful and they displayed a remarkable collection of different head gear. I particularly noticed three men wearing hats which could only be fashionable amongst pixies. Short and with commendably thick beards, they could have been actors relaxing after filming a scene from *Snow White and the Seven Dwarfs*, but if they had been filming it must have been some hours ago as they were now most definitely 'in their cups'. Over by a window, I saw my first Saami in his full national costume, a kaleidoscope of colour, with a hat of many points and reindeer shoes with curly toes. He was playing a fruit machine. Whilst the dress of those about me may have differed from that of American cowboys of the Wild West, I was struck with the comparison of this open bar to the film sets depicting such places as 'The Last Chance Saloon' of Tombstone, Arizona. Let me hasten to say that the Inari Hotel was ideal for my purpose. It provided clean, comfortable, efficiently run and remarkably reasonably priced accommodation, and I formed a favourable first impression.

I turned to the young man behind the bar.

'Where is the reception?' I asked.

'I'm the reception,' he replied as he pulled some glasses of draft lager for a customer. 'What do you want?'

I told him I had booked a room. He nodded and, as soon as he had taken money from a man who had poured himself a cup of coffee and taken a selection of Danish pastries, he attended to the formalities of my registration and told me where to find my room. I was glad to shed my belongings and equipment and take stock of my situation. My room was on the second floor, facing towards the little town and not towards the lake, which was a pity. The furnishings were simple, but it was clean, warm and had all that I required of it. The *en suite* bathroom was unusual in that the shower was without curtains or other protection to stop the water splashing about, but the bathroom floor sloped to a drain in the middle and, when I tested it later, this simple arrangement caused no problems. In my bedroom, and throughout all the public rooms and corridors, were 'No Smoking' signs. These signs did not simply *ask* patrons to refrain from smoking, but positively threatened dire retribution to anyone caught smoking. The warnings were strictly observed, because I later noticed that anyone who could not go without a cigarette stood outside in the Arctic winter for their dose of nicotine.

Just across from the hotel were a few shops and a tourist information centre. The girls at the information centre told me what I needed to know about the area and the shops supplied me with a selection of provisions and other necessaries.

The next morning dawned fine and bright as I set out to explore this little community and its environs. The hotel was on the lakeside at a point that seemed to be a major junction for the official snowmobile routes that criss-crossed the lake. I walked down the bank onto the lake. The ice was thick and as solid as concrete but the snow was variable. The snowmobile routes were reasonably compacted, but off the tracks the snow would not hold my weight and I did not want a repeat of my experience outside the 'Artkium' in Rovaniemi. I put on my snowshoes for the first time and set off to inspect the shore line and the various homes around the lakeside. Without those snowshoes I would have fared no better than I had in Rovaniemi but the technique of walking with them was something that I had to learn. They are attached only to the toe of each boot so that the heel is left free to be lifted.

This movement can cause them to swing about and it is very easy to trip. To prevent this they have long tails that trail in the snow and keep them in line. The technique requires a toe-up walk or shuffling gait. To spread the weight over the snow, the shoes are relatively wide, so, to prevent the shoes clashing as one walks, the wearer has to adopt a stride that keeps the legs wide apart. It took a little getting used to but the net effect was, as I recorded in my diary, 'a little like doing the goose-step whilst wearing a heavy nappy'.[6] It was all right for short distances but I found the exercise very tiring. For longer journeys across open areas skis would have been more effective and easier to use. However, my snowshoes served their purpose: they gave me some measure of confidence and allowed me to get to places that would otherwise have been inaccessible.

It was a lonely walk across this section of the lake. A few people passed on skis or, more usually, snowmobiles. Almost everyone stuck to the official snowmobile routes. Tracks running off them were rare and where I came across the tracks of wild reindeer I saw that they too had generally stuck to the compacted snow of the routes. Praying that my snow-shoes were going to be reliable I did deviate once or twice to get a better look at the houses dotted about the shore. Some were grand, brightly painted buildings, others small and quaint. All were attractive to the eye and all were made of timber. Each had a big pile of firewood stacked nearby under the shelter of trees. I had the impression that most were summer holiday homes, now shut up for the winter. I could imagine how pleasant it must be to spend a summer up here in such attractive houses, reading, fishing and boating but, of course, the midges and mosquitoes would be a problem.

The girls at the local tourist office arranged for me to visit a local reindeer farm. I told them I wanted to get some photographs of a Saami farmer looking after his herd and it would be preferable if he were wearing the Saami traditional costume.

'I'll see what I can do,' said one of the girls in the office, whose name was Heidi. After a few phone calls all was arranged for the

---

[6] US – diaper

following morning. Heidi was to accompany me in a taxi to the farm and act as my interpreter.

In the morning, I discovered that Heidi was a Saami and had donned national costume. This was a double bonus for me. The drive to the farm took only twenty minutes and we were met by the farmer with a big smile. He was, as promised, in costume. Heidi worked with him as he moved his reindeer about the farm. His favourite animal was a beautiful white creature with a perfect set of antlers and he glowed with pride as he walked him around me to be photographed. Unfortunately, the day was overcast and the light hazy; there was a gentle fall of snow. It wasn't a 'white out' but, without contrast, the beauty of his white reindeer was lost against the snow. I didn't have the heart to ask him for another reindeer with a dark coat so that my photographs had more punch. I struggled to make the best of what was available to me. The tour included a demonstration of a reindeer pulling a small boat-like pulk.[7] This time the reindeer had a darker coat and the pulk was as brightly coloured as the national costumes. It stood out prettily, even in the prevailing conditions. The farmer led it around the paddock with Heidi in the pulk, and then gave a demonstration with himself as a passenger. I was intrigued to notice that the pulk was pulled by a single rope that went between the legs of the reindeer to the harness about its neck. There were no reins but he did have a light whip.

'How do you control the animal?' I asked.

'Well, if you want to turn left, you hit the reindeer on its right side and it turns left to get away from what ever is causing it pain, and if you want to go right, you hit it on the left.'

I supposed a tap on the centre of its hind quarters got it moving forwards, but I couldn't work out how to make it stop and Heidi was not up to translating the answer to that query. I presume that if you stop goading the beast forward, it will naturally stop. I never did learn the answer, but I concluded that, although the reindeer is a beautiful creature, it is remarkably stupid.

---

[7] From the Laplander word 'pulkke', meaning a travelling sled, traditionally made of wood and reindeer hide

I learned a little about the Saami costume and dress. Whilst the Saami usually dressed in modern Western clothing, many still wore their exotic national dress on festive occasions, particularly if they were engaged in the tourist industry. My host was in his full regalia as he showed me about his farm. The base colour of the costumes was a dark blue but both were trimmed with broad red and yellow strips that stood out brightly. Both wore reindeer-skin shoes with curly toes and at their throats, large ornamental brooches made of gold. The farmer complemented his costume with a colourful woollen scarf and a many-pointed hat hung with red tassels. Heidi wore a red patterned shawl and a white knitted bonnet decorated with red pom-poms. My Saami friends confessed that there was no special significance in the spiked design of the headgear. It was purely decorative, but their colourful costume made identification easy in the snow. The curly, pointed shoes, however, were more practical than decorative. The fur of the soles was carefully arranged so that the hairs lay in a line, giving the best possible grip on ice yet still permitting easy walking. The curly point to the toe had two practical uses. The first was for easy attachment of skis, but, more important, where the foot had sunk deeply into the snow, the curl above the toe was helpful in cutting a way out to the surface. I recalled the length of the Eskimo mukluks, made of sealskin, which came over the knee. Here the Saami shoe barely reached the ankle. How did it keep out the deep snow? The answer seemed to be that, no matter how high a boot could be made, the snow in Finland was likely to be deeper and almost bound to get in over the top. What the Saami use is a form of puttee so that the shoes are sealed into the leggings of the costume. The risk of snow ingression is thus reduced to a minimum.

'Are they warm?' I asked.

'Oh yes, very warm,' they answered. 'But in particularly cold conditions we wrap our feet in wool before putting on the shoe.'

They described the technique. It was identical to that which I had learned from the Russians in Chukotka when they wrapped their feet against the cold. A New Zealand Maori had once described to me a similar technique that he had used to wrap his boots in hessian sacking so as to stop himself slipping on the lanolin of the wool when sheep shearing. How did these skills transfer themselves around the world? I wondered. When I had tried to teach English outdoor men the advantages of this method of foot wrapping over the conventional Hi-Tec socks, I had been ridiculed. Here, where the people really knew about survival in the cold, they preferred the ancient method of wrapping their feet even though such socks were available to them.

When it was time for us to leave, the wife of the farmer kindly gave us a lift back to the Inari Hotel. By comparison, instead of an ornate hat, her black curly hair was in an exotic coiffure and she was dressed in tight denims. Her knee-length leather boots looked like something out of a production of *Puss-In-Boots*, or perhaps *The Pirates of Penzance*. They were black, high-heeled and turned over just below the knee, more suited to the fashion cat-walks of Paris or Milan than a reindeer farm in northern Finland. This contrast between the man and his wife was so marked it was almost comic, and I smiled to myself.

It wasn't until we were back at the Inari hotel that I discovered it had not been part of her employment duties for Heidi to accompany me to the farm. It was her day off and, out of the goodness of her heart, she had generously donated her time to helping me, knowing that without her I would have been unable to communicate with the farmer. I don't think she had any other motive because when I insisted on paying her a modelling fee she was overcome with embarrassment.

That evening I joined the throng at the hotel, got a beer from the bar and went to sit on my own at a table in a corner so as to observe the crowds. It wasn't long before others joined me. They were most welcome. I was happy to have their company and find out more about the people. My 'guests' were a young Finnish gold prospector, two young ladies – one a Fin and the other a Saami – and a Norwegian couple. The Norwegian couple were just passing through the region but the others were local residents. Fortunately for me, all but the Norwegian woman spoke good English. I felt like a Tudor king with his retinue. The Norwegian man was the oddest of the bunch. When he realised I was English, he seemed to hold me personally responsible for the attitude of the world's anti-whaling lobby and, in particular, for the part played by Britain in pressing for stricter regulations on whaling. He berated me for the damage it was doing to the Norwegian industry. I allowed his admonitions to float over my head. Instead, I absorbed the passion of his feelings.

'Are you in the whaling business?' I asked.

'No.'

When I pushed him further to learn his profession, he stated, with what seemed to me to be extraordinary pride, that his government regulations prevented him from working. I gathered that his family home had been in the south of Norway. In an endeavour to maintain the country's population in the north the government paid him a generous allowance to live there. If he found work in the north, he would lose that allowance, and as the allowance was greater than any income he could earn by working, he was effectively paid not to work. Any penalties there may have been for his failure to look for work did not seem to enter the argument. I must admit that I had great difficulty understanding everything he told me and I'm sure I missed some of the finer points but, in view of what he perceived to be my personal responsibility for Norway's difficulties with their whaling industry, any attempt on my part to rationalise what he had been saying would have been construed as hostile. I held my counsel but my Finnish companions were my allies and they teased him unmercifully.

To change the subject and, more importantly, to glean local knowledge, I asked the Finns and the Saami about travel in the forest and, in particular, about snowmobile travel. What were the 'dos' and 'don'ts'? All were emphatic that it was not safe to take a snowmobile off the approved routes. The snow was generally two metres deep and off the route quite uncompacted. If the front ski runners dug into the snow, the snowmobile would tend to drive itself deeper in. As there was no means of reversing the machine, the only way would be forward and down. The lakes were still frozen over with thick ice, but this late in the year there would be a layer of water – maybe half a metre deep – sandwiched between the snow and the ice. When off track the snowmobile was perfectly capable of sinking through into the layer of water and losing all traction. I made a mental note never to leave the official route when I took out a snowmobile.

Thinking of the specialised survival skills of the Inuit of Canada and Greenland and the Inupiat of Alaska in that harsh and empty wilderness they call home, I asked the Saami lady what particular precautions she would take if she went into the forest alone.

'I would never,' she said, 'go into the forest without a knife and matches – so that I could make a fire and I would always take with me my Nokia mobile telephone so that I could call for help if I was in trouble.'

Technology has certainly come to this part of the Arctic.

I personally could not spot any general physical distinction between the Finns and the Saami. What differences there were seemed to be more cultural than genetic. I learned from my friends that there was harmony between them. Earlier dissatisfaction at the cultural restraints placed on the Saami was now in the past. The feeling in my little party was that there was less harmony between the Norwegians and their Saami. Whereas much better integration had taken place between the Finnish and Russian Saami since *glasnost*, it was said that the Russian Saami 'seemed to be very influenced by their Soviet past.' Exactly what all this meant I am not too sure, but certainly we were a happy little group of mixed nationalities at my table and having aired his resentment for my part in the restrictions on Norwegian whaling, even the Norwegian became affable.

The next day I took delivery of my hired snowmobile and sledge. The weather was dull and overcast.

'Have you ever driven a snowmobile before?' the hirer asked.

'No,' I admitted, and was given a briefing on the controls and a long, stern lecture about not leaving the official route. I also carried a more than adequate supply of extra fuel and oil for the two-stroke engine. He listed the few places where fuel was available and it was impressed on me to manage my fuel usage and replenishment carefully. Having satisfied himself that I was suitably briefed, he indicated a track through some woodland that would lead to the lake and the official routes that would take me to Nellim which had been described as a very pretty place with a most unusually attractive church. It was my first place of interest. Once again, he cautioned me to stay on the official route.

I set off carefully through the wood. The hazy light made seeing the track particularly difficult in the snow. Everything merged into a white, featureless mist. The snowmobile seemed a truculent machine with a mind of its own but, as I had spent nearly 30 years flying complex aircraft, I certainly was not going to be defeated by such a basic two-stroke machine. I was determined to master the noisy, unruly little brute. Where the track came out of the wood and onto the lake I could see no sign of the official route and had no option but to carry along what track there was until, to my consternation, this minor pathway divided. There was no indication of the correct route. I had wanted to get to Nellim which was to the east. One track curved away west around a headland. I turned to the east on the other track, but within 100 yards this track looped round on itself into a deep snow bank on the edge of the wood and I sunk in. Having travelled less than half a mile, I was now stuck fast. My rage at my own incompetence and consequent embarrassment knew no bounds. It didn't help when I stepped off the machine and sunk into the snow up to my armpits. I felt that the day was not going particularly well. The snowmobile now towered above me and it was with considerable difficulty that I dragged myself back onto it. From the sledge, I extracted my snowshoes, put them on and made my way back to the hirer of the machine. I didn't know how to look him in the face when I explained my predicament. He didn't flinch but got out another machine and took me back to the scene. With a combination of brute force and skill he extracted my snowmobile from the bank and got it facing in the right direction. He then led me down the other fork in the track and onto the official route.

Pointing to the east he said, 'Nellim is that way.' I don't think I could have borne it if he had reminded me not to leave the official track. He must have wondered whether he was ever going to see me or his machine again.

Perhaps that unhappy start to my travels was for the best.

Henceforth, I was devoid of overconfidence – and that is a very good thing. Equally, I was determined not to let this little machine defeat me. I am happy to report that I eventually brought the uncomfortable brute to heel. It took a couple of days of travel through the woods and over the lakes before that snowmobile and I came to a sullen understanding but, in the end, I was confident that I could make it do what I wanted. I did not lose my respect for the risks involved and, needless to say, never left the official route. Without it I could not have experienced the pristine beauty of the winter woodlands – the trees dressed in snow and endless lakes through which the routes took me. For the most part, I was alone in this white world and the scent of the air was delicious.

As my travels took me past the large town of Ivalo, I found a family group fishing through the ice. I had always wanted to see that activity so I parked my snowmobile on the edge of the track and gingerly walked over to them. The snow was not deep. They had an enormous hand-cranked auger for cutting holes through the ice; then, using remarkably short fishing rods, they lowered their baited hooks into the water. It was not long before the line was removed with a fish on the end. Whilst I watched, they collected quite a few fish, but all were small and I doubt they would have made a very satisfying meal.

I pressed on, hoping to be at Nellim well before nightfall. There I found the delightful little wooden church with Russian Orthodox golden crosses on the twin domes. The craftsmanship was superb, Set as it was in deep snow on the edge of the forest, it was stunningly beautiful. Everything was constructed in wood and most of the fittings were well polished. Unfortunately, the doors were locked and I could only guess at the simple splendour of its interior. I had come a long way to see this church, but it was worth it.

I asked a local woman in the village of Nellim where I could camp for the night.

'Oh, wherever you want – but not in someone's private garden.'

Such freedom of movement is a pleasure. As I had no intention of camping in someone's private garden, I headed back out of the village and found an attractive little island in the lake. It wasn't big, only a few hundred yards across, and for this night it was going to be mine – all mine – to enjoy in perfect isolation and solitude. I erected my tent and cooked myself a warm and substantial meal. With my reindeer skins and down sleeping bag, I made myself a very comfortable bed which I slipped into as the daylight faded away. Like the caribou skins I had used in Canada, one went under my legs and one over the lower part of my sleeping bag. Although Finland in March could not compare with the savagery of February in Canada's north, the skins were still a comfort providing me with exceptional warmth and, I confess, a sense of primitiveness that comes from wrapping oneself in the pelt of an animal to exclude the elements. With the door of my tent open, I could lie in my sleeping bag and watch the stars move between the trees across the lake. The night sky would occasionally put on a display of the aurora. Eerie, variable and beautiful, it would mesmerise me for an hour or two, then vanish as quickly as it had appeared. Breakfast after an Arctic winter's night under canvas is always a meal to remember.

My only disappointment was that I could not get close to that point where the countries of Finland, Norway and Russia meet. No official routes went near that spot and it was an area visitors like myself would not be encouraged to approach, so that ambition had to be abandoned.

My final night in the wilderness was spent in one of the shelters that are scattered about Finland's forests. It was a little log cabin equipped with a wood-burning stove, simply furnished with a table and two benches. A window looked across the frozen lake. In a nearby lean-to shed was a supply of cut logs and, next to that, the supreme luxury of the wilderness – a lavatory. These wilderness shelters are maintained by the State and intended for transit shelter rather than accommodation. When I arrived in the late afternoon, a party of German ski tourists under the control of a local guide and his assistant were just tidying up and getting ready to leave. They left me the remains of a big pot of coffee, which was much appreciated. Their tour guide was a heavily built man of middle years with a good sense of humour. I don't know whether my inexperience showed – or perhaps it was because I'm

English and my years are beginning to be obvious – or just his general sense of responsibility for all who travel in the northern forests in winter – but he took it upon himself to examine my snowmobile and equipment.

'Why haven't you covered your sledge with a tarpaulin? You have too much snow in it,' he observed. He shook my fuel containers. 'Do you have enough fuel? There's nothing between here and Inari.'

I explained my fuel calculation and reserves and he nodded in satisfaction. Then, reading my intentions, he reminded me that the huts were not meant for accommodation. They were only for rest and shelter.

'You must leave it open for anyone else who wants to stop.'

Satisfied that I was not going to be an embarrassment to anyone, he sent his party of skiers off down the track and mounted his own massive machine.

'Well, enjoy your trip. Don't get off the official route,' he shouted, as he set off with his young assistant.

A silence descended around my domain. I went out and chopped some logs so that a reasonably generous stack of ready fuel would remain available by the stove after I departed the next morning. Who knew if the next arrival might not be an exhausted traveller escaping a savage return of winter weather? It was not only good housekeeping but the least I could do in return for the benefits I was receiving. As evening set in, the light in the sky turned pink, then through various shades of darkening grey until it faded. There should have been an inky blackness to the moonless night, but with the broad covering of snow it was possible to see the low hills on the other side of the lake just by the reflected light of the stars. Except for the gentle crackling of the log fire in the stove, there was perfect silence; it made me feel I was on some higher, more ethereal plane. I cooked myself a hot meal, threw a few more logs into the stove and placed a long-life candle to burn in the window. Then, with a large mug of hot coffee by my side, I opened a book to read. I remember turning the pages, but I don't remember reading any of it. My mind was absorbed by my environment and the variety of experiences in the Arctic.

## THE WARM ARTIC

When, many years ago, I had seen Greenland from the air, and planned my first adventure to visit the world of the great explorers such as Knud Rasmussen, Peary, Amundsen and Byrd, and experience the ferocity of the Arctic at its dramatic worst, I was already too old to consider seriously taxing feats of endurance. I had neither the money nor strength to equip and haul a sledge 600 miles or more to either of the poles. I was content simply to see and feel something of the harshness of the land. Very quickly this desire for rough adventure had matured to a deep appreciation of a pristine and lonely world that has yet to succumb to the ravages of mankind. I don't know which I enjoy most of this Arctic world: the silence and isolation of the wilderness; or the occasional and unexpected encounters with others who share my feeling for this natural environment. In my wanderings around the Arctic Ocean, I had indeed experienced something of Arctic savagery, its isolation and beauty. It is in the Arctic that I have felt at one with God and nature. The people I have met in that pristine world have formed an important facet of that experience. I asked myself which region and which individual had impressed me most? I thought of Spitsbergen, Greenland, Nunavut, Alaska, Russia and now Finland. How could I compare the mountains of Spitsbergen and the endless expanse of Nunavut with that extraordinary, dishevelled little town of Provideniya in Chukotka, or the grandeur of Greenland with the vast combination of lakes and forest in which I now sat in contemplation? Each has its unique features and still there is a uniformity that allows me to think of it all as one. How can I compare little Zhenya, who had tried to give me her watch as a gift, with Mr Geosah, who had shown me how to build an igloo and been so upset when he discovered that his wife had forgotten to pack the sandwiches for our lunch? Where did the enthusiasm of that Polish research team on Spitsbergen fit into this hierarchy of comparisons? There was also the generosity of young Heidi who gave up her day off to help me, a perfect stranger, see a Saami reindeer farm. All share an equal niche in my affections. As I have been a lone traveller for most of the time, people were always ready to approach me, or accept my approaches to them. The people I have met have been of all shapes, sizes and colours, men and women, old and young. Some have been physically strong, others apparently puny. If they shared one thing in common, it was the ordinariness of their appearance which allowed them to pass unnoticed amongst the Kabloona of the south, yet each possessed stoicism and a kindness and quality of mind that raised them head and shoulders above the rest of mankind as I know it. In their sparsely inhabited world, they are relatively free from the suspicions that urban man entertains of his neighbours. I find that Arctic people are not frightened to catch my eyes and return my smiles. In the south, similar gestures from a stranger would have urban man adopting a defensive attitude. The Arctic people are reliable in times of strife – open, warm and easy to approach. Perhaps others have had different experiences of the north, but I always get a tingle of excitement and a glow of warmth whenever I am reminded of the lands that surround the Arctic Ocean and the human beings who inhabit them.

# Chapter 10

# ICELAND AND EAST GREENLAND

*An amazing adventure with a grandson.*

With my visit to Russia's Kola Peninsula and Finnish Lapland, I had circled the lands surrounding the Arctic Ocean and completed what I had set out to do, but I hadn't taken into account how the lure of the Arctic and its people would continue to tug at my thoughts.

I had not yet visited Iceland. The authoritative book, *The Circumpolar North*, written 'for those with more than a superficial interest in the northern regions of our planet,' states that it includes Iceland 'more on account of its relationship with other northern lands than for its own attributes, for it is the least "Arctic" of the countries we are considering.' Only one little island, Grimsey, off its northern coast had a latitude just north of the Arctic Circle. For completeness, I felt that I too should include that country with the magical name 'Iceland', and if I were going to Iceland it seemed a short distance to cross the Denmark Straits and visit East Greenland. The east coast of Greenland has, I was assured by my reading, a character quite distinct from the communities of the western side of the land mass. That alone was exciting enough to warrant a visit. There were two communities to consider: the larger centre at Ammassalik and the small, remote Ittoqqortoormiit, well north on the edge of Scoresbysund. Ammassalik was easier to get to and had more facilities. Ittoqqortoormiit was much more complicated a venue, but what had really fascinated me for many years was the name: 'Ittoqqortoormiit'. Who could resist a name like that? I certainly could not imagine how it should be pronounced! The name of a place is a strange reason to plan a visit but, for me, an important one. The third and most powerful reason for my return to the north came from within my family – my eldest grandson Ben. Although born in England, he was now a New Zealander. A true Kiwi, he was making a profession of adventure and outdoor pursuits but his opportunities to visit the Polar North were few.

'Grandpa,' he asked on more than one occasion, 'will you take me with you next time you go to the Arctic?'

Ben is exceptionally fit and strong and at the time I began planning this visit he had just turned 20 – some 53 years my junior. We were certainly going to make an odd couple sharing a small two man tent for three or four weeks. Therein lay the only serious danger. Such proximity would either destroy our relationship or create a bonding between us that would be the envy of all who treasure personal closeness with their family. Avoiding the former and achieving the latter would be something both of us would have to work hard at. I could not match his physical prowess and I knew he wanted to stretch himself. On the other hand, he had yet to develop an interest in the warmth that could be generated by making friends with people of different cultures in remote areas, something that, as I hope I have made clear, lies at the root of my love of the North. None of my trips up north could be described as mundane but this trip was going to be a new and challenging experience.

Iceland is a dynamic land. It sits astride both the European and American tectonic plates and is subject to considerable volcanic action. The junction of the two plates runs roughly diagonally across the island from south-west to north-east and the two sections of the island are tearing apart at, in geological terms, the incredibly high rate of about 2 centimetres per year. In places the ground is scarred by stretch marks and it is possible to walk along these scars with their high rock faces, Europe on one side and America on the other. The culture and history of the island is fascinating as I had discovered when making a brief holiday visit to Iceland on a cruise ship with my wife. We had a tantalisingly short, one day visit to the capital, Reykjavík, and one to the north coast city of Akureyri. Customs and legends abound and each tale is both educational and an entertainment in itself. We had found the people friendly and charming, their Nordic origins obvious in their naturally fair hair, blue eyes and clear skin.

But Ben was from New Zealand and there he had already experienced the drama of a volcanic land. He didn't want to repeat that and, whilst he may have been interested in the history and culture, this was not the reason he had made his way to the North. He wanted to stretch himself in challenging country. In the north west extreme of the country the coast is heavily cut with fjords and the land stretches out like three fingers towards, and almost touching, the Arctic Circle. It was the most northerly of these three fingers that was to be our Icelandic objective. From the town of Ísafjörður we would be able to take a boat across the wide Isafjarðardjûp to the nature reserve of Hornstrandir. The population of Iceland is sparse, only two persons per square kilometre, but 87% of that population live in the urban areas.[1] Hornstrandir is decidedly unpopulated and that was just what we wanted. Fishermen and whalers had inhabited this nature reserve, but they had all drifted away, leaving only a few holiday homes used by Icelanders in the summer. A boat from Ísafjörður would drop us off at the tiny hamlet of Hesteyri, tucked into yet another of the many fjords.

After our arrival in Iceland and an overnight stop at the international airport of Keflavik, we made our way to Ísafjörður. This town certainly had the flavour of the Arctic. Like the rest of Iceland, it was virtually devoid of trees. There were high, rolling hills surrounding the fjord and although it was July these carried many large patches of snow down to quite low levels. There was a small airport and a harbour. The town was spotless and the air a joy to breath. Traffic was light.

We went to a small campsite in the grounds of a little hotel. Ben said he wanted to 'hang about'; I wanted to go for a walk, so I left him and strolled up the side of the fjord. When I got back a young German girl had arrived and was putting up her somewhat

---

[1] *Philips' Universal Atlas* (London: G. Philip & Son, 1981)

unusual tent. We were the only two sets of campers on the site. Ben had started to cook supper, so we invited her to join us. Her name was Gisela Funk, a second year student at Edinburgh University reading Architecture, and she was spending four weeks travelling and camping in Iceland. We mentioned that we had two nights before our boat left for Hornstrandir.

The next day we checked in to the operators of the ferry to be sure our passage was in order.

'Yes, it's all OK for tomorrow,' they said, 'but do you want to leave this afternoon at two p.m?'

We jumped at it, but first we had to buy our provisions and fuel supplies. Ísafjörður was well stocked and we got everything we wanted: food from the little supermarkets and fuel from the petrol station. With the passing years, my demands for food had diminished, but Ben was still building his already powerful body. In any event, he had a naturally high metabolism and we both knew that our supplies had to be generous. I gave him his head with the shopping and fell in with his selections. I just wondered how we were going to carry it all plus our equipment. Whilst we hurriedly lugged our provisions back to our campsite to pack up and go, we commented on the number of attractive girls in the town with beautiful blond hair. My own hair had been a dark brown but was now grey. Ben had very curly hair, worn almost shoulder length, and his time in the New Zealand outdoors had bleached it so that it was more like a golden mane. As we hurried along, I noticed a pretty girl walking toward us down the road. Like the other young girls we had commented on, she had a mantle of silky blond hair. Her eyes were cast down and she seemed oblivious to us but as she passed I saw her eyes quickly lift and flash a glance at Ben. It was the sort of glance I hadn't seen in many decades! Fortunately, Ben had not noticed this and I smiled to myself, thinking it was probably a good thing we were heading for a deserted wilderness.

Back at the little camp site, Gisela's tent was there, but she was nowhere to be seen. She would think it odd our suddenly vanishing without saying anything, but that was too bad. In all probability, we would never see her again. We quickly broke camp and set off for the quayside.

The boat that took us across to Hesteyri was a fast launch. There were a few other passengers, I judged to be day trippers, together with a few campers like ourselves. Not all were for Hesteyri. The boat would continue to other landing places around the nature reserve. The person in charge of this motley collection of passengers told us of a woman, known as the Queen of Hesteyri, who kept open a small establishment offering coffee or lunches to the summer visitors who passed through the hamlet. Her family had lived there when it had been a living community. Now she was the only resident, happy to remain there in isolation when there were no passing visitors. I later learned that her name was Birna Pálsdóttir. Ben and I had plans to live rough in the wilderness and did not think that the monarch, Birna, was going to be a person of much interest to us. We were wrong, however.

Ben and I chose to sit in the open, rather than the cabin of the boat, where we could enjoy the smell of the salt and feel the wind blowing about us during the crossing. Whilst the day was not cold, (my diary had recorded a temperature of $+12°C$), the forward motion of the boat made it deliciously cool and fresh and we were happy to sit and ponder our own thoughts as we viewed the dramatic scenery. Steep cliffs dropped straight into the fjord. The Drangajökull glacier glistened off to the east. The sea was calm and the boat made good speed across the deep clear water.

The tide was in at Hesteyri and the boat was able to dock at the small landing jetty. Rather than the houses being clustered together as they would be in England, the dwellings in this hamlet were spread well apart. All were built of wood with corrugated iron roofs. They were small, yet seemed to have two storeys. The most striking feature was that the whole area was covered with wild flowers of many hues. As the passengers dispersed into this nature reserve, I could see that the flowers were tall, sometimes reaching to waist height. The place was surrounded by high hills – some of which qualified as mountains. With remarkable speed, the passengers dispersed. Maybe some went to have coffee with Birna, but others vanished into the surrounding country, or returned to the boat.

Because of the weight of supplies and provisions we were

carrying, I thought it would be a good idea to set up a base camp on the edge of the hamlet where we could make a 'stash'; from there we would be able to take excursions with lighter packs to the locations we chose to visit. Ben had other ideas. At the back of the hamlet was a high ridge, its upper slopes covered in boulders. From the top there would be a commanding view across the hills and fjords.

'That's the obvious place to camp,' he said, 'up there.'

He headed straight for the ridge. It was going to be a steep climb without packs, but our rucksacks weighed in excess of 20 kilos each. Dear God, I thought, he's trying to kill me. I had done all the planning and arranging of this expedition, but I wanted Ben to take the lead, so I said nothing. I did my best to keep up with him, but I was finding it very difficult indeed and my breathing was getting heavier and heavier. Whether it was the sound of my rasping breath, or the realisation that, whatever the view, it was not really an ideal camp site, Ben relented and stopped. There would be no shelter from the wind and none of the many rivers in the vicinity flowed *up* to the ridge, so collecting water supplies could be a problem. We retreated to a path that led from the hamlet and up a gentle rise away from the coast. We followed it for about a quarter of a mile, then moved out to a very acceptable level area out of sight of the hamlet and within easy reach of a fast-flowing river. That's more like it, I thought.

The site was most attractive. We had space and water. When the time came to leave, it would not be far back to the jetty and, although the land was open, we had seclusion. We set up our camp and pitched the tent. The last time I had used that tent had been on the Mackenzie River Delta when the temperature was at or below $-40°C$. Here the temperature was in double figures above freezing. This was genteel. Now we could relax and get the feel of the place. Tomorrow we would start to explore.

We both had excellent maps of the area and each had an essential compass and our own satellite navigation unit. We planned our activities. Ben made it clear he wanted to do a circular walk of about five days and he wanted to do this alone. He didn't actually say that I would hold him back. He didn't have to. He also needed some space from me, and this I appreciated, but I was a little concerned that he had had no previous experience of the terrain and the route he was setting out would be lonely and rugged. It would be easy for a lone walker to have an accident and not be found for a very long time. He's a big boy now, I thought. He must do as he wants. For my part, I decided I would walk over the mountain to Nordur Aðalvík on a bay facing out into the Denmark Strait, where I would stay a couple of nights before returning to camp. At least Ben's route would coincide with mine some of the way. The tent, our only tent, would stay at the base camp. I had supplied Ben with a modern breathable survival bag into which he could crawl with a sleeping bag if the weather turned rough. I carried an ancient plastic survival bag. It had been with me since my first trip to Greenland some twenty years previously. There I had slept out in the open and simply used it as a ground sheet. It would do in an emergency, though there was always the danger of condensation from within if I had to get inside.

It had rained during the night, the air was fresh and the sky showed signs of clearing. It was a perfect day for our respective excursions. We enjoyed a substantial breakfast, secured the camp and set off following the track up a gentle incline. It took us north-west, directly towards my objective at Aðalvík. It was easy walking until we got to the plateau at the top. It is not high, only about 1,000 feet. There the surface was covered with boulders of various sizes. If it wasn't for the lichen on the boulders, the only vegetation, and the patches of snow, we might have been standing on the surface of Mars. It was bleak and unattractive, a huge contrast to the extensive wild flowers that surrounded Hesteyri. It was only about two miles across the plateau and the path we were following picked a way through the worst of the boulder field. However, some of the patches of snow obscured the path. The snow was compacted and firm to walk on but it was difficult to pick up the path again after clearing the snow, though in such terrain as this, one didn't really need a path. It was sufficient just to head in the right direction. There were even cairns pointing out the general route, but the path did make walking a good deal easier.

At the far side of the plateau, beauty returned. There, an escarpment led down into meadowland. It must have been four or five miles across to the mountains on the other side. In this bowl, nearly a thousand feet below where we stood, there were two lakes and a river flowing gently towards the sea, which was somewhere on our left. As in Hesteyri, the meadow was ablaze with wildflowers. Whilst we stood in clear air, there was a light shower of rain across the far side of the meadow and, through it, a full rainbow added a further colourful touch. I felt as Dorothy must have when searching for the Wizard of Oz and she first saw the Emerald City. Here, however, there was no city. At first we thought the area devoid of humanity but, as we studied the vista, Ben spotted a tiny blob of red close to the river and not far from the lakes. Straining our eyes, we saw that this was a little house. We presumed it was a holiday home as there was no farming in the area and it was too far from the sea to be useful for fishermen. It seemed to us that Icelanders craved isolation when on holiday. I didn't think they could be accused of being gregarious, but in this I was to be proved wrong.

Ben and I descended the escarpment a little way and stopped at a point where we had some shelter. It was a convenient time to have a lunch break. After lunch we continued the descent to where our paths would diverge. I was going north-west and Ben was going to head due north to the hills on the other side of the meadow, which he intended to cross, and then pick his way around the north coast, circling back to our base camp. I was already developing a high regard for Ben's ability to look after himself. He had a quiet confidence that was reassuring, but I could not rid myself of the fear that a nasty accident might result in having to go back to his mother, my daughter, and tell her that something awful had happened to Ben and he would not be coming home. I was even more terrified by the prospect of having to tell my wife that I had lost our eldest grandson.

'Are you quite confident in finding your way around?' I asked

'Absolutely,' he responded.

'Well, if you're not back at camp by Friday, I'm calling out the emergency services,' I said.

## ICELAND AND EAST GREENLAND

Ben made no comment but grinned at me. We picked up our rucksacks, shook hands and parted company. As I headed northwest, I watched Ben striding off to the valley floor and away to the north. The last I saw of him was a tiny figure picking his way across one of the little rivers that flow into the larger of the two lakes.

I was quite happy on my own and I took my time on the remainder of my journey. Down by the river I could see the tracks of one or more four-wheel all-terrain vehicles. So that's how the holiday makers in that little house get there with all their supplies for their vacation, I reasoned. I presume they take one of the launches, complete with supplies and all-terrain vehicles to Aðalvík and then drive the five miles or so to their lonely dwelling. For those who like their home isolated, this little spot must be the Land of Beulah. Whilst I had the urge to meet whoever chose to live in such a spot, I realised that I would be destroying their whole objective were I to call for a chat. Instead, I turned away and followed the river downstream to a suitable crossing point. There being no bridges in such a wilderness, I stripped from the waist down and waded across to the other side, carrying my trousers, underwear, boots and socks above my head. At this moment, modesty required that I too had seclusion.

Once across the river, I had a few miles of sand dunes to traverse to get to Aðalvík. It had taken me seven hours to get there and I was very tired. The only feature at Aðalvík was an emergency hut. There were no other buildings. There was a narrow beach, but with virtually all Arctic coasts, it was littered with drift wood. Above me towered a massive hill called Baejarfjail. Its cliffs fell adjacent to the bay but there was a road up it to an abandoned US military post. I think it was from up there in 1941 that the World War II battle between the Royal Navy and the Nazi battle cruiser, *The Bismarck*, was observed. When HMS *Hood* was sunk with massive loss of life, the smoke from the explosion was easily visible from the land. As history records, the Royal Navy sunk *The Bismarck* just three days afterwards. It was sad to stand on so peaceful a spot and contemplate such carnage.

There were two tents at Aðalvík. One contained a family of two adults and three children and the other looked familiar to me. It couldn't possibly be Gisela's, could it? Then I spotted a girl heading towards the road that ran up Baejarfjail. It was Gisela! How odd that we should meet again in such a wilderness. She had made a landing further round the coast, walked to Aðalvík and made her camp. I caught up with her and chatted for a bit. I also apologised for our sudden disappearance from Ísafjörður without explanation.

'I wondered what had happened to you,' she responded.

I left her to walk up the old military road while I picked a spot to camp and made myself a hot meal. I was too weary to take trouble. If I remember correctly, my fare consisted only of reconstituted mashed potatoes and gravy. A bit simple, but it had bulk and filled my belly with warmth. I got into my sleeping bag. It was only 7.30 p.m.

At this latitude, south of the Arctic Circle in July, the sun may set, but it never gets dark. The twilight lasts all night. It also means that children never really know when it's bed time and they play late into the evening. The children at this camp were well behaved and their happy chatter did not stop me falling asleep. I was tired enough to sleep through a revolution. Judging that there might be rain, I decided to use my plastic survival bag as a bivouac and prayed that there would be no significant condensation. It was a mistake; I should have moved into the emergency shelter but had been reluctant to do so as I had assumed it was for emergencies, not for ordinary camping accommodation. As I drifted into sleep, I wondered how Ben was getting on.

The call of nature awoke me at 10.00 p.m. The children were still up and playing. There had been condensation and my sleeping bag was decidedly damp. Sleeping bags filled with artificial material can cope well with moisture but down filled bags are disasters if they get wet. They lose all loft and with it all thermal properties. My bag was filled with down. I tried to brush off the condensation with my shirt and moved outside the plastic survival bag. I hoped the dampness would evaporate. I went back to sleep but awoke again at 2.00 a.m. The sky was now crystal clear and the temperature had dropped significantly. It was only +3°C and, because of this, there had been a heavy fall of dew to add to my already wet sleeping bag. Before I left England, I should have bought myself a breathable 'bivi' bag, like the one I had given to Ben. It was too late now to have regrets. What to do? I had had some seven hours sleep and was quite refreshed. As I was reluctant to let my sleeping bag get any wetter and there was ample light in the sky, I decided to break camp and return to Hesteyri. By 2.30 I was on my way. As I left, I saw that the children were now inside the family tent but still awake for I could hear them talking. When did they get their sleep? I wondered. Gisela's tent was dark and quiet. Once again, I had departed without warning.

I took my time walking back. I draped my sleeping bag over the top of my rucksack rather than compress it in its present wet condition, hoping the movement of air might help to dry it. It was pleasant to be on the move. The early morning air smelt delicious. The sun was now over the horizon, but low in the sky and hidden behind the hills, outlining them in a warm glow of fiery light. I walked on, crossed the river and started to climb the escarpment. I was waiting to feel the sun's rays on me before stopping for breakfast. That point was reached when I got to the spot where Ben and I had had lunch together the previous day. I spread out my sleeping bag to catch the growing warmth of the sun and spent the rest of the day at a leisurely pace. After a satisfying bowl of hot porridge and a cup of tea, life felt very good indeed. It took seven hours to get back to Hesteyri, but the remainder of the day and the return journey were unremarkable.

I now had the tent to myself until Ben's return. It was a period of relaxation and long daily walks in this fresh, green and dramatic landscape. I studied and photographed the wildflowers and deep, thick mosses that grew on the banks of the many streams and rivers flowing across the tundra. One day an Arctic fox walked past the door of the tent and looked in whilst I was writing my diary. He was not alarmed but trotted off before I could reach for my camera. My walks were of about four hours' duration. I travelled on the trails and paths, leaving them only where the surface was hard, firm and clear, or covered with rocks and boulders. On the very flat areas it was easy to walk into deep, boggy patches without warning. There was never a need to carry water; the streams and rivers were readily available and the water clear and fresh. From the beach I picked up and kept a large scallop shell which I used for scooping up and drinking the abundant supply of water. On one of my excursions I took a circuitous route to the top of the ridge that Ben had selected for our camp on the first day. He was right about the view – it was quite spectacular. I discovered the remains of an old whaling station further up the fjord and in my wanderings I would often pass the little house where Birna provided coffee and lunches for the occasional visitor. I frequently saw her about the house, carrying out such non-regal duties as washing up or hanging clothes out to dry. I would wave, and she would wave back. She seemed very friendly and it was remiss of me not to try and make more personal contact with her.

I lacked intellectual stimulation and longed for something to read. I found that the labels on packet foods were hardly great literature! I should have brought a few paperback books, but the dread of additional weight had dissuaded me. Memories of trying to pull that overloaded sledge across the Mackenzie River Delta still scarred my mind.

The weather had been very variable and it was raining quite hard when I climbed into my sleeping bag. I wonder how Ben is coping with this, I mused. I was sound asleep when I was roused by movement in the tent and something shifting around. I awoke with a start and found that it was Ben. He had returned earlier than expected and was trying to get into the shelter. I was delighted to see him safely back. He had been caught in some very bad conditions and had spent one night huddled under a rock overhang in his 'bivi' bag whilst a storm raged about him. He had decided to return to base and chose a direct, but unrecognised, route back to camp devoid of paths or markers, using his compass and the satellite navigator I had given him. On the map he showed me the way he had taken. It looked awful.

'What was the terrain like?' I asked.

'Couldn't see much of it,' he replied. 'I spent all the time in low cloud and rain, but it was very rocky and covered in boulders.'

It was a good effort on his part and I realised I didn't have to worry about him any more. Ben knew how to look after himself in the wilderness.

I told him I had met Gisela at Aðalvík. Ben said that he too had met her near some rescue hut on the north coast. Gisela had reported that she had seen me fast asleep when she went to bed, but that I had vanished by the time she got up. It was certainly odd how we kept meeting the same individual in such a large area of wilderness; and she must have been puzzled by the way we appeared and disappeared without warning.

The following day Ben and I went down to the old whaling station for a picnic. It was a ruin, for it hadn't been used for over a hundred years. I noticed a large hole in the tall chimney still standing, but could not think what had caused that particular damage. I later learned that the commander of an Icelandic patrol gun-boat had decided to use it for target practice. What a daft thing to do! You would think a grown man would have more sense. There was not too much left of it to examine but it made a focal point for us. On the little beach beside this ruin we gathered scraps of wood and made a fire. We had a brew up and then Ben grilled some pitta bread with cheese and salami. Whether or not it was because I hadn't had a civilised meal for some time, I don't know, but that grilled sandwich was fabulous. After even a short period of rough living, my level of culinary discrimination had seriously declined. It was very peaceful and we certainly had the place to ourselves. This isolation was broken only when another Arctic fox came to inspect us. He kept his distance as he sniffed around before trotting away.

It was a nice day, so I stripped off and went into the fjord for a swim. The water was not too cold; it was, in fact, surprisingly warm for this latitude (66°N). Ben joined me and we splashed about for a bit stretching our limbs and refreshing and cleansing our bodies. As we got out, to our amusement two seals popped their heads out of the water to see what had been causing the commotion. It was all very relaxing.

As we still had a couple of days before our return to Ísafjörður Ben wandered out by himself for a stroll. I followed him a little while later and found him down in the hamlet talking to a woman in the doorway of Birna's house. Her name was Pálina and she was Birna's daughter. She invited us in for coffee, and to meet her mother.

'I've seen you about frequently,' Birna said. 'Why have you not called before to say "hello"?'

They could not have been more hospitable.

'We have a large group of friends arriving tomorrow and I have to open the old school house for their accommodation,' Pálina said. 'They are coming to help us build an extension to the house, but there will be plenty of room for you. Why stay in that tent with all the rain about?'

We accepted gratefully. It would be good to have a bit more space and very nice to be in dry accommodation. It would also be an opportunity for me to get socially involved with Icelandic people.

Ben and I packed up our camp and moved into the schoolhouse. The downstairs consisted of a long hall and the area upstairs was partitioned in two and formed a dormitory. Real beds! Downstairs there was a kitchen area, bathroom and lavatory. Such luxury!

It was a Friday afternoon and Pálina's friends arrived later in the day in what looked like an offshore rescue craft. Her husband, Halldór, had also returned with some children. Earlier, he had cut his left hand very badly whilst shifting building material and been rushed to hospital for emergency treatment. They evidently had good communication with the outside world and an efficient rescue service. Neither Ben nor I forced ourselves upon their company, but they invited us to join them. With the one exception, a Dutchman who had married Pálina's sister, they were all Icelandic, but as a courtesy to Ben and me, they spoke in English.

There were five or six of them and they came from different professional backgrounds. Pálina's husband and one other were carpenters, one was a computer expert, one was a pilot. All had turned out this weekend to help Pálina's injured husband. The

Dutchman passed round cans of beer and we mingled and chatted. I spent quite a bit of time playing strange card games with two young girls. I have no idea what the rules were, but I seemed to be winning most of the time; at least, the girls kept telling me I had won.

The next morning, I was up early and had breakfast. The carpenter was the first down, followed by the others. Later, they all went out onto the building site. Ben and I decided to offer our help and were given odd jobs to do, Shifting and stacking building material, passing tools and supplies to those on the roof – generally, we did our best to contribute. When they stopped for lunch they invited us to join them.

'Be one of the family' they said.

It was lovely to do just that. Conversation, for our benefit, was almost entirely in English and ranged over many topics: the building work, domestic issues, the war in the Middle East and the recent al Qa'eda attack on London, amongst other things. It was certainly very entertaining. What wasn't mentioned was the three year fishing dispute between England and Iceland in the early seventies, known as 'The Cod War.' They were such splendid and genial fellows that any sort of conflict with them seemed unthinkable.

When work resumed after lunch, Ben and I were deployed to help with setting up and concreting in the piers on which the building extension would stand. The day finished at about six and again we were invited to join them for a meal. Paula and her mother provided an enormous bowl of spaghetti and another of stewed meat. There were seven of us but there was sufficient for twice that number.

That evening, another party of seven Icelanders joined us in the school house. Although friendly, they did not mix with us. We drank more beer, chatted and played cards with the children late into the night. The new group slept on the floor downstairs. The place was beginning to resemble a refugee camp.

The next day, when Ben and I had made sure that our kit was dry and ready for the next phase of our travels, we went back to see if we could help further. We really were redundant to the

# THE WARM ARTIC

building work other than to oversee a bonfire for disposal of rubbish. Later, Ben got involved in some activity with a couple of young boys and I asked Pálina if I could help in any way. I did not want anyone to think I was accepting their hospitality without any contribution.

'Yes,' she said. 'We have a party of fifteen tourists coming in for coffee and lunch and I would be grateful if you could help me clear the kitchen.'

Being the weekend, there were usually summer day trippers. I was pleased to do my bit and for the next couple of hours I washed and dried the dishes, pots and pans, and helped clear the table after the visitors. Such domesticity may seem incongruous on an Arctic adventure, but it's a wonderful way to bond with people and I felt very close to Pálina and her family.

That was our last day in the Hornstrandir reserve. I was pleased to be on our way to Greenland, but sorry to have to leave this very convivial group. It turned out, however, that our Icelandic adventures were not yet over. Pálina was taking two of the young girls back to Ísafjörður on the same boat as Ben and me. On board she asked, 'Where are you staying in Ísafjörður?'

'We planned to stay at the camp site so we can make an early start for the flight back to Reykjavik.'

'No,' she responded. 'You are family. You come and stay with me. I'll take you to the airport tomorrow.'

This was a little overwhelming but we gratefully accepted. Her home turned out to be in the next fjord, in the town of Bolungarvik, about half an hour's drive from Ísafjörður.

'I must stop to buy something for dinner' she said.

No matter how I pleaded, she would not let me into the supermarket to buy anything by way of contribution.

'Don't leave the car before I return,' she ordered in such a firm tone that I dared not disobey her. The town was compact and well appointed, her home comfortable and well furnished.

'Have a shower. There are plenty of towels, and leave out any clothing you want washed. There are some beers for you in the living room when you've finished. I'm going to start cooking supper.'

I don't know about Ben, but I was flabbergasted. I have never before or since been treated to such hospitality from a relative stranger.

Dinner was in the dining room rather than the kitchen. Pálina served roast lamb and a selection of vegetables, including roast potatoes and roast onions. A bottle of red wine stood on the table and there were crystal goblets by each place. Such elegance! Such grace! Swilling beer out of the can and eating packet food in an old school hall is all very well on an Arctic adventure, but drinking good red wine from crystal goblets at a stylish dinner table made this a meal fit for a king. You can be sure none of it was wasted.

After dinner I got up to help clear the table. It was about nine o'clock.

'No, leave that. I want to show you our little town.'

Reluctantly, I put down the plates I had collected and we got in her car. First we drove onto a winding mountain track that went up and up until we reached a radar complex on the top of a mountain. We were some 1,500 feet up and could see for miles in all directions. There was a rope to keep people away from the cliff edge which dropped sheer to the sea below. The sun was setting but there was still ample light to study the panorama of fjords and mountains. After this, she took us to a pretty little church where her father was buried. He was a fisherman who, despite his experience in Icelandic waters, had been lost at sea, aged 58, when his boat was overwhelmed in severe weather. Pálina then took us to the fisherman's museum, a reconstruction of stone and sod buildings, and a collection of tools and work benches from a bygone era.

It was, by this time, getting on for 1.00 a.m. The sun was below the horizon but the light was a constant sunset and this, together with the polychrome sky, lent the scene an eerie atmosphere. I was beginning to fret because we had an early start the next day to catch our flight but I didn't like to say anything. I was relieved when we got back in the car to return to her home. But we were not finished yet. Despite the hour, Pálina wanted to visit her sister whose parents-in-law should have arrived from Holland. They were still up when we arrived and were welcomed in. By 2.00 a.m. another sister and her husband had called and a regular party was developing, Pálina and her sister singing traditional Icelandic folk songs. That was a bit of interesting culture I hadn't expected. Pálina took a leading part in the local music scene we learned. Her songs were quite different from any folk songs I had heard before. I'm not going to get much sleep tonight, I thought and I worried whether Pálina was really going to be able to take us to the airport and what I could do about it if she let us down. I needn't have worried. We were back in her house and in bed by 3.00 a.m. True to her word, the next morning Pálina had us at the airport in plenty of time for our flight out – complete with our washing.

Ben and I now had two days in Reykjavik before flying to Greenland. We went to the city's camp site. Though unaccustomed to the crowds of other campers who pressed upon us, we were grateful for the facilities and its proximity to the city airport for the early morning Wednesday flight to Ittoqqortoormiit. Ben decided he wanted some time on his own and I left him to his own devices, being content to relax and chat to fellow campers or explore the city.

Nothing remarkable occurred until the second evening. I was sitting in a little multinational group when I noticed a cooking stove go out of control in the communal cooking area. A three foot ball of flame shot up and the owner of the little stove leapt back. I grabbed the nearest fire blanket and rushed forward to help, but by the time I got there, the malicious little stove had been brought back under control. I then turned to its owner, a young woman, to ask if she was all right. Much to my surprise, it was Gisela Funk – minus her eyebrows and the hair above her forehead. She might have been a little shaken but she was uninjured and remarkably calm. The missing hair would, no doubt, quickly grow back before she returned to her studies in the civilised world. How strange that, here in Iceland, we kept unexpectedly meeting!

I now focused my attention on Greenland. It's a magical country. I was heading with Ben quite far north on the East Coast; to Ittoqqortoormiit at the mouth of Scoresbysund.

Colonisation here began much later than on the west of Greenland and was not on the same scale. Although the East Coast has been populated for more than four thousand years, during periods of unfavourable climatic conditions the isolated communities died out and the area would be deserted until the next immigration. It was not until 1884, when the Greenland explorer Gustav Holm succeeded in getting to the area where Ammassalik now stands, that conditions for the 400 or so people living there improved. A Trading and Mission Station was founded in 1894. The health and general level of nutrition of the population improved and the mortality rate fell.[2] Ammassalik was then the only real settlement on the East Coast. The population had grown dramatically to around 3,000 and the area could no longer support the number of traditional hunters in the community, so a decision was made to establish another settlement at Scoresbysund, now known by its Greenlandic name of Kangertîtivaq. In 1925, the new settlement was set up and became known as Ittoqqortoormiit: 'The Place with the Large Houses'. The community had a shaky start, but the hunting conditions were far better than anticipated and the present population, now made up mostly from descendants of the first settlers, has grown to over 500. The nearest landing site suitable for a commercial aircraft was on a promontory of land known as Constable Point in the adjacent fjord. To get from Constable Point to Ittoqqortoormiit in the summer necessitated a service provided either by boats, which was notoriously unreliable because of the constant pressure of ice being forced into the main fjord, or by a helicopter provided by a Danish company, which was very much cheaper. I had been advised by Karina, my contact in Ittoqqortoormiit, to take the latter. Ben and I would eventually learn something about the difficulties of pack ice during our stay.

The flight from Reykjavik took place in clear weather in a very comfortable Fokker operated by Air Iceland. We saw something of the Hornstrandir where we had met and become entwined with Pálina and her family, then flew roughly northwards across the

---

[2] East Greenland Tourist board

Denmark Straits. Amongst the other passengers was a party of twelve British climbers who were going to climb the mountains of Liverpool Land. I think Ben would have liked to be one of them but he didn't say as much to me. I was more interested in seeing the community. As we watched, the ice floes moving south along the Denmark Strait from their origins in the Arctic Ocean became progressively more compact and a number of large tabular icebergs could be seen. These were from sections of ice that had broken free, from the ice shelves in northern Ellesmere and had drifted with the currents down the east coast, whereas the ice around the west coast was mostly formed from huge chunks of ice calved from the snouts of glaciers. As we approached Kangertîtivaq we could see the wide entrance to the sound was virtually blocked by the pack. We circled the town a couple of times before landing at Constable Point.

I was very excited to be back in Greenland, particularly in that corner of the island I had had my eye on for so many years. Ben was intrigued but, for the moment, kept his emotions to himself. Whilst we waited for the helicopter, I talked to a Danish lady who had lived in the area for many years. I tried to get her to teach me how to say 'Ittoqqortoormiit'. As there were Greenlanders about us, she was a little embarrassed as she struggled to get me to say it correctly. A couple of them within earshot grinned broadly. I was obviously not being a good pupil. I chose not to embarrass her further and left the lesson for another person on another occasion. Ben seemed happy sitting outside in the sun. It was not until we were in the helicopter as it climbed over the hills and across Walrus Bay that he revealed his excitement.

This part of Greenland is unique. All around us, away from the main fjord, were rolling hills, vast and treeless. The colours were in the rocks, their grey relieved by reds, yellows, greens and blues. Tundra covered the ground between, but the vegetation was very sparse and barely evident from the air. Across the main fjord to the south were high mountains covered with snow. They shimmered in the strong light as their glaciers followed their languid course into the waters of the fjord. It was all quite breathtaking. I was surprised at the size of Walrus Bay. I thought it was going to be a little cove, but it was enormous. A river came from between the mountains. It changed from deep and fast-flowing to shallow and meandering as it spread out into a delta which covered most of the bay, finally finding its way into a narrow body of water behind a big sand bar. This was where Ben and I were going to camp for the duration of our stay.

The heliport for Ittoqqortoormiit was on the top of a little hill overlooking the town. A tall Dane called Martin easily picked us out from the other passengers and introduced himself. He was Karina's partner and together they ran a fledgling travel organisation, Nanu Travel.[3] It was through them I had got the necessary details and they had been extraordinarily helpful. He gave us a lift the short distance to his little office in the town. This town may be known as 'The Place with the Large Houses', but all we could see, apart from the church, store and community hall, were small, compact wooden houses on stilts, arranged in some disorder about the area. I suppose everything is relative. Compared to the tiny traditional houses of stone and sod or walrus skin, they were indeed large. Most of them could have done with a good lick of paint. Martin and Karina were going to provide us with a rifle, ammunition and a dog to warn us of any polar bears that might approach. This was polar bear country and camping outside the town we would be at risk from attack. Martin taught us that the dog might bark at anything that disturbed it and the bark would sound like any other bark, but if the dog recognised something dangerous, his warning would be deep throated, low and more like a cough. With my bad hearing, I would probably have to rely on Ben to hear it and relay the warning to me! I love this sort of place, but not being top of the food chain was a little unnerving for me. He handed over the rifle and ammunition, supplied us with fuel for our stove, then took us to his home where their dogs were kept. This was perched high on some rocks overlooking the sound. There we met Karina, a young and attractive Danish girl with whom I had been in e-mail contact over the year of my planning.

---

[3] Nanu Travel, Box 04, 3980 Ittoqqortoormiit. Tel: +299 991280 Fax: +299 991070 e-mail: nanu@greennet.gl; www.nanu-travel.com; 'Nanu' is the Greenlandic word for polar bear

What a challenge it must be for this couple, living in a remote community and trying to build up a tourist trade with such limited facilities! It had nothing for the tourists who wanted to be spoon fed; it had everything for those with a proper sense of adventure.

Martin also warned us about musk ox, large beasts with thick shaggy coats and impressive horns. I think of them as Arctic bison, but this is probably an incorrect description. They move in herds and are quick to form a defensive ring if the herd is threatened. We were told that they would not be aggressive as a herd, but a solitary male could be very dangerous.

'Don't try and shoot it at the top of its head. The bone and horns are so dense that even this high powered rifle would not stop it. Go for the neck. If you feel you have to make a run for it, don't run uphill. Its chest and fore-legs are very powerful and you won't escape it. Run down hill as it is very poor at doing that.'

I had always thought musk ox were benign and peaceful creatures. I didn't realise they were going to be an additional hazard.

Karina introduced me to another character who was to make a great impression on me and steal my affections.

'He is my favourite,' Karina said. 'And his name is Tank.'

'He' was one of their husky sledge dogs and was the one selected to guard us. It was better for the dog to be with us and exercising than being tied up for the summer, which is the fate of most sledge dogs. Tank was young, maybe three years old, thick set and immensely powerful. Many of the other sledge dogs had faces only their mothers would call loveable, but Tank's was broad and intelligent and his eyes trusting. His coat was wonderfully dense and he had a mane any lion would be proud of. We were given a supply of dog biscuits.

'Feed him with half a kilo of these every evening, and ignore him if he asks for more. He's a bit greedy,' Martin said. 'Make sure he can reach water when he's tied up. That's very important.'

Tank's lead was more of a long rope tether than anything else. Martin pointed the way out of town and onto the rugged track leading to Walrus Bay. I am genuinely fond of animals, have a natural empathy with them and pride myself on being quick to

## ICELAND AND EAST GREENLAND

build up a good rapport. I was, however, soon to discover that Tank's look of intelligence was a complete misrepresentation of the truth.

We were heavily loaded with supplies and equipment that now included the rifle. It was about three miles to Walrus Bay. Other sledge dog teams were tied up for the summer and whenever we came near them they howled in fury, not at Ben and me, but at Tank's insolence at walking past them. Tank kept his dignity and held his head high. His sister, a slim and graceful husky, followed. In this community, the dogs were generally tied up, but the bitches and puppies were allowed to run free. Out of town, the track followed the edge of the ice-filled water. The water was so tightly packed with ice that the spaces in-between could barely be seen. The sun was strong and the light glared brilliantly off the white surface. I was grateful for the very dark glasses I had bought specially for this trip. Tank trotted happily and trustingly with us. He had one quite infuriating habit, however. He would pull on his leash going down hill and drag us back going up hill. It was most unhelpful. Tank's sister roamed more widely but generally stayed with us.

At Walrus Bay we noticed two tents pitched close to the road. Were these tourists or locals? I would not have been particularly surprised had one of them belonged to Gisela since she had so unexpectedly peppered our travels. There was no sign of life. We moved further on, looking for a suitable spot close to one of the many rivers and with some sort of bank – any sort of bank – that would give us shelter if there was wind. There wasn't much to choose from one spot to another so we soon stopped and set up camp. The view was impressive. Behind us were mountains, to the left a sparkling lake of clear, fresh water. Before us was the wide stretch of tundra crossed by the streams of the delta. Beyond that, a sea full of ice and beyond that, far in the distance, the range of snow-capped mountains on Volquart Boon Kyst[4] with their many

---

[4] Kyst is the Danish word for coast. The name was suggested in 1938 to commemorate the original discovery of Scoresbysund by Volquaart Boon, a Danish whaler sailing aboard a Dutch or German ship. When following the coast from 76°30'N to 68°40'N in 1761, the ship reported being swept by a strong current into a wide and deep fjord 70°40'N. There is no doubt that this was the present day Scoresbysund

glaciers. Above all this hung a deep blue sky. Ben sat, stripped to the waist, on the tundra beside the tent gazing about him.

'What an amazing view!' he exclaimed. The temperature was about +10°C in the shade and more than +30°C in the sun. Although the day was getting late, the sun was still high in the sky. We were at latitude 70°30' N. The sun would not set for a further three weeks and it was going to be more than a month before we had any darkness. I was very contented. I was now where, for many years, I had often dreamed of being.

The two tents we had passed earlier were still in our view and we saw that their occupants, Greenlanders, had returned. Shortly afterwards, two children appeared beside us, A boy and a girl aged somewhere between eight and ten years. We smiled a greeting and they were not shy to make themselves at home amongst our meagre possessions, quickly delving into bags and packets. We were intrigued by their total lack of inhibition, which we presumed was a cultural difference. Through them we were making local contact. They soon found my sheath knife, which I had earlier bought in Finland. It is unusual in its Saami design and made for hunting and living in the wilderness. I keep its blade keenly sharp. Their eyes lit up as they pulled it out of its sheath but I stepped in and took it away from them. It was much too dangerous in the hands of children. They showed no disappointment but turned their attention to our other bits of kit. Then they spotted my Nordic walking poles, very popular for walkers and hikers of all ages in Europe. Ben had been scathing about them.

'I've seen them used by people of your generation,' was his dismissive comment.

These two children were fascinated by them. They picked them up and looked questioningly at us. I demonstrated their use and the young boy grabbed them with delight and started walking around in circles. It was a comic sight. I had them set for my height and this young chap had not really started growing. I then made a big mistake and readjusted them for his height. He watched me intently as I made the adjustment. His joy knew no bounds and he raced about with them, his sister in hot pursuit.

Ben and I watched with amusement. The two children ranged further a field and were sometimes out of sight.

'Are you sure they are safe with those kids?' Ben asked.

I was anxious to establish any sort of a link between us and the local community.

'I hope so. The people of the North truly respect the property of others. I'll take the risk,' I replied.

The next time the children came into view, they each had one of the Nordic poles and were following the line of the nearest river, trying, or pretending, to spear some of the young Arctic char that live in the lake. They disappeared behind some rocks and next time we saw them, the young boy was walking towards us, obviously in some distress as he waved the Nordic pole above his head. The young girl followed sheepishly behind. Neither of them spoke English but his gestures made it clear that he had loosened the adjustment of the pole in his play and, when pretending to spear a fish in the lake, the top half had remained in his hand, and the bottom half had flown into the deep water and was now somewhere amongst the rocks on the bottom. They didn't speak English and the only Inuktitut word I knew was for 'Thank you'. That word didn't seem appropriate for the occasion but they had no difficulty in understanding me. I made my annoyance very clear. Sheepishly they returned what was left of my Nordic poles and slunk away. My first attempt at intercourse with the local community had been a dismal failure and it was my fault that I now had only one pole. However, the young lad was truly repentant. Moreover, instead of running back and hiding with his parents, he had shown commendable courage and maturity in coming to me to confess the accident and try to explain what had happened. It was not long before I was feeling very guilty for my anger.

The afternoon had progressed. Tank, tethered to a large rock between us and the river was looking expectantly at me. I measured out his food and gave it to him. That dog had the appetite and table manners of a Tyrannosaurus rex. 'A bit greedy' was a masterpiece of understatement! I thought he was going to take off my hand as I emptied the bowl of biscuits onto the ground. He positively 'hoovered' them up, crunching them in his powerful jaws. I'm sure he took in some pebbles with the biscuits and crunched and swallowed them too. I'm sad to record that Tank's table manners did not improve the whole period we were together. I learned how to feed him without putting my hands at risk and, for his part, he recognised that I was the one who fed him – which made me the Alpha male. Our friendship blossomed.

We planned to spend the next day, Thursday, at Walrus Bay, then Friday and Saturday walking around to Kap Torbin where Kangertîtivaq joins the Denmark Strait. On Sunday and Monday we would walk back to Walrus Bay, then have a day to ourselves and fly home on Wednesday. After supper, Ben decided to go off on his own; he had no set plans and he didn't know where he was going or when he would be back. I was content to sit with Tank and watch the sun move round to the north as midnight approached, though it remained above the horizon and shining brightly. Strangely, despite the fact that the sun was still high in the sky as evening approached, the temperature dropped significantly. Ben had not returned by the time I turned in and went to bed, but when I woke up at 8.30 the next morning, he was in the tent fast asleep.

I took Tank for a four hour walk. At first I kept him on the tether, then I took the risk and released him, watching him bound away across the tundra, but although he remained some distance from me, he continued to range in my vicinity. I judged that he would not leave me. I was happy with my camera, photographing the ice in the sea and other features of interest. The lake was a tranquil spot. Fed by melting snow, its water was pure and clear. I have never before or afterwards tasted such delicious fresh water. I did try swimming in it. I had swum amongst the ice of the Ilulissat Fjord in West Greenland, and in the Billifjorden of Svalbard at nearly 80°N and in the icy waters of Lake Baikal in Siberia, but this was the coldest I had ever experienced and it broke the record for being my shortest swim ever! When I had stopped shivering, I felt very smug and very clean. I had chosen the spot where the lake flows out into a river, so any pollution I might have caused would quickly drain away to the sea. Tank clearly thought the whole exercise an absurdity and waited patiently for me to dress and continue our walk.

Ben didn't wake up until mid day. We walked into town together to ask about a suitable route to Kap Torbin and collect some more dog biscuits for Tank. What with the appetites of both Ben and Tank we really should have had a team of porters or pack horses to haul our provisions. Martin and Karina had a cabin at Kap Torbin. They usually went down by boat, but when the ice was too closely packed they might walk to it. One could not walk around the shoreline because there was no continuous beach. High cliffs went straight down into the water in several places. We would have to circle back inland and cross two high ranges of hills before descending onto the level tundra where the going would be easy.

'We usually take about five or six hours for the journey,' Martin assured us.

That sounded very reasonable; two days each way would be leisurely indeed.

We wandered down to the little store. Except for a good supply of canned beer, it was devoid of stock. We invested in some beer. Karina had previously told me they had only two supply ships a year, at the end of July and at the end of August. The ice conditions would not permit shipping at any other time. This community was still very dependent on its hunting – supplies brought in by sea were a bonus to the hunters but a lifeline to other residents. The sea seemed to me to be very congested with ice still but the supply ship was already on its way. How strange to live in a community where you are cut off from supplies for ten months of the year! We were also told that an adventure cruise ship, *The Explorer*, was expected tomorrow. I knew this ship was a regular visitor to most Arctic and Antarctic spots on the edge of a reliable tourist operation. It had come into Provideniya when I was in Chukotka.[5]

Ben and I moved down to the jetty to drink our beers and make ourselves some simple lunch. There was a little activity going on

---

[5] Chapter 7

around us. A small boat was carried down to the water on the prongs of a large earth-moving vehicle. It was taken down the slope and gently floated off the prongs as it was lowered into the sea. Another person was carrying out some maintenance work on his boat. Then a thick-set chap, a Greenlander, climbed up onto the jetty from his boat and introduced himself to us. He was of middle years and told us he had been a hunter most of his life, but now, with age, he chose to make a living from the little store. He was ready to chat and we were more than ready to listen. He talked about the hunting. There had not been too many bears recently, but they were about.

'What do you do if a bear approaches and you are unarmed?' I asked. It was a question that I have asked more than once.

'Well, don't be like a tourist and try and take photographs of it,' he answered. 'They are not very brave, so make yourself bigger. Hold your rucksack over your head and try to look more powerful.'

Interesting, but I think I'll be sure that I am armed when in polar bear country. I then asked him how to pronounce 'Ittoqqortoormiit'. He took the challenge and on my fourth or fifth attempt he seemed to be satisfied – or else decided I wasn't going to get any better! I now can roll the name off my tongue with great aplomb – but, in truth, I may well be deceiving myself.[6]

We talked about the ice.

'Very difficult,' he said. 'There is the ice from the Arctic Ocean being forced into Kangertîtivaq by the currents of the Denmark Strait; there is the glacier ice coming from the head of the fjord and there is the wind. Everything depends on how they react with each other. It can be packed one minute and gone the next.'

He told us of how he had got trapped out at sea by ice and had only got back by charging the low level ice and cutting the motor as his boat slid over the top into the next patch of water, then repeating the process until he got past the main pack. His boat must have been very tough to withstand that sort of pounding. He told us that when any ship enters the area, one of the local men

---

[6] 'Eet-two-caw-toor-me'

went out to pilot it through the ice, and again when it came time to leave. But as the ice changes so unpredictably these pilots occasionally find they cannot get back into the harbour and finish up stranded at Kap Torbin for up to a week waiting for the ice to move.

'What sort of weather do you think of as cold?' we asked him.

'Oh, we don't think it is cold until the temperature is below minus forty and the wind is more than fifty miles per hour.'[7]

On the question of whether the Greenlanders are part of the Eskimo group, he was very prosaic.

'I prefer to be called Inuit,' he said, 'but I don't mind if I'm called Eskimo. Even if it does mean "eaters of raw meat", it doesn't offend me. I do eat raw meat.'

That seemed to be about as far as I could take the subject. He asked where we were staying.

'I'll get my nephew to run you back,' he said, and summoned a young lad sitting with some other youngsters by a large inflatable craft. The lad brought the boat over and we climbed aboard. Tank managed to jump in when we called him and we were whisked back to Walrus Bay. It was exhilarating, twisting and turning between the blocks of ice at high speed. Ben sat leaning forward with the wind blowing his long curly hair about his shoulders. He was clearly enjoying the ride. So was I. Tank was a little dubious, however, and seemed happier when we had disembarked. We ambled back to the tent and had supper. I fed Tank, then Ben went off again by himself for some hours and I took Tank for a long walk before bed.

The next morning, I was up early and saw the cruise ship, *The Explorer*, circling an iceberg out in the sound. It stopped and, shortly afterwards, six zodiac craft laden with tourists came roaring through the ice towards the sand bar. They landed them at the far end and the zodiacs returned empty. Apparently, the tourists were going to walk back to town before rejoining the ship. I was out with Tank and I had the rifle over my shoulder. To get from the sand bar to the point where the track back to town

---

[7] I calculated that to be a wind chill of −67°C (−88°F)

started, the tourists had to ford a section of water, so I thought I would wait for them at the crossing point and take some photographs. I perched on a rock with Tank sitting beside me. By the time the leaders had reached the ford, the others had become very strung out along the sand bar. The first of them approached the ford at what appeared to be the obvious spot. Had they tried to wade across there, the water would have been about chest deep. I knew where it was wider but shallow, only about a foot deep, and I pointed out the crossing. They hesitated before taking off their boots and wading in. The first ones over stopped for a chat, but all were very friendly and Tank was a great attraction. A lady who bred Huskies was much impressed by him. Tank took it all in his stride and graciously accepted the admiration of those who petted and talked to him.

'Do you live here?' they asked. 'Why have you got the dog?'

I pointed out our tent in the distance and told them it was Tank's duty to warn us if a polar bear approached. My reason for carrying a rifle became obvious. I think that their tour operator had sold them Scoresbysund and Ittoqqortoormiit as a wild and inhospitable place that could only be visited by *The Explorer*. Their dreams of adventure may have been a little deflated by finding an old age pensioner camping there, complete with rifle and guard dog. I hope I didn't spoilt their holiday. The guide who accompanied them from the ship was not so friendly.[8]

This was the day that Ben and I were due to walk over to Kap Torbin. Ben emerged at about 11.30 a.m and we packed up to go. We lightened our load by asking Martin and Karina if we could leave excess equipment and supplies with them and set off on this next adventure taking only what was necessary for the four days. The day had started fine and clear, but we became conscious of a steadily increasing wind as we climbed the hill the other side of town. At first the going was quite easy but the hill became steeper, the terrain more difficult and the wind stronger. By the time we reached the top of the hill, the wind must have been blowing at 40

---

[8] On November 23, 2007, just two years after the ship visited Ittoqqortoormiit, it hit a submerged object whilst cruising in Antarctic waters and sank

miles per hour with gusts up to 60 miles per hour. The boulders were also bigger and more tightly packed, so that it was no longer possible to walk between them. Progress could only be made by stepping or climbing from one boulder to another. Ben had no difficulty, Tank was managing well, but I was finding it exhausting. A level area on the top eased the stress of moving from one boulder to another but it was still hard going. If from this present position we could progress down to the tundra on the other side I was going to be able to cope, but that didn't seem to be the case. We stopped for a rest and took off our rucksacks. Ben went ahead to see the lie of the land.

'Not so good,' he reported. 'There is no way down to the tundra from here. We will have to route down through that valley and then over those far hills before getting down. What do you think?'

As far as we could make out, the whole journey would be strewn with these large boulders. Is this the route Martin and Karina take for a five or six hour walk to Kap Torbin? I asked myself. I seriously began to doubt my ability to complete the journey to the tundra where we could set up camp and rest, but I was tormented by two pressures. The first was to avoid yet another failure – the abandonment of my trek from Inuvik to Aklavik[9] had seriously dented my self-esteem. The second, and more pressing, was that I didn't want to let Ben down, and this is what made me tenacious. He needed more than our tranquil base at Walrus Bay.

'Let's not throw it away too quickly,' I answered. 'I'll give it a go.'

'Are you sure? There's still a long way to go before we are out of these hills and I don't want you finding you're stuck up there and can't move.'

He looked hard at me.

'I'll give it a go,' I insisted.

We pressed on. The buffeting of the wind whilst trying to get from one boulder to another was no help at all. After what

---

[9] Chapter 5

seemed like half an hour I admitted defeat. I knew I wasn't going to make it. I would drop exhausted in very difficult terrain; it would be stupid to carry on.

'Ben. I'm really sorry, but I'm not going to make it. I think we should turn back.'

'That's the best possible decision,' he replied.

Our roles were now reversed. Ben had become the leader and taken control. It had been obvious to him much earlier that the journey over this terrain was too much for me but he was biding his time, waiting for me to acknowledge the fact. I hope he gave me credit for trying not to let him down.

The return to Walrus Bay seemed to take for ever. The wind was blowing from the north and, as we came over the top of the hill, we could see that all the ice clogging the north had dissipated southwards. In the town, we called in to see Martin and Karina and collect the extra equipment and supplies we had left with them. They offered us some coffee and, before we left, gave us a musk ox T-bone steak for our supper. Although we were their clients, they treated us as friends.

I could barely recognise Walrus Bay without the ice. It had lost its magic. The other Greenland Camp had been vacated, their tents collapsed and weighed down with rocks to save them from the wind. We moved close under the rocks of the hill next to the lake, which was in the lee of the wind, and got some shelter. This wind was still a problem for us and made it difficult to erect the tent. We secured it by stacking flat rocks on the valance in the same way as I had secured the tent with snow in the winter. We cooked ourselves the musk ox steak, packet mashed potatoes and packet gravy. In addition to his supply of dog biscuits, we presented Tank with the bone from the T-bone steak. He had earned it. I just wished he had better table manners.

I awoke relatively early the next morning to the sound of Tank whining. It didn't sound like the warning call that Martin had taught us to listen for, but I got up to investigate. After gnawing on his T-bone, Tank had stashed it away by some rocks before settling down and then, in moving restlessly about, he had wound his long tether around the rock so tightly he was stuck fast. It wasn't the tight restraint which was upsetting him – he had often suffered that – it was the fact that two crows had somehow discovered his bone and were trying to unearth it while he was unable to protect it. Much to Tank's relief, I chased off the crows and untangled him.

The wind had dropped and the sky was again clear and bright. I left Ben sleeping and, after breakfast, took Tank for another walk, this time to find and explore what was left of the old meteorology and radio station that the Americans had set up and operated during the Second World War. All that remained was scattered rubbish, lengths of steel guy ropes that had steadied the radio masts against the elements, and parts of the masts themselves. I wondered how popular, or unpopular, a posting to it was during the war. It certainly wasn't in a combat zone but although the summer weather we were experiencing at Walrus Bay was really very pleasant, I knew that the winters would be savage and the men who manned the station, particularly if they were from urban homes in the States, would have found the isolation very hard indeed. The remoteness of the station would have made frequent rotation of the crew well-nigh impossible, so the men would have been stuck here for many months at a time, if not for the duration of the war. Claustrophobia and personal conflicts would have been endemic; discipline would have been difficult to maintain.

I picked my way around and tried to feel the ghosts of those who had served here. I could just imagine their homecoming to wives and children after the war.

'What did you do during the war, Daddy?'

'Well, son, I sat in a wooden hut in the Arctic and told Air Force headquarters that it was cold, dark and windy.'

Not very inspiring, but at least no one was shooting at them and, provided they could avoid the occasional polar bear, in the summer they might have been able to enjoy watching the herds of walruses that once pulled themselves up onto the sand bar. That was, after all, how the bay had got its name. Neither Ben nor I saw any walrus during our stay and we were told by the local community that they were no longer seen in large numbers.

Ben and I continued our 'out-of-synch' routine. I was up early and spent many hours walking with Tank. He would sleep late, then go for even longer walks and return very late. On one occasion, he was gone for just over eight hours. He had crossed the bay and climbed a high range of hills at the far end which had been intriguing him. From there he had enjoyed the most dramatic view across the whole sweep of the bay and the little peninsula leading down to Kap Torbin and out into the Denmark Strait. On this walk, the female husky, Tank's sister, who had followed us on the first day, had been paying us one of her occasional visits and she accompanied Ben all the way, some seven or eight miles, to the hill. She even followed him up the difficult terrain of the slope but, in Ben's words, she didn't much enjoy it.

On one of my walks towards the town I came across many little groups of hunters and their families sitting on the rocks some 50 to 100 feet above the Bay. With the loss of the wind, the currents had forced the ice back close inshore and the hunters were after seals, or the occasional walrus, that rose to breathe between the blocks of ice. The technique was to shoot them with high powered rifles, then scramble down with grapples and recover their dead bodies from the sea bed. It was a technique that seemed to work. Each of the little groups had their 'harvest' of kills – maybe two or three. Some had more. The hunters didn't take their eyes off the patches of open water, but they were ready to talk to me. I braved the tactless question.

'Do any of the kills fail to be recovered?'

'Oh yes,' came the honest reply, 'we lose many'.

What a sad waste of life! But these folk really depend on their hunting, and in the summer it is the only way they can 'harvest' seals. I had to remind myself that the seals were not endangered, but these people were. Their way of life does not mesh easily with the rest of the world.

There was a large group of hunters at one point and a great deal of activity going on around a broad patch of open water below them. I saw the bodies of some seven or eight seals laid out on the ice. Two or three men were standing on a big patch of ice, casting grapples. Another was in a very small boat, casting a grapple into the same water but from another angle. I watched for about an hour during which the hunters were tenacious in their search for whatever was on the sea bed. The tension among the group was electric. I later learned it was a walrus which had been shot, a very valuable commodity for them, which they eventually recovered successfully.

One morning I sat on a rock by the little lake with Tank at my side. It was early and Ben was still asleep. The sun was warm on my back as I watched a number of young hatchlings of the Arctic char that populate the lake searching for food in the shallows. I looked across to the ice and the mountains on Volquart Boon Kyst and tried to discern any movement of the larger icebergs in the sound. The few clouds in the sky seemed to hang motionless. I thought with quiet amusement of the time when Ben and I were in Iceland and I had been desperate for intellectual stimulation in the form of something to read. Now I was perfectly happy sitting where I was with Tank beside me. I felt that God also sat with me. It was a change effected by the passage of time. All of a sudden, I noticed with surprise that Ben was up and I looked at my watch. I had been sitting on that rock ruminating for more than two hours, but I felt no shame.

I made myself some hot soup while Ben had his breakfast. I had been thinking how I might temper Ben's disappointment at the loss of the walk to Kap Torbin and I suggested that perhaps we could charter a small boat to take us across to the tundra between the mountains that had defeated me and the cape. I think Ben was pleased by the idea, so we walked back into, town to see what could be arranged. It proved impossible.

'We might be able to get you there,' they said, 'but if that ice shifts we won't be able to get you back and you may have to wait for several days.'

We only had another day before we flew out so it was not a risk we could accept. Kap Torbin would have to remain beyond our reach.

We walked back. The day was warm and the air still. When we got to the sand bar we each, with one accord, decided to go swimming between the floating ice in the bay and waded over to the sand bar. Ben wanted me to take a photograph of him standing on a large chunk of ice. He stripped off to a pair of shorts and waded in. He was quickly out of his depth and swam over to a flat shelf where the edge was at water level. He hauled himself out, much like a walrus, stood up and walked a few feet further on. He then turned his back to me, dropped his shorts and put his hands behind his neck. The pose was perfect. He was facing the sun and the light etched his form. I quickly fired off some photographs before the moment was lost. He possessed a fine physique – there wasn't an ounce of fat on him and, with his legs astride, his body formed a perfect X. He then pulled up his shorts, lowered himself into the water and swam back. It was now my turn. I stripped naked and strode forth.

Behind me I heard Ben say, 'I think this is all rather funny.'

It must have been a comic sight for him, watching his aging grandfather, naked, wading into the water and swimming over to the same patch of ice. Tank tried to follow, but decided against it. The water was deep and I was well out of my depth so I could not push off from the bottom to get up onto the ice. I tried to drag myself up onto the same shelf but it collapsed when I got my full weight onto it and I sank back into the water with chunks of ice on top of me. I wasn't hurt and I resurfaced laughing. It was, as Ben had said, 'all rather funny'. After a little swim, I returned to the beach and got dressed.

Whatever others may say or think about the escapade, it played an import part in the bond of respect and friendship that was developing between us.

On the way back to camp, Tank was ranging freely. He was several hundred yards ahead when I saw a Greenlandic couple having a picnic on the tundra. To my distress, Tank turned towards them. I broke into a run, trying to call him back. Whilst the Greenlanders keep dogs, they do not have them as pets and don't have the same affection for them as I have for many animals. As Tank approached, the woman picked up a stone and threatened him with it. To my relief, he backed off. I caught up with them, panting and wheezing.

'I'm so sorry he disturbed you,' I said, and I put Tank on the tether and started to haul him away.

## ICELAND AND EAST GREENLAND

'That's OK,' the man replied. 'He didn't do any harm.'

We talked for a minute or two, whilst I kept Tank closely reined in. Then, as we turned to go, the man offered us some of his musk ox meat. There must have been about two pounds of it.

'I shot it last year and it has been in my deep freeze since.'

What a nice gesture! Ben carried the meat back to camp. I didn't want any of it but Ben thought it would make a nice snack before supper. I sat fascinated as he made a two pound fried musk ox steak sandwich and wolfed it down before we had our usual fare of packet food.

That evening, as we stood talking outside the tent, four hunters crossed the tundra heading for the hills. Three were of average size, the other quite short. They had small knapsacks and carried rifles. They were going to pass by about one or two hundred yards from our tent, so Ben and I gave friendly waves. The shortest waved back, then broke away from his companions and came directly towards us. He resembled an animated garden gnome with his assortment of clothing and his bobble hat. He came up to us, bowed formally, shook our hands as he muttered something unintelligible in Inuktitut, bowed again and hurried off to catch up with his companions. What a friendly little chap! I hoped his hunting was a success.

The next day was intended to be very lazy. It was our last on Walrus Bay. Neither of us went for walks. The weather was perfect. Ben picked up his sleeping mattress from the tent and climbed up the rocks behind our camp to a favourite spot of his where there was a level area. There he could stretch out and doze in the sun. I was busying myself cooking lunch on our little stove, Tank, as ever, lying by my side but still tethered to a very big rock. We had become quite inseparable and I was quietly dreading having to return him to Karina the next day. The little cooking stove was hissing away and I had my back to the tundra. Tank was fast asleep.

The next thing I knew, Ben came leaping down the rocks yelling, 'Musk ox, behind you. It's only a hundred and fifty yards away.'

I looked round, but saw nothing.

'It's moved off behind those boulders,' he said.

Ben dived into the tent and came out with the rifle. I turned the stove off and grabbed my camera. Tank opened his eyes and looked questioningly, but we decided to leave him where he was and set off in pursuit of the musk ox we could now see picking its way between the boulders and moving away from us. Tank tried to follow and, when he found he was tethered, let out a howl of anguish. I looked back hesitantly to make sure he was firmly anchored to the rock. It was a big one and I had tied it securely. I turned and ran after Ben. We took care we didn't run blindly into the musk ox if it stopped behind a boulder. As we moved further and further away from our camp, Tank's howls rose in pitch and fury and, looking back, I saw that he was dragging the rock behind him as he tried to follow. His progress was desperately slow, of course, and he strained every muscle. I didn't think he would get far and continued the pursuit of the musk ox. We didn't want to kill it. We just wanted to get close enough to photograph it. The rifle was in case it turned nasty. The musk ox knew we were following because it kept finding vantage points to stop and watch our progress. The animal was moving much faster than we were and it soon became very clear we weren't going to get close enough for a photo, so we abandoned the chase and returned to camp. It had been very stimulating and exciting. As we approached, we found that Tank had dragged the rock as far as the middle of the river and was sitting there looking very sorry for himself. Our reprimand for his failings as a guard dog fell on deaf ears, but it was very easy to forgive him.

 The next bit of excitement came that night. We were lying in our sleeping bags talking somnolently when the tent shook. It could only be an animal. We knew Tank was tethered beyond reach of the tent, so it couldn't be him. He had already demonstrated that his qualities as a watch dog were limited and unreliable, so what sort of animal was it? The tent shook again. Ben picked up the rifle and we gingerly peered out through a ventilation chink. It was only Tank's sister who had decided to pay us an evening visit. She had curled herself into a comfortable ball and was leaning on the doorway of the tent. It was a bit of an anti-climax, but I'm very glad it wasn't a polar bear. That really would have complicated our evening.

The next day, we sadly packed up our camp and returned to Ittoqqortoormiit. We went to the tourist office where Martin and Karina were at work, handed back the gun and ammunition and said goodbye to Tank. I really had become very fond of that animal. Subsequently, when back in England, I sent an e-mail to Karina to thank her for all the good work she and her husband had done for us. I added that I was missing Tank. In her reply she said that Tank had been very quiet since we had left and she thought he was pining.

Part of the travel experience is the combination of joy at returning home and sadness at leaving a place where you have found excitement, happiness and new friends. Leaving Ittoqqortoormiit brought forth both those emotions. On the helicopter flight to Constable Point I had an excellent view of Walrus Bay, our campsite, the sand bar from which Ben and I had swum, the area we had covered in our walks and the lake beside which Tank and I had lazed away tranquil hours. It also crossed my mind that during our stay in Greenland we had not had another chance encounter with Gisela.

Our flight back to Iceland and then on to England was to route from Constable Point to Ammassalik and then across the Denmark Strait to Reykjavik. The weather was perfect: no wind and not a cloud in the sky. Visibility was unlimited. We ought to get a good view of the mountainous coast on the flight to Ammassalik, I thought. I did not expect to enjoy the most spectacular flight in my 55 years experience of aviation. Just after take off, the captain announced that, after crossing the sound, he would descend to a low level to get a better view of the mountains. During my career I had crossed the Andes on a number of occasions and flown over the Alps many, many times, usually at high altitude because the big jets were hideously uneconomic at low levels. We were now in a turbo prop aircraft and they were less affected in that way. The captain levelled off a few hundred feet above the tops of the mountains and we were treated to a view of the endless expanse of the inland icecap stretching away to the west. Great Nunataks poked out of the surface and it was easy to pick out the course of the glacier ice as it flowed around the pinnacles of rock. The mountains themselves were arranged in ridges rather than peaks, and the ridges were razor sharp. I had expected wind erosion would have rounded their ridges to blunt crests. In fact, it was thermal shock and fracturing of the rocks that gave them their keen edge. Summer heat and moisture get into the crevices, then the bitter cold of winter expands that moisture so that the rocks flake away. In much the same way Stone Age man sharpened his flints by chipping away the edges. Between these mountain ridges were snow fields and glaciers streaked with glacial moraine which gave them the appearance of streaky marble. One could readily follow the course of the glaciers down to the fjords and see the newly formed icebergs that calved from their snouts and flowed out into the Denmark Strait. I tried to imagine what it would be like to traverse that territory, the dangers and the hardships that would have to be endured. Now I could not even contemplate such an exercise, yet the Danish military Sirius patrols[10] have done that for many decades and I had read that men once trained to do the work would not contemplate any other. They loved it. Had I been young and unattached, I would have longed to join that force.

We followed these mountains for their 500 mile stretch down to Ammassalik. After Constable Point, Ammassalik's little airport seemed huge. Instead of a terminal consisting of two 'portacabins' and a coffee vending machine, it had a restaurant, gift shop, lounge and not one, but two check-in desks. It was positively metropolitan. There were quite a few tourists about and I felt oppressed by the crowd. I had become too accustomed to small communities and, although I probably am being a bit unkind to the town, I was very glad I had made the decision to go to

---

[10] From among the *Frømandskorpset* (and other Danish military volunteers) are selected the personnel of one of the most extraordinary of armed units – the *Slæde-patuljen Sirius* (or Sledge Patrol [1]). Using dogsleds and the simplest of equipment, Sirius Patrols cover all of northeastern Greenland. In the brief Arctic summer, kayaks are used to skirt the coastline. The rest of the year, Sirius Patrols criss-cross the Greenland icecap asserting Danish sovereignty. See: http://www.sfu.ca/casr/id-arcticviking4.htm

Ittoqqortoormiit rather than take the easier option of settling for Ammassalik. I was filled with a great sadness as we left Greenland behind. The rest of the return journey was unremarkable, save for the pleasure of being greeted by my wife back in England, which was immeasurable.

Before I could consider the expedition at an end, I had to see Ben off on his flight to New Zealand, which I did two days later. My doubts as to whether Ben had been disappointed with his first Arctic experience were resolved at the airport. He turned and embraced me.

'Grandpa, we've had the most amazing experiences together.'

His eyes were shining and I knew we had won. We had cemented a relationship that any grandparent would treasure. He picked up his rucksack, now additionally laden with my tent, my mountaineering boots, GPS unit, lightweight multi-stove, Yeti Super Gaiters and all the other bits and pieces I would no longer need, and strode into the terminal. They couldn't be going to a better home.

# POSTSCRIPT

Without ambitions and goals our lives can be pointless and empty. We must strive to achieve, but sometimes in the striving, life can be a little like holding onto the tail of a tiger. Once you start chasing the goals they become difficult to abandon and it is easy to lose track of what is really important.

There is an old Inuit song that seems to get life into better perspective and perhaps expresses what I have learned from the Arctic:

> *I think over again my small adventures,*
> *My fears;*
> *Those small ones that seemed so big*
> *For all the vital things*
> *I had to get and to reach,*
> *And yet there is only one great thing,*
> *The only thing*:
> *To live to see the great day that dawns*
> *And the light that fills the world.*

I owe an enormous debt of gratitude to many people: to the Arctic people with their warm and open hearts; to the experience of men like Commander Chris Furse RN, Robin Hanbury-Tenison and Charlie King whose knowledge, advice and encouragement prepared and guided a way through the physical hazards and many logistical difficulties that lay in wait for me; to Grazyna Callan who stoically struggled to drum some basic Russian into my addled head – and she is in no way responsible for my ineptitude in that amusing language; without her teaching

I would never have managed that simple relationship with little Zhenya.

I must also thank those who helped to contain my enthusiasm and put logical order into the editing of the manuscript for this book without crushing the passion in which it was tendered. In particular, I must mention my daughter, Professor Cathy Price, who put many hours of her busy working life into proofreading and commenting on the text. Most of all, however, I must express my undying gratitude to my wife, Janet – a true 'Arctic Widow' – who not only gave copious advice in the writing of this book but generously gave me love and understanding and the freedom to indulge in the Arctic, the only mistress she would ever tolerate.

Norman Price

# INDEX

Aðalvík 215–17
Acid Rain Project, Svalbard 9, 14–27, 30–1
Aklak Air flight 91–3
Aklavik 81–2, 83, 101, 103–8
  aborted trek to 84–9
Aklavik Fur Factory 103
Alaska 117–42
Alaskan Rose 43
alcohol 50, 139, 153
Ammassalik 207, 225, 246
Amundsen, Roald 30, 127, 139
Anadyr 144, 158
Anchorage 119–22
Andreas, German photographer 132, 133, 134
'Animal Rights' movement 54
Anvil City (later Nome) 126
  *see also* Nome
apatite 173
Archangel Airlines 173
Arctic area, geographical 1
Arctic foxes 2, 11, 145, 217, 219
Arkhangelsk 171–2
Artika Hotel, Murmansk 175, 176–7, 182, 186

Baejarfjail 215
Baffin Bay 41
Barents, William 11
bear bells 119
bears *see* black bear; grizzly bear; polar bear
Beaufort Delta Region Career Fair 114–15
beluga whale 96
Ben, Norman Price's grandson 208, 209–15, 218–27, 230–1, 232–40, 241–7
Bering Strait 130, 143, 144–5
Bering, Vitus 162

Beringia 143
Big Diomede Island 144
Billifjorden 12, 13
birds 2, 13, 24, 27, 115–16, 137
*Bismarck, The* 215
black bear 119, 120
Bolungarvik 222–4
brown bear *see* grizzly bear
Brucebyen 12, 21, 27
Buryateya people 165–6

Canada 53–5
  Mackenzie river delta 81–116
  a spring among the Inuit in Nunavut 70–80
  a winter among the Inuit in Nunavut 55–70
career opportunities 115
caribou 2, 5, 90, 96, 98–9
  skins 54, 60–1, 113
caviar 168
children
  cultural gulf 65–6
  education *see* education
  Inuvik 102–3
  Iqaluit 71–2
  Provideniya 155–6
  Resolute Bay 63
  Saami 189
  Saqqaq 45–6
Chukchi tribe 145
Chukotka 143–70
churches
  'igloo church', Inuvik 101–2
  Nellim 201
  New Apostolic Church, Murmansk 181–2
  St Jude's Cathedral, Iqaluit 71, 101
Cliff (a Kabloona) 62

# INDEX

climate change 99
  *see also* global warming
coal 11, 47, 151
cold protection 59–61, 76, 78–9, 85, 189–90
  foot wrapping 166–7, 196–7
  Saami techniques 196–7
Constable Point 225, 226
copper-nickel 173
Council (village) 134–6
crab fishing 5, 138
crime 50–1, 66–7, 131, 156
currency 148

David, proprietor at Polar Bed and Breakfast 84, 89
Davis Strait 34, 39, 42
Dempster highway 108–9
Dempster, W.J.D. 109
Denali National Park 118
Denmark 6, 36
  Straits 226, 234, 246
Dezhinevo, Cape 144, 145
Disko Bay 37, 39, 41
Dorset culture 3
Drangajökull glacier 211
driftwood 5
drugs 62, 66–7, 97, 131

education 19, 63–4, 65–6, 97, 101, 189
  music 159
Egede, Hans 36
Elina, Yupik woman 152
Emma Bay 148, 162, 163
employment 115, 130
entertainment 102–3, 159–60
Eric the Red 6, 35, 52
Eskimos
  Alaskan 118–19, 120–4, 125, 130–1, 132–42
  as collective Western Culture 3–5
  Eskimosy tribe *see* Yupik Eskimosy
  use of the name 3, 4, 119, 235
*Explorer, The* 233, 235, 236

Finland 187–205
fishing 2, 6, 41, 46
  beach fishing camps 121–2, 123
  crab 5, 138
flora 1

Alaskan tundra 137
of Greenland 37–8, 43–4
of Spitsbergen 14, 22
food storage 94
Forel, Mt 34
Fort Macpherson/Macphoo 108, 109, 110
foxes, Arctic 2, 11, 145, 217, 219
Frank, Inuit in Aklavik 107
Franklin, Sir John 53, 162
Frobisher Bay 70
Frobisher, Sir Martin 35, 53
frost bite 89–90
fulmars 13, 24
Funk, Gisela 210, 216, 219, 224
fur trade 54, 117–18

Geosah, Mr (Inuit of Iqaluit) 72–4
Germany 188
global warming 51, 99
gold mining/panning 125–7, 128–9, 136, 140–2
Great Slave Lake 81
greenhouses 19, 43–4, 101
Greenland 6, 33–7
  East Greenland 207–8, 224–47
  exploration of west coast 37–52
Greenpeace 114
Grimsey island 207
Grise Fjord 55
grizzly bear 83, 99, 119–20, 129–30, 136
Gulf Stream 10, 171
Gunnbjørn, Mt 34
Gwich'in people 81, 103, 106–7, 110

Hal, environmental consultant 84, 90
Halldór, son-in-law of Birna Pálsdóttir 220
Heidi, Saami girl from Inari tourist office 194–5, 197
heliographs 14, 25–6
Hesteyri 209, 211
  'Queen of Hesteyri' *see* Pálsdóttir, Birna
Holm, Gustav 225
homes, Inuit 5
*Hood*, HMS 215
Hornstrandir nature reserve 209, 211–22
Hudson Bay Company 110
hunting 2, 5, 46, 133

252

# INDEX

and the Animal Rights and Greenpeace movements 54, 114
with dogs 71
Greenland culture 47
in the Mackenzie river delta 96, 114
Norton culture 3–4
polar bear 68, 69
seal 3, 5, 11, 46, 76–8, 138–9, 240
at Walrus Bay 240–1
whaling 47, 96, 99, 198
huskies 99–100
Tank 228–9, 231–3, 235–6, 238–9, 242–3, 244, 245

Ibyuk pingo 82, 94
ice 4–5, 234–5
 ice cap of Greenland 33–4
 icebergs 34, 41–2, 49–50, 226, 246
 winter ice roads 98, 103–4
Iceland 207, 208–24
Iditarod Run 125, 127, 139
igloo building 72–4
Ilulissat 47–9
Ilulissat Fjord 49–50, 51
Inari 191–9
Inari Hotel 192–3
Independence Day, in Alaska 139–40
indigenous people
 'Eskimo' as a collective name 3, 4
 Eurasian group 2–3
 of Greenland 34–5
 Western Arctic group 2, 3–7
 see also specific tribes
Inland Ice (of Greenland) 33–4
Innukie (an Inuk) 62
insects 2, 37, 191
Inuit people 4, 235
 and the Animal Rights and Greenpeace movements 54, 114
 in Canadian Armed Forces 115
 communities 5–6
 drugs 62
 education 63–4, 65–6, 97, 101
 experiences among the Inuit in Nunavut 55–80
 fur trade 54
 in the Mackenzie river delta 105–8, 110, 112–14 see also Mackenzie river delta
 nationalism 55

 song 249
Inuktitut 66
Inupiat people 4, 118
Inuvialuit people 4, 81, 90, 103
 at Tuktoyaktuk 93–4, 95–7
Inuvik 82, 84, 89–90, 100–3
 aborted trek from 84–9
 airport 91–2
 igloo church 101–2
Iqaluit 65–6, 70–4
 St Jude's Cathedral 71, 101
iron 173
Ísafjörður 209–10
Isfjorden 13, 24
*Iskongen, The* 12, 13, 14, 25
Ittoqqortoormiit 207–8, 224–5, 236, 245
ivory carving 145

Japan Current 143
Jerry, theatre company owner 102–3
Jesudason, Bazel 56, 60–2, 68
Jesudason, Terry 56, 61–2
jewellery making 72
Johnson, Albert (Mad Trapper of Rat River) 110–12

Kabloona people 7, 53, 82, 110
Kalaallit Nunaat 36
 see also Greenland
Kangertîtivaq 225, 226, 234
Kap Farvel 33
Kap Morris Jesup 33
Kap Torbin 233, 235
Karina, contact in Ittoqqortoormiit 225, 227–8, 233, 238, 245
KGH (Kongelig Grølandske Handel) agency 47
Kittigazuit 90
Kola Peninsula 171–86, 189
Komi tribe 2
Komsomolskaya Bay 148, 162, 163
Kotzebue 121–3, 128
Kuroshio current 143

language 2, 65–6, 149, 189
Lapland 187–205
 Kola Peninsula 171–86, 189
Leaf Ericsson 35
lemming 2, 41
Lena, River 144

253

# INDEX

Lenin Prospect 179
Lenin statue 151
Little Diomede Island 144
Longyear, Alfred 11
Longyearbyen 9, 11–13, 28–30
Louis, Spanish base camp manager 75–6

Mackenzie river delta 81–116
Maoris 94, 167, 196–7
Martin, a Dane, partner of Karina 227–8, 233, 238, 245
Mary, proprietor's wife at Polar Bed and Breakfast 103, 106, 107–8, 110, 112
McKinley, Mount 118
minerals 11, 55, 173
mining 11–12, 47
    gold mining/panning 125–7, 128–9, 136, 140–2
Mitrofanov, Adik 149, 167–8
Mitrofanov, Stanislav 143, 146, 147, 148–9, 150, 151, 154, 157–8, 166–7, 168–9
Mitrofanov, Yadvega 148, 149, 150, 152, 154, 157–8, 168–9
Moore, Captain T. 162, 163
moraine 22, 23, 27, 246
mosquitoes 37, 124
Murmansk 171–86
    New Apostolic Church 181–2
music 159
musk ox 228, 243–4
    meat 243

Na Kaa Tak (sighting instrument) 113–14
NANA (Northwest Arctic Native Association) Museum 122
Nanu Travel 227
nationalism 66–7
nature *see* birds; flora; trees; wildlife
Nellim 201
New Chaplino 167
Nome 125–31, 139–42
Nome, Cape 126, 138–9
Nordenskiöldbreen glacier 12, 21
Norma, hotel manageress 93
North West Passage 53, 81, 162
Northwest Mounted Police (NWMP) 108–9
Norton culture 3–4
Norway 11, 36, 187, 188, 198
Norwegians

in Inari 197–8
police 14, 17, 18–19
in Svalbard archipelago 10, 11–12, 14, 17, 18–19, 30
Nunataks 10, 14, 26, 245–6
Nunavut 55, 67, 69, 80
    a spring among the Inuit 70–80
    a winter among the Inuit 55–70

oil 55
Olga, Russian school teacher 19, 20
Osborn, John 136–7
Oyashio current 143

Page, Dick 157–8, 168, 169, 170
Pálina, daughter of Birna Pálsdóttir 220, 222–4
Pálsdóttir, Birna 211, 218, 220
Paris, Treaty of (1920) 11, 28
Paul, Natural Resources Officer 93, 96–7
Pijamini, Inuit hunter 76, 77–80
Pilgrim Springs 132
pingos 82–3, 90, 93–4
Plover Point 163
Plover, The (British brig) 162–3
polar bear 2, 10, 11, 27, 69, 234
    Inuit advice 74
    skins 54, 67–8, 69
    'tag' control of killing 67, 68, 98
Poles 22
Provideniya 144, 145–63, 167–70
Provideniya Bay 162, 163
puffin 24
Pyramiden 14, 16, 19–20

Qeqertarsuaq 37, 38–40, 41, 47
Qutdligssat 47

raven 115–16
Red River 109
reindeer 27, 133
    farm 194–5
    skins 189–90, 202
Reindeer Roses 14
Resolute Bay 55
    experiences among the Inuit at 55–70, 74–80
Reykjavik 224
roads, winter ice 98, 103–4
Rovaniemi 189–91

# INDEX

Roy, Inuit community elder 113–14
Royal Canadian Mounted Police (RCMP) 66, 67, 83, 111–12
Russia
  and Alaska 117–18
  Chukotka 143–70
  and Finland 187–8
  Kola Peninsula 171–86, 189
  Murmansk 171–86
  Russian revolution 187
Russian–American Company 117–18
Russian people
  of Chukotka 145–70
  Eskimosy tribe *see* Yupik Eskimosy
  Eurasian group 2
  immigrants to the Arctic 6–7
  of Murmansk 174–85
  on Spitsbergen 11–12, 16–20, 30

Saami (Lapps) 2, 171, 172, 173, 188–9
  at Inari 192–3, 194–7, 198–9
  national costume 196
Safety Lagoon 134
Salmon Lake (Alaska) 131–2
Saqqaq 42–4, 45–6
Sasha, Provideniyan photographer 164
Scoresbysund 225, 236
sea life 2
seal
  'Animal Rights' protection 54
  furs 54, 113
  hunting 3, 5, 11, 46, 76–8, 138–9, 240
  meat 123
Semmermiut 49, 51
Seward Peninsula 125–42
Seward, William Henry 117, 118, 125
shamans 6
shellfish 40
  crab fishing 5, 138
shops 153, 179
  shopping booths 180–1
shrimp 40
Siberia 144
Skookum pass 134
sledges 5, 22–3
  dog sledge 36, 125, 127
  Iditarod Run 125, 127
Sliney, Florence 63, 64–6
Sliney, Ray 63, 64–6
Small Tool people 3

snow 4–5, 58
  in Chukotka 143
  snow-clearing techniques 183
  walking on 190–1, 193–4
snow house villages 5
snowmobiles 70–1, 198–9, 200–1
Solomon (ghost town) 134
Solomon River 136
Sønder Strømfjord 37, 51
spirituality 6
Spitsbergen 10–12, 26–8
  Svalbard Acid Rain Project (1987) 9, 14–27, 30–1
Split pingo 82, 94
supernatural 6
Svalbard Acid Rain Project (1987) 9, 14–27, 30–1
Svalbard archipelago 10–11
Svetlana, Provideniyan woman 160–1
Sweden 187
swimming 16, 21, 39, 50, 219, 232, 241–2

tern 27
theatre 102–3
Thule people 35, 74–5
tourists
  in Greenland 37, 51, 235–6
  at the Hornstrandir reserve 222
  in Provideniya 158–9
  in Svalbard archipelago 9–10, 21
  Taiwanese 125, 142
transport
  Alaskan 127–8
  Finnish 191
  *see also* snowmobiles
trees 37
Tsiigehtchic 108, 109–10
Tuk Hotel Inn 93
Tuktoyaktuk (Tuk) 82–3, 90–1, 93–100
tundra
  Alaskan 124, 126, 128–9, 132, 137
  Kola Peninsula 172
  Mackenzie river delta 81
  navigation 4–5
  plant life 44, 53, 137

Uelen 145
Ureliki 148, 162

Vienna, Congress of (1815) 36
violence 66–7

# INDEX

Volquart Boon Kyst 229–30

walrus 239, 240, 241
  tusk ivory 145
Walrus Bay 226–7, 229–30, 235–6, 238–45
weddings
  Aklavik 105–7
  Greenland 48–9
whaling 47, 96, 99, 198
White Sea 171
wildlife 2
  birds *see* birds
  management 55
  national parks 118
  *see also specific animals*

wolf 5, 83, 98–9, 114
wolverine pelt 121

Yakuty tribe 2
Yukon River 118
Yupik Eskimosy 2, 4, 122, 145
  communities around Provideniya 152, 163, 165–6, 167, 169

Zhenya, Provideniyan girl 160–2
Zyeninhan, Provideniyan girl 155–6